LIVING THE SACRED ORISA PATH

A COMPLETE GUIDE TO THE ORISHAS, YORUBA WISDOM, & THE 256 SACRED ODU IFA

AWO IFAGBEMI

First Edition: 2026.
Print. ISBN: 979-8-9909018-5-8
LCCN: 2026911475
Published by Michael Perez, Erie, PA, U.S.A.

Limit of Liability/Disclaimer Notice
By reading this book, the reader acknowledges and accepts the following.
This book describes certain traditional practices of Yoruba culture, including animal sacrifice and divination. The information provided herein is solely for educational and entertainment purposes. It is not intended to replace the advice of a qualified professional in any regulated field, such as medical, legal, or financial services. This information is not intended to diagnose, treat, cure, prevent illness, or predict future events. By choosing to read this book, the reader acknowledges that the Author does not offer legal, financial, medical, or any advice requiring professional licensure. This book does not substitute for such advice. Readers also understand that neither the Author nor the Publisher can guarantee the reliability or accuracy of the information presented in this book. Therefore, readers are strongly advised to consult legally licensed professionals in their respective jurisdictions before attempting any techniques outlined in this book. Furthermore, readers are urged to discuss any alternative remedies, herbal use, or spiritual practices mentioned herein with qualified and legally recognized professionals beforehand. It is essential not to disregard professional advice or delay seeking it due to the direct or indirect influence of the information contained in this book. By continuing to read this book, the reader acknowledges that neither the Author nor the Publisher shall be held liable for any losses, whether direct or indirect, incurred from the use or misuse of the material presented within this publication.

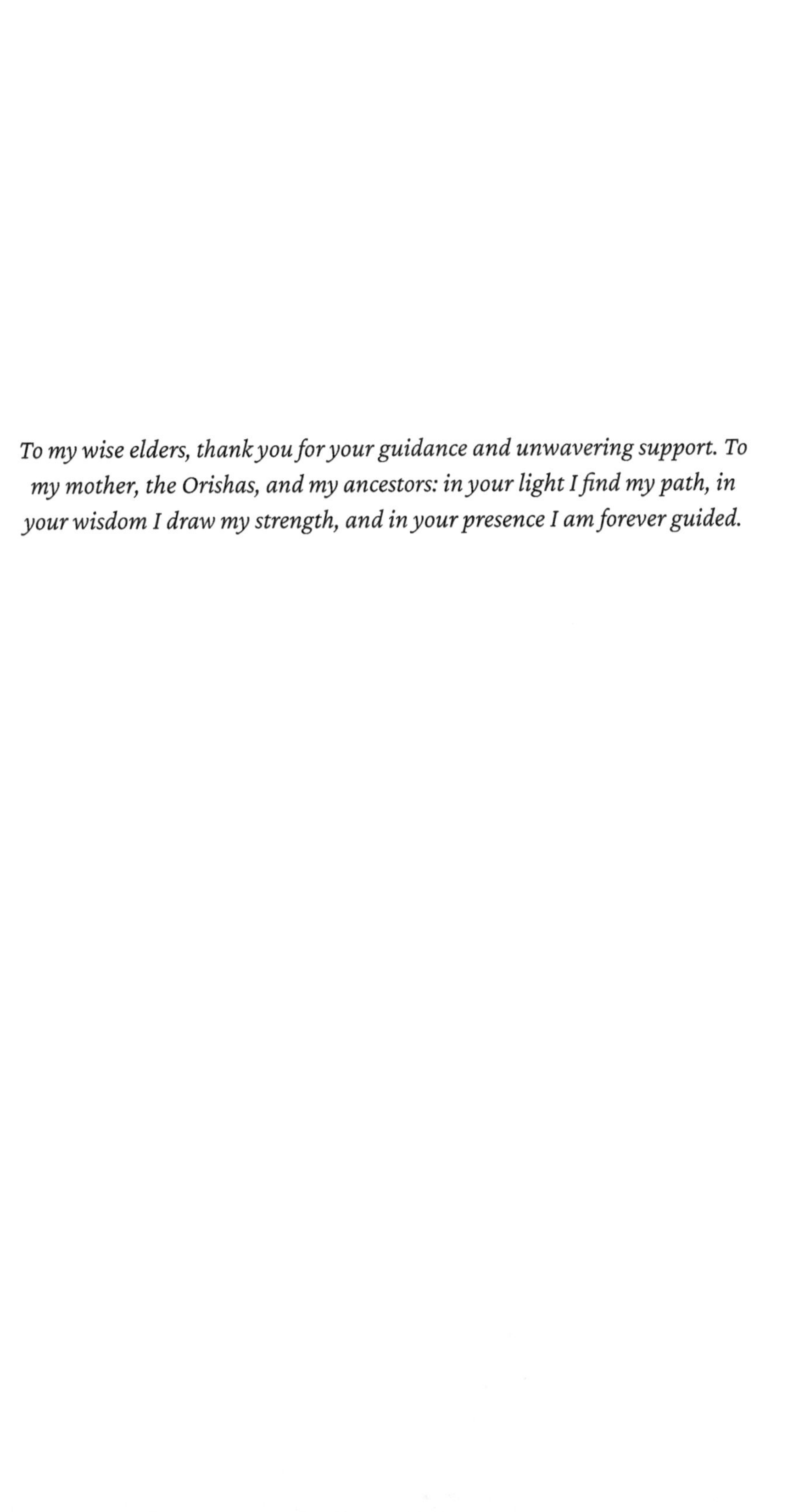

To my wise elders, thank you for your guidance and unwavering support. To my mother, the Orishas, and my ancestors: in your light I find my path, in your wisdom I draw my strength, and in your presence I am forever guided.

INTRODUCTION

This book is a collection of essays and personal reflections gathered over many years. I never intended to publish these writings, but as I revisited my journals, notes, and essays on Yoruba philosophy, I realized they formed a body of work worth sharing. When I wrote *The Yoruba Spiritual Training Manual* and *The Sacred Teachings of the Orishas*, my goal was to provide structured guidance, clear frameworks, and lessons to help students understand and practice the Yoruba tradition. Those books reflect the teacher in me: organized, intentional, and focused on presenting wisdom in a way others could follow. *This book is different.* What you're holding is the result of years of quiet reflection and writings that were never originally meant to be shared. They began as private thoughts, moments of insight, and attempts to make sense of my experiences.

Over time, I came to realize that these fragments were not random, but part of a larger pattern that was taking shape. Gradually, they formed something meaningful: a map of the Orisha path as I have come to live and understand it, not a fixed doctrine, but a lived journey shaped by practice, reflection, and personal transformation. Within these pages, elements of the Yoruba spiritual tradition are woven together with the psychological and philosophical insights that have guided my own growth and healing. Each reflection stands on its own, yet together they create a deeper, more personal exploration of the path. It is my hope that this work offers guidance, inspiration, and clarity to others walking a similar journey. This book invites you to experience Yoruba spiritual philosophy as a living tradition, one that explores enduring questions of destiny, balance, adversity, and harmony, while also speaking to the modern search for meaning in a world often disconnected from sacred rhythms. Within these pages, you will encounter the Orishas, gain a basic understanding of the 256 Odu Ifa, and find practical ways to bring spiritual awareness into everyday life. Some chapters are designed as a reference, offering descriptions of the Odu, plant associations, and other key elements of the tradition. Others are more reflective, focusing on personal growth, self-examination, and spiritual development.

I do not present these essays as a complete or authoritative account of Yoruba tradition. Instead, they reflect my own experience as a Babalawo, an ongoing effort to live in alignment with its teachings. This path has shaped how I face challenges, honor my ancestors, and move toward my destiny. If something in these pages resonates with you, sparks insight, or deepens your understanding, then this book has served its purpose.

May the Orishas guide your path.
May the ancestors walk beside you.
May the flow of Ashe move through your life with clarity, balance, and peace.
- The Author -

CONTENTS

THE FOUNDATIONS OF YORUBA THOUGHT
PART I

CHAPTER 1

THE YORUBA PANTHEON

AN INTRODUCTION TO THE ORISHAS

AN OVERVIEW OF THE ORISHAS

In the Yoruba spiritual tradition, which originated with the Yoruba people of southwestern Nigeria, Benin, and Togo, as well as among the Yoruba diaspora across the Caribbean and the Americas, all life is understood to flow from a single, Supreme Source. This Source is called *Olodumare*, sometimes also known as *Olorun*. Olodumare is the ultimate Creator, the origin of all that exists, and the force that sustains life and maintains balance. From this sacred Source, the universe comes into being, moves, and eventually returns. Flowing through all creation is *Ase* (pronounced *ah-shay*), the divine energy, life force, and spiritual power that animates every part of the universe. While it is often translated as "power," Ase is far more than strength or ability. It is the force that enables change, sustains growth, and connects people, animals, plants, objects, and moments into a living, unified whole. Ase is also the Creator's energy for performing miracles and shaping reality, and it is believed that those who align with it can work with it in their own lives.

Practitioners often speak of "accumulating Ase," which means increasing one's spiritual energy and effectiveness through positive actions, discipline, and alignment with the divine. When a person loses connection with this flow, their Ase can become blocked, leading to obstacles, challenges, or a sense of disconnection. Understanding Ase is essential to grasping the foundation of the Yoruba spiritual system, as it shows how devotees can consciously participate in life and strengthen their spiritual and personal well-being. To enhance their Ase and invite blessings, practitioners often turn to prayer, meditation, and ritual, seeking guidance, protection, and support from the Orishas, the sacred spiritual beings of the Yoruba pantheon.

The Orishas act as intermediaries between humans and the Supreme Creator, Olodumare, helping to guide, protect, and influence the world on Olodumare's behalf. Olodumare is often described as distant and without gender. The Orishas were created to assist in managing the many aspects of creation. It is believed that Olodumare broke off pieces of divine essence and shaped them into primordial beings called the Irunmole, who became the first Orishas. These sacred spiritual beings helped form the physical universe under Olodumare's guidance. Devotees believe they carry and express Olodumare's energy, maintaining the spiritual laws of creation. Each Orisha is a distinct expression of divine energy, representing a particular aspect of life, nature, or human experience. They are caretakers of creation, overseeing its daily workings while guiding, protecting, and inspiring humanity. The Yoruba honor the Orishas through rituals, prayers, dances, offerings, and divination, creating a living connection with their energy. By working with an Orisha, a person can navigate life's challenges more effectively, develop personal strengths, and deepen their understanding of themselves and the universe.

This chapter primarily serves as a reference guide to the Orishas, introducing who they are, what they govern, and how they are understood in the Yoruba tradition. Below, many of the Orishas in the Yoruba pantheon are presented to help you better understand their nature, qualities, and roles as you continue your studies and deepen your connection to this spiritual path.

* * *

ORISHA AJE

- **Description:** Aje is the Orisha of wealth, prosperity, and abundance. She governs financial success, material blessings, commerce, and the flow of resources. Closely associated with cowrie shells, markets, and feminine power, Aje also represents fertility, intuition, and the ability to manifest prosperity. She is deeply respected not only for bringing riches but also for her wisdom and healing energy.
- **Frequency:** Prosperity, intuition, and manifestation of material and spiritual abundance.
- **Manifestation:** Generosity, resourcefulness, and financial empowerment.
- **Purpose:** Teaches how to harness natural abundance, manifest prosperity, and balance giving and receiving.
- **Domain:** Wealth, money, markets, fertility, material and spiritual abundance, feminine power.
- **Colors:** White, silver, gold.
- **Symbols:** Cowrie shells, coins, the moon.
- **Common Offerings:** Pigeons, flowers, jewelry, cowries, money, incense, candles.

AGANJU

- **Description:** Aganju is a powerful Orisha closely linked to Shango and sometimes viewed as a historic king of the Oyo Empire. He rules over wild and challenging landscapes such as volcanoes, deserts, caves, and mountain peaks. Associated with fire, lava, and untamed nature, Aganju empowers his followers with strength, resilience, and the ability to overcome hardships. He also guides and protects travelers, embodying transformation, stability, and grounding through raw natural forces.
- **Frequency:** Strength, resilience, and endurance.

- **Manifestation:** Courage, determination, and mastery over challenges.
- **Purpose:** Guides personal fortitude, grounding in nature's raw power, and transformation through struggle.
- **Domain:** Volcanoes, deserts, fire, strength, untamed nature, transformation, resilience.
- **Colors:** Brown, red, dark earth tones.
- **Symbols:** Volcanoes, the desert, machete.
- **Common Offerings:** Palm oil, red wine, candles or bonfires (firelight), hot peppers.
- **Catholic Syncretism:** Saint Christopher - Feast Day: July 25.

BABALU-AYE

- **Description:** Babalu-Aye is the Orisha of the earth, illness, and healing. He governs infectious diseases and their cures, embodying the dual power to both cause and heal sickness. Deeply connected to death and the natural cycles of life, Babalu-Aye is seen as a force of nature who teaches respect for the body and the earth through his power over health and disease.
- **Domain:** Illness, healing, disease, death, earth, natural cycles, transformation through suffering.
- **Personality:** Stern, compassionate, patient, powerful healer.
- **Colors:** Purple, brown, black, and earth tones.
- **Symbols:** Straw mats, broom, healing herbs.
- **Common Offerings:** Grains, palm oil, goats, pigeons, roosters.
- **Catholic Syncretism:** Saint Lazarus - Feast Day: July 29 (traditional observance).

INLE / ERINLE

- **Description:** Inle, also called Erinle, is the Orisha of health, medicine, hunting, and the estuary where fresh water meets the sea. He is known as a skilled healer and herbalist and is often regarded as the protector of deaf and LGBTQ+

individuals. Inle is depicted as a strong, androgynous warrior and hunter who embodies compassion and skill.

- **Domain:** Healing, medicine, water, hunting, estuaries, and protection of marginalized communities.
- **Personality:** Compassionate, skilled, protective, nurturing.
- **Colors:** Blue, white, coral.
- **Symbols:** Snakes, fish, shells.
- **Common Offerings:** Fish, shells, herbs, water, pigeons, guinea fowl, flowers, candles.
- **Catholic Syncretism:** Saint Sebastian - Feast Day: January 20 (traditional).

EGBE

- Spiritual companions, destiny, collective soul, and personal fate. Egbe represents the invisible spiritual double or group of spiritual allies connected to each individual, guiding and protecting their life path. It embodies community, balance, and the unseen forces that influence one's destiny.

EGUNGUN

- **Domain:** Ancestral spirits, ancestral wisdom, protection, and community connection.
- **Personality:** Revered, mysterious, powerful, and protective.
- **Colors:** White, blue, and purple.
- **Symbols:** Masks, flowing robes, ancestral costumes.
- **Offerings:** A wide range of foods and drink, Egungun can be given almost anything.
- **Days/Associations:** Honored during Egungun festivals as the link between the living and the ancestors.

ESU / ELEGUA

- **Description:** Esu (also called Elegua) is a vital Orisha who serves as the messenger between Olodumare (God) and all other Orishas. Known as the guardian of roads and crossroads, he is always honored first in ceremonies, as he opens the way and delivers offerings. Esu is both a divine trickster and a wise gatekeeper, capable of influencing fate and revealing the past, present, and future.

- **Domain:** Crossroads, destiny, communication, fate, spiritual access, and divine justice. He is the gatekeeper between the human world and the Orishas.
- **Personality:** Clever, unpredictable, mischievous, and deeply wise.
- **Colors:** Red and black.
- **Symbols:** Keys, crossroads, cowrie shells, roads.
- **Common Offerings:** Palm oil, rum, cigars, roasted corn, candy, roosters.
- **Catholic Syncretism:** Saint Anthony of Padua - Feast Day: June 13.

IBEJI

- **Description:** Ibeji are the divine Orisha twins, also known as the Jimaguas. In Yoruba tradition, twins are considered sacred and believed to carry strong spiritual power. Ibeji represents duality, harmony, joy, and the balance of masculine and feminine energies. They bless those who honor them with protection, happiness, and good fortune, especially children and families.
- **Domain:** Twins, duality, balance, joy, childhood, and protection.
- **Personality:** Playful, loving, joyful, balanced.
- **Colors:** Bright and varied - often red and blue or other joyful combinations.
- **Symbols:** Twin figures, dolls, paired items.
- **Common Offerings:** Water, fruit, candies, cake, sweets, toys, candles.
- **Catholic Syncretism:** Saints Cosmas and Damian -Feast Day: September 26.

IYAMI OSORONGA

- **Description:** The Iyami Osoronga are believe to be a collective of ancestral female spirits, known as the *spiritual Mothers*. They embody feminine power, mystery, and transformative energy, overseeing the hidden and sacred aspects of creation, spiritual law, and destiny. Revered as powerful custodians of cosmic balance, they are associated with birds, particularly nocturnal species, and are honored through ritual, offerings, and divination to maintain harmony, guidance, and protection. They are not a single being, but a unified force representing the strength and wisdom of ancestral women.

NANA BULUKU

- **Description:** Nana Buluku is one of the oldest and most revered primordial deities, especially honored by the Fon people of Benin and in Dahomean cosmology. She is seen as the supreme feminine force and the mother of all. In Vodou traditions, she helped create the universe. In the Yoruba diaspora, Nana Buluku is respected as a powerful feminine aspect of Olodumare, embodying the divine in her forms as maiden, mother, and grandmother. She governs the cosmos, fertility, and the natural cycles of life, representing ancestral wisdom, the earth's rhythms, the seasons, and the sacred feminine.
- **Domain:** The ground, the earth, fertility, the seasons, stages of life, the moon cycles
- **Personality:** Ancient, nurturing, mysterious, wise.
- **Colors:** Deep purple, earth tones, white, and indigo.
- **Symbols:** Moon, earth, sacred ground, old woman's walking staff.
- **Offerings:** seeds, planting, various fruits and vegetables, water
- **Days/Associations:** Traditionally honored on July 26 (Feast of Saint Anne); also venerated on days sacred to *Orunmila, Esu, Oshun, Yemoja, Aje, Olokun, Egbe, and Oshumare* in the traditional Yoruba calendar.

OBA

- Description: Considered the oldest of Orisha Shango's wives, she was tricked into cutting off her ear to win his love. Out of grief, she is said to have turned into the Oba River in Nigeria. She rules over marriage and relationships.
- **Domain:** Marriage, loyalty, sacrifice, endurance, and feminine strength.
- **Personality:** Devoted, resilient, emotional, misunderstood.
- **Colors:** Pink, burgundy, white.
- **Symbols:** Crown with one ear missing, rivers, flowing water.
- **Offerings:** Beans, white rice, shea butter, red wine, flowers, and sweet foods.
- **Days/Associations:** Wednesday; associated with the Oba River in Nigeria and invoked for matters of love, fidelity, and emotional healing.
- **Catholic Syncretism:** Saint Catherine -**Feast Day:** November 25 (in many traditions).

OBATALA

- **Description:** Obatala is revered as the father of all Orishas and the divine sculptor of humanity. He is the Orisha of purity, wisdom, and creation, embodying justice, peace, patience, and clarity. Associated with the color white, Obatala brings calm, balance, and spiritual authority. As a gentle and compassionate deity, he teaches humility, self-discipline, and righteousness. He is believed to govern all heads (consciousness) and is called upon in times of confusion or need for ethical clarity.
- **Domain:** Purity, creation, wisdom, justice, peace, and clarity of mind.
- **Personality:** Compassionate, patient, serene, wise, principled.
- **Colors:** White.
- **Symbols:** Snail, white cloth, mountains, sky.
- **Offerings:** White foods such as coconut, white rice, milk, cassava, bananas, and no salt. Other offerings include silver items, shea butter, and white candles.

- **Days/Associations:** Associated with the sky and high places such as mountains. Regarded as the father of the Orishas and protector of those with physical or mental challenges.
- **Catholic Syncretism:** Our Lady of Mercy - **Feast Day:** September 24.

ODUDUWA

- **Description:** Oduduwa is both a legendary ancestor and a powerful Orisha in Yoruba tradition. He is known as the first King (Ooni) of Ife and is honored as the founder of the Yoruba people and their civilization. Oduduwa represents divine kingship, ancestral wisdom, and the foundation of social order and leadership.
- **Domain:** Kingship, leadership, creation, ancestry, civilization.
- **Personality:** Noble, wise, foundational, dignified.
- **Offerings:** Yams, palm wine, kola nuts, and traditional Yoruba foods.
- **Days/Associations:** Honored by rulers, elders, and those seeking leadership or wisdom.

OGUN

- **Description:** Ogun is one of the most revered Orishas, known as the fierce warrior and master of iron, war, labor, hunting, and technology. A powerful blacksmith and pathfinder, Ogun is credited with clearing the way for the other Orishas at the dawn of creation. He taught humanity how to forge tools, build civilizations, and master technology. As the patron of blacksmiths, warriors, and workers, Ogun represents strength, endurance, transformation, and innovation.
- **Domain:** Iron, war, hunting, labor, technology, transformation, agriculture, craftsmanship.
- **Personality:** Strong, determined, protective, hardworking, intense.
- **Colors:** Black and Green (sometimes red).
- **Symbols:** Machete, iron tools, chains, dogs.

- **Common Offerings:** palm oil, rum, plantains, guinea pepper, red pepper, water, alcohol, iron items, metal trinkets, metal jewelry.
- **Catholic Syncretism:** Saint Peter (often with Saint Paul) - Feast Day: June 29.
- **Associations:** Patron of blacksmiths, soldiers, hunters, mechanics, and laborers.

OKO

- **Description:** Oko is the Orisha of agriculture, farming, and the fertility of the land. He is the patron of farmers and is honored for bringing abundance, good harvests, and prosperity to those who work the soil. Oko also symbolizes the ability to cultivate not only crops, but also the growth and prosperity in one's life.
- **Domain:** Agriculture, fertility, harvest, land cultivation, scarecrows.
- **Personality:** Nurturing, patient, generous.
- **Colors:** Brown, green.
- **Symbols:** Farming tools, crops.
- **Offerings:** Fruits, vegetables, and other harvest items.
- **Days/Associations:** Honored by farmers and those seeking abundance through cultivation.

OLOKUN

- **Description:** Olokun is the powerful and mysterious Orisha who dwells in the deepest parts of the ocean. Associated with immense spiritual and material wealth, Olokun is revered as the keeper of hidden treasures, ancient wisdom, and transformative healing. Often connected with Yemaya as a sibling or counterpart, Olokun's energy is vast, enigmatic, and capable of great force sometimes said to be chained to contain their power. This Orisha also governs dreams, the unconscious, and mystical knowledge.
- **Domain:** Ocean depths, mystery, wealth,

- **Personality:** Mysterious, ancient, wise, powerful, deep, sometimes feared and greatly respected.
- **Colors:** Dark blue, black.
- **Symbols:** Seashells, coral, masks, ocean currents.
- **Common Offerings:** Coins, cowries, melons, colorful beads.

ORI

- Ori literally means "head" and symbolizes the essence of personal destiny, spiritual consciousness, and inner wisdom. Ori is the divine spark within each person that governs their fate, intuition, and life purpose. It is the ultimate Orisha of self-realization and spiritual authority over one's path.

ORO

- **Description:** Oro is the Orisha of justice, law, secrecy, and male authority. He is known for his stern and authoritative nature, upholding fairness and moral order. Oro is often called upon during legal disputes and ethical decisions.
- **Domain:** Justice, law, secrecy, authority, moral order.
- **Personality:** Stern, just, authoritative, disciplined.
- **Colors:** White and black.
- **Symbols:** Sacred knives, ritual staffs.
- **Offerings:** White foods, kola nuts.
- **Days/Associations:** Invoked in matters of law, justice, and morality.

ORUNMILA

- **Description:** Orunmila is the Orisha of wisdom, divination, and destiny. He possesses the divine knowledge of all things and helps people understand their life paths through the sacred Ifá divination system. As a calm and patient guide, Orunmila plays a vital role in Yoruba spirituality, offering insight and clarity in times of decision and uncertainty.

- **Domain:** Wisdom, destiny, foresight, divine records, and the sacred teachings of Ifá.
- **Personality:** Wise, serene, all-knowing, patient, and observant.
- **Colors:** Green and yellow (or green and brown in some traditions).
- **Symbols:** Opele (divination chain), ikin (palm nuts), books, scrolls.
- **Common Offerings:** Coconut, palm oil, gin.
- **Catholic Syncretism:** Saint Francis of Assisi - Feast Day: October 4.

OSAIN- OSANYIN
Ray of Herbal Wisdom and Nature Medicine

- **Description:** Osain is the Orisha of herbs, healing, and natural medicine. He knows the spiritual and healing power of every plant and is called upon by healers, herbalists, and spiritual workers. He lives in the forest and helps people heal through nature.
- **Domain:** Herbal medicine, healing, plants, nature, forests.
- **Personality:** Wise, mysterious, powerful, connected to nature.
- **Symbols:** Leaves, herbs, one-legged figure, staff.
- **Offerings:** Healing herbs, leaves, flowers, tobacco, alcohol.
- **Saint Day:** Saint Joseph - March 19

OCHOSI

- **Description:** Ochosi is the Orisha of hunting, justice, truth, and the forest. A skilled tracker and marksman, his arrows never miss their target. As the patron of hunters and seekers of truth, Oshosi is often invoked in legal matters and situations involving injustice or oppression. He brings swift and fair resolution, embodying precision, focus, and divine justice.
- **Domain:** Hunting, justice, truth, law, morality, the forest, protection of the innocent.
- **Personality:** Focused, just, fair, quiet, swift, observant.

- **Colors:** Green and blue.
- **Symbols:** Bow and arrow, forest animals, horns, hunting gear.
- **Common Offerings:** Plantains, pears, mangoes, avocados, papayas, gin or other spirits, fruits, a glass of water, candles.
- **Catholic Syncretism:** Saint Norbert Feast Day: June 6 (regional tradition).
- **Associations:** Patron of hunters, justice-seekers, and those facing legal battles

OSHUN

- **Description:** Oshun is one of the most cherished and radiant Orishas, governing rivers, streams, and all fresh water. She is the Orisha of love, beauty, sensuality, fertility, and attraction. Oshun brings sweetness into life, offering abundance, joy, wealth, and emotional healing. She is also a fierce protector of women and children and is known for her powerful presence in matters of the heart and spirit.
- **Domain:** Love, beauty, fertility, emotional healing, rivers, wealth, sweetness, and feminine power.
- **Personality:** Sensual, kind, flirtatious, nurturing, generous, but can be vengeful when disrespected.
- **Colors:** Yellow, gold, amber.
- **Symbols:** Mirror, fan, honey, river water.
- **Common Offerings:** Honey (always tasted first), oranges, yellow flowers, sweets, white wine.
- **Catholic Syncretism:** Our Lady of Charity (La Virgen de la Caridad del Cobre); Feast Day: September 8; Day of the Week: Friday or Saturday (varies by tradition).

OSUMARE

- **Description:** Osumare is the Orisha of rainbows and serpents, embodying transformation, renewal, and balance. Often appearing as a rainbow serpent, Osumare represents the bridge between earth and sky, matter and spirit. His presence signals new beginnings, healing, purification, and the release of negativity. Osumare protects children, artists, and those who exist outside traditional gender roles, including transgender and non-binary individuals.

- **Domain:** Rainbows, serpents, transformation, renewal, balance, cycles of nature, and spiritual cleansing.
- **Personality:** Harmonious, protective, transformative, serene yet powerful.
- **Colors:** Multicolored (rainbow hues), white.
- **Symbols:** Rainbow, serpent, umbilical cord.
- **Common Offerings:** Fresh water, honey, flowers, fruits, incense, candles.
- **Associations:** Linked to natural cycles, creativity, and the harmony between opposites.

OYA

- **Description:** Oya is the fierce Orisha of wind, storms, tornadoes, and hurricanes. She governs powerful forces of change and transformation. Oya is also the protector of the marketplace and the guardian of the dead, guiding ancestors safely to the afterlife. She blesses her followers with intuition, clairvoyance, and the ability to communicate with spirits. Her energy brings sudden shifts that clear the way for new beginnings and growth.
- **Domain:** Wind, storms, change, transformation, death, ancestors, marketplace.
- **Personality:** Fierce, powerful, intuitive, transformative.
- **Colors:** Burgundy, purple, rust, brown.
- **Symbols:** Buffalo, sword, lightning, copper coins.
- **Offerings:** Plums, eggplants, grapes, raisins, copper coins, female goats, jewelry.
- **Catholic Syncretism:** Saint Theresa (commonly St. Theresa of Lisieux) Feast Day: October 1 or October 15 (varies by tradition).

SHANGO

- **Description:** Shango is the fierce and majestic Orisha of thunder, lightning, fire, drumming, and masculine virility. Once a mighty king of the Oyo Empire, he embodies strength, charisma, passion, and justice. Shango is known for his booming presence, love of music and dance, and his role as a protector of the oppressed and punisher of the wicked. He is often called upon for courage, power, and fairness in battle or life challenges.
- **Domain:** Thunder, lightning, fire, masculinity, justice, leadership, and personal power.
- **Personality:** Passionate, bold, charismatic, fierce, just.
- **Colors:** Red and white
- **Symbols:** Double-headed axe (oshe), thunderstones, drums.
- **Common Offerings:** Roosters, red wine, rum, tobacco, red and white candles, roasted yams, cornmeal, red peppers, bitter kola, porridge, okra, bananas, palm oil, water, incense.
- **Catholic Syncretism:** Saint Barbara - Feast Day: December 4 (commonly observed).
- **Associations:** Protector of warriors, dancers, leaders, and those seeking justice or personal empowerment.

YEMAYA

- **Description:** Yemaya is the nurturing and powerful Orisha of the ocean, motherhood, and creation. As the mother of many Orishas, she embodies maternal love, protection, fertility, and emotional healing. Her energy is vast and soothing like the sea, yet capable of great power when stirred. Yemaya watches over women, children, and all life that begins in water, offering deep emotional support and strength.
- **Domain:** Ocean surface, motherhood, fertility, nurturing, creation, and protection.
- **Personality:** Gentle, loving, protective, calm, yet immensely powerful.
- **Colors:** Blue, white, silver.

- **Symbols:** Seashells, fish, the moon, water vessels (pots).
- **Common Offerings:** Melons, molasses, seashells, white and blue flowers, fish dishes.
- **Catholic Syncretism:** Our Lady of Regla; Feast Day: September 8 (date may vary by region); Day of the Week: Saturday or Monday.

YEWA

- **Description:** A mysterious Orisha associated with the earth and the ground, residing inside the cemetery. Yewa is very much linked to the mysteries of death and is said to rule over the decomposition of corpses. Both Oya and Yewa ensure the barriers between life and death are kept separate.
- **Offerings:** Cowrie shells, flowers, water, incense, candles, pigeons, and female goats.
- **Saint Day:** Saint Clare of Assisi - Feast Day: August 11 (traditional)

* * *

CHAPTER 2

DIVINE FORCES WITHIN AND BEYOND
AWAKENING THE INNER PANTHEON

In the Yoruba spiritual tradition, as discussed in the previous chapter, the Orishas are manifestations of Olodumare's infinite power, sacred expressions through which the Divine engages with the world. Olodumare can be imagined as pure, undivided light. Like sunlight passing through a stained-glass window or a prism, the light changes form and color, yet its source remains the same; the brilliance we see comes from the light itself, not from the window or prism. In the same way, each Orisha is like a unique color of that divine light, distinct yet inseparable from Olodumare.

Each carries its own force, vibration, and purpose while remaining fully connected to the one sacred origin. The Orishas sustain the natural order, guide human life, and illuminate the spiritual pathways of the cosmos. Through them, Olodumare's infinite energy becomes tangible: in rivers and mountains, in storms and winds, in the courage of the warrior, the wisdom of the elder, and the joy of the celebrant. They serve as both mirrors and teachers, revealing the Divine within creation and within ourselves. In this way, Olodumare's unity is never diminished by multiplicity. Instead, it becomes visible, vibrant, and experiential through the manifold presence of the Orishas, allowing the Divine to touch and shape every aspect of life.

The Orishas can be understood on multiple levels, reflecting both their external presence and their inner influence. From the traditional devotional perspective, the Orishas are independent spiritual beings with distinct personalities, domains, and stories. They exist beyond human thought and actively guide, protect, and influence the world. Devotees honor them through prayer, offerings, rituals, and ceremonies, cultivating spiritual growth through relationship, reverence, and alignment. This is the most ancient and widely practiced understanding of the Orishas as real, external beings. At the same time, the Orishas' energy manifests within us.

From this perspective, they are archetypal forces or universal patterns of consciousness that shape human behavior, emotions, and character. The same energies that govern nature storms, rivers, courage, wisdom, and abundance also exist within the soul. By recognizing and harmonizing with these inner energies through introspection, discipline, and alignment, practitioners foster personal growth, balance, and transformation. In essence, the Orishas are both external guides and inner archetypes: real beings whose energies resonate through the world and within each individual, offering multiple paths to connect with the Divine and live in harmony with creation.

THE ORISHAS AS ARCHETYPES OF THE PSYCHE

The idea that the Orishas manifest as inner forces is not widely understood, yet it offers a powerful way to explore their meaning. From this perspective, each Orisha represents a natural function of the human mind and spirit. The framework below presents one interpretive approach, not a fixed doctrine, but a lens for examining the relationship between Orisha traditions and human psychology. It explores how different Orishas may correspond to dimensions of human consciousness and inner development.

1. Olodumare (The Supreme Being)

1. **Archetype:** Pure Consciousness / Source Awareness
2. **Psychological Role:** The field of unified consciousness from which all mental states arise. The ground of being itself.
3. **Inner Relationship:** The transcendent Self that holds all Orishas in balance. The ultimate observer within the psyche that witnesses without judgment.

2. Orí (Inner Head)

1. **Archetype:** Higher Self / Destiny / Executive Integrator
2. **Psychological Role:** The central organizing intelligence of the psyche moral compass, the sense of purpose, and the selector of destiny. Your essential nature and life path.
3. **Inner Relationship:** The master key through which all Orishas express themselves. When Orí is aligned and clear, the entire inner pantheon operates harmoniously.

3. Eshu (Elegba)

1. **Archetype:** Trickster / Catalyst / Shadow Integration
2. **Psychological Role:** The unconscious disruptor that provokes awareness by challenging assumptions. The force of change, irony, paradox, and unexpected opportunity. Opens doors and creates crossroads.
3. **Inner Relationship:** Opens communication between all Orishas. Activates transformation by stirring up what needs to be seen. Balances order (Obatala) with chaos (Ogun).

4. Obatala

1. **Archetype:** Wisdom / Moral Clarity / Higher Reason
2. **Psychological Role:** Represents order, purity, self-discipline, and ethical reasoning. The super-ego, purified of judgment, conscience guided by wisdom rather than fear.

3. **Inner Relationship:** The "cool head" that balances Ogun's aggression and Sango's passion. The father of harmony, the mentor to impulsive forces.

5. Ogun

1. **Archetype:** Warrior / Builder / Willpower
2. **Psychological Role:** Represents drive, focus, perseverance, and the capacity to overcome resistance. The archetype of action, determination, and the ability to cut through obstacles.
3. **Inner Relationship:** Works with Sango to externalize vision; tempered by Obatala's calm and Osun's empathy. When unbalanced, it can turn destructive or rigid.

6. Shango

1. **Archetype:** Fire of Will / Justice / Emotional Power
2. **Psychological Role:** Passion, charisma, leadership, self-assertion, and moral force. The capacity to stand in one's truth and demand justice.
3. **Inner Relationship:** Complements Ogun's determination with charisma and vision; needs Osun's sensitivity and Obatala's wisdom to avoid pride or destructive anger.

7. Oshun

1. **Archetype:** Love / Intuition / Emotional Intelligence
2. **Psychological Role:** Embodies empathy, sensuality, intuition, aesthetic appreciation, and relational intelligence. The capacity for sweetness, flow, and connection.
3. **Inner Relationship:** Softens Ogun and Sango's intensity. Balances Yemoja's deep emotion with lightness and joy. Supports Ochosi's creativity through inspiration.

8. Yemoja

1. **Archetype:** The Oceanic Mother / Emotional Depth / Subconscious
2. **Psychological Role:** Represents emotional and ancestral memory, the deep reservoir of feeling, instinct, and nurturing capacity. The waters from which all life emerges.
3. **Inner Relationship:** Source of nourishment for all other Orishas. Works closely with Osun (surface emotion) and Oba (loyalty).

9. Ochosi

1. **Archetype:** Hunter / Focus / Intuitive Intelligence
2. **Psychological Role:** Symbolizes insight, attention, and discernment, the capacity to find truth and aim the mind precisely toward what matters.
3. **Inner Relationship:** Works with Ogun (who clears the path) and Eshu (who opens it). Represents goal orientation balanced by intuition.

10. Oba

1. **Archetype:** Devotion / Sacrifice / Emotional Strength
2. **Psychological Role:** Represents commitment, endurance in love, and the psychology of self-sacrifice. The capacity to stand by what and whom one loves.
3. **Inner Relationship:** Complements Osun and Yemoja, forming a triad of feminine archetypes each embodying different emotional responses: joy, depth, and loyalty.

11. Oyá

1. **Archetype:** Change / Transformation / Breath of Life
2. **Psychological Role:** Represents the psychic force of transition endings, rebirth, and personal evolution. The wind that clears away what is dead to make room for new life.

3. **Inner Relationship:** Works with Eshu to provoke change, with Yemoja to purify emotion, and with Orunmila to translate chaos into wisdom.

12. Orunmila / Ifa

1. **Archetype:** Wisdom / Intuition / Divine Intelligence
2. **Psychological Role:** Embodies insight, discernment, and the higher reasoning that transcends logic. The archetype of deep knowing and prophetic understanding.
3. **Inner Relationship:** The mind's link between Orí and experience interprets destiny's lessons. Balances Obatala's intellect with Osun's intuition.

13. Olokun

1. **Archetype:** Depth / Mysticism / Collective Unconscious
2. **Psychological Role:** Symbol of the abyssal self, representing mystery, creativity, and the hidden dimensions of being. The depths that cannot be fully known.
3. **Inner Relationship:** The deeper, more mysterious counterpart of Yemoja. Unites with Orunmila to reveal esoteric wisdom through dreams or trance.

14. Babalu-Aye

1. **Archetype:** Healing / Mortality / Transformation Through Suffering
2. **Psychological Role:** Represents illness, vulnerability, and the wisdom that arises from healing. Teaches acceptance of impermanence and cultivates empathy for suffering.
3. **Inner Relationship:** Balances Obatala's perfectionism with compassion. Works with Yemoja and Orunmila to purify karmic or ancestral wounds.

15. Oshumare

1. **Archetype:** Renewal / Polarity / Cyclical Energy
2. **Psychological Role:** Symbolizes transformation, the unity of opposites, and the integration of masculine and feminine energy within the psyche. The rainbow that bridges heaven and earth.
3. **Inner Relationship:** Mediates between Oshun and Shango, uniting passion and harmony. Represents the psyche's ability to regenerate after conflict.

16. Erinle

1. **Archetype:** Provider / Inner Healer / Abundance Consciousness
2. **Psychological Role:** Represents nourishment, healing through nature, and harmony between body and mind. The quiet, steady force of provision.
3. **Inner Relationship:** Partner of Oshun and servant of Yemoja; connects the inner emotional world with physical well-being.

17. Osanyin

1. **Archetype:** Herbalist / Knowledge of Nature / Mind-Body Medicine
2. **Psychological Role:** Represents the subtle intelligence of nature, the healing power of attention, plants, and consciousness. The wisdom of the natural world.
3. **Inner Relationship:** Works closely with Babalú-Ayé and Orunmila; governs the psychosomatic interface between mind and matter.

18. Ibeji (The Twins)

1. **Archetype:** Duality / Playfulness / Balance
2. **Psychological Role:** Symbolize the balance between opposites,

joy and sorrow, innocence and wisdom, spontaneity and seriousness. The sacred play of existence.

3. **Inner Relationship:** Mediate between Òshun (pleasure) and Obatala (discipline). Represent the psyche's ability to regenerate through play and paradox.

19. Egungun (Ancestors)

1. **Archetype:** Ancestral Memory / Collective Past
2. **Psychological Role:** Represent inherited memory, trans-generational patterns, and the psychological DNA of one's lineage. The voices of those who came before.
3. **Inner Relationship:** Work through Orí and Orunmila, influencing the subconscious. Healing ancestral wounds realigns the entire inner pantheon.

Together, these forces form a living system of psychological and spiritual energies within the human being, an inner pantheon that, when balanced, allows for wholeness, clarity, and alignment with one's destiny.

* * *

Practices for Restoring Inner Balance

Each Orisha represents a natural force within the human psyche. When these energies are out of balance, we may notice disruptions in our thoughts, emotions, or behaviors. The following practices provide practical ways to restore harmony not through formal religious rituals, but through everyday actions that awaken, nurture, and strengthen each inner energy. Below are examples of how we can cultivate these spiritual forces within ourselves when they feel diminished or dormant.

OSHUN
Cultivating Oshun Energy
Passion, Joy, and Self-Worth

Oshun is the energy of love, sensuality, creativity, and self-esteem. When this force is balanced, you radiate confidence, attract positive relationships, and experience genuine joy. When weak, you feel unworthy or emotionally numb. When excessive, you may seek constant approval or lose yourself in pleasure.

Practical Ways to Strengthen your Oshun Energy

Beautify Your Environment and Body: Speak daily affirmations to yourself: "I am beautiful. I am worthy. I am enough." Adorn yourself with flowing clothing, jewelry, or beads that make you feel radiant. Keep your surroundings clean, vibrant, and filled with fresh flowers or beautiful objects. Light a candle simply because it pleases you.

Practice Gratitude for Simple Pleasures: Each day, notice one small joy: the warmth of sun on your skin, the taste of honey, the sound of water. Pause for three breaths and let yourself fully receive the pleasure. Keep a small jar where you drop notes of gratitude for beautiful moments.

Engage in Self-Care Rituals: Take time for rest without guilt. Prepare nourishing meals and eat them slowly. Create bathing rituals with natural oils, salts, and conscious presence. Move your body in ways that feel good gentle stretching, sensual dance, flowing movement.

Learn to Receive: When someone compliments you, simply say "thank you" without deflecting. Let kind words land in your heart. Practice accepting help, gifts, and affection. Remind yourself daily: "I deserve to receive."

Express Creativity Without Judgment: Paint, write, sing, or dance without worrying about the outcome. Let yourself play with color, sound, or movement. Create something just for the joy of creating. Silence your inner critic for 15 minutes and make something imperfect.

Connect with Water: Spend time near rivers, streams, or any flowing water. If you can't be near water, play recordings of rivers or rainfall. Add a small fountain to your home or workspace. When you bathe, imagine the water washing away unworthiness.

Wear Yellow and Gold: Incorporate these colors into your clothing, jewelry, or surroundings. Notice how they affect your mood and confidence. Hold a piece of gold or brass as a reminder of your inherent value.

Sweeten Your Inner Voice: Notice when you speak harshly to yourself. Reframe negative self-talk into loving affirmations. Speak to yourself as you would speak to someone you deeply love. End each day by naming one thing you appreciate about yourself.

Celebrate Yourself: Get dressed up and go out, even if alone. Choose an outfit that makes you feel confident and beautiful. Move through the world knowing you deserve to be seen. Dance, laugh, and enjoy your own company.

* * *

YEMAYA

CULTIVATING YEMAYA ENERGY
Nurturing and Emotional Depth

Yemaya is the energy of motherhood, emotional depth, protection, and unconditional love. When balanced, you nurture yourself and others with wisdom, maintain healthy boundaries, and move through emotions without drowning. When weak, you may feel emotionally disconnected or unable to receive care. When excessive, you may lose yourself in caring for others or become overwhelmed by feelings.

Practical Ways to Strengthen your Yemaya Energy

Practice Emotional Self-Care: Set aside time daily to check in with your feelings. Journal without editing let your emotions flow onto paper. Ask yourself: "What do I need right now?" and honor the answer. Create a safe space to cry when needed.

Offer Forgiveness: Write a letter of forgiveness to yourself, even if you don't send it. Release resentment toward others through ritual: write it down, then tear it up or burn it. Speak compassionate words to yourself about past mistakes. Remember that forgiveness is for your freedom, not for them.

Establish Healthy Boundaries: Practice saying no without over-explaining. Communicate your needs clearly and calmly. Notice when you feel drained by others and take space. Protect your energy as you would protect a child.

Allow Deep Feeling Without Drowning: When emotions arise, acknowledge them fully. Ground yourself while feeling feet on floor, hands on heart, deep breathing. Remind yourself: "I can feel this and still be safe." Let emotions move through you rather than holding onto them.

Connect with Large Waters: Visit the ocean, a lake, or a large river when possible. Sit by water and simply observe its movement. Listen to recordings of waves or ocean sounds. Collect stones or shells as reminders of her presence.

Practice Self-Mothering: Hold yourself as you would hold a distressed child. Speak gentle, reassuring words to yourself. Tend to your needs with patience and love. Wrap yourself in a warm blanket and offer comfort.

Create Nourishing Rituals: Prepare food with care and intention. Light candles as a way of honoring yourself and loved ones. Offer blessings to your home, your body, your day. Set a place at your table for ancestors or loved ones.

Honor Natural Cycles: Notice the phases of the moon and how they affect you. Accept that emotions have seasons some days full, some days empty. Be patient with your own growth and healing. Recognize that rest is as important as action.

Protect What You Love: Identify what and who matters most to you. Take concrete steps to safeguard your relationships and values. Speak up when something threatens your well-being. Create physical and emotional safety in your home.

* * *

Shango is the energy of leadership, passion, courage, and righteous anger. When balanced, you stand in your power, speak your truth, and protect what is right. When weak, you may feel passive, fearful, or unable to assert yourself. When excessive, you may become aggressive, domineering, or quick to anger.

Practical Ways to Strengthen your Shango Energy

Reconnect with Personal Power: Stand before a mirror for 2–5 minutes each morning. Place feet firmly on the ground, shoulders back, head high. Look yourself in the eyes and speak: "I am strong. I am capable. I am in control of my life." Feel the truth of these words in your body.

Take Daily Courageous Actions: Each day, do one thing that challenges fear. Speak up in a meeting when you usually stay silent. Assert a boundary you've been avoiding. Try something new that scares you a little. Notice your courage growing with each small act.

Move Your Body Powerfully: Engage in activities that awaken vitality: drumming, dancing, martial arts, weightlifting. Spend 15–30 minutes releasing physical energy. Feel your strength and aliveness. Let movement clear stagnant energy.

Channel Anger Constructively: When angry, write down everything you feel without editing. Shout into a pillow or release tension through physical movement. After releasing, ask: "What action would actually address this?" Take one constructive step to address the injustice or frustration.

Seek Justice in Small Ways: Notice situations where fairness is lacking. Take clear, calm action to address inequity. Speak up when someone is treated unfairly. Support those who are vulnerable. Let your actions reflect your values.

Use Symbolic Practices: Light a red candle when you need courage. Wear red clothing or beads to connect with his energy. Drum or listen to drumming for 5–10 minutes. Hold a stone that represents strength to you.

Meditate on Inner Fire: Sit quietly and visualize a flame in your chest. See it growing, warming, empowering you. Imagine this fire guiding your decisions with clarity. Let it burn away fear and hesitation.

Balance Power with Humility: Before reacting in conflict, pause and breathe. Ask yourself: "Am I acting from strength or ego?" Choose responses that protect, inspire, or help rather than dominate. Remember that true power serves, not controls.

Speak Your Truth: Practice saying what you really think, kindly but directly. Stop softening your words to make others comfortable. Let your voice be heard in matters that concern you. Trust that your perspective matters.

* * *

<u>OGUN</u>

CULTIVATING OGUN ENERGY
Willpower, Action, and Discipline

Ogun is the energy of focus, determination, and the ability to cut through obstacles. When balanced, you complete what you start, move through challenges steadily, and manifest your vision. When weak, you procrastinate, feel stuck, or lack follow-through. When excessive, you become rigid, work-obsessed, or burn out.

Practical Ways to Strengthen your Ogun Energy

Act with Purpose Each Morning: Before checking your phone, state your primary intention for the day. Choose one meaningful task and commit to completing it. Let this be your blade what cuts through everything else. Make your bed immediately to build momentum.

Complete What You Begin: Identify unfinished tasks and projects. Choose one and finish it this week. Notice how completion feels in your body. Train your will through follow-through.

Build Consistency: Dedicate time daily to a skill, habit, or craft. Even 15 minutes a day builds momentum. Let small, consistent efforts accumulate. Trust the power of showing up.

Break Obstacles into Steps: When facing a large challenge, write down each small action needed. Take one step at a time without looking at the whole mountain. Celebrate each small completion. Move steadily rather than rushing.

Balance Effort with Rest: Work intensely for focused periods, then pause. Schedule rest as part of your discipline. Notice when you're pushing too hard and ease back. Remember that the forge must cool.

Work with Your Hands: Engage in practical, physical tasks. Build, repair, craft, or create something tangible. Let your hands shape the material world. Feel satisfaction in visible results.

Create Order: Clear clutter from your workspace. Organize your tools and environment. Let your outer order support inner focus. Channel discipline through your surroundings.

Honor Your Tools: Care for the instruments of your work. Clean, sharpen, maintain what you use. Treat your tools with respect. Let this care remind you of your craft.

Take the First Step: When resistance arises, commit to just five minutes. Anyone can do anything for five minutes. Often, starting creates momentum. Let the first action led to the next.

* * *

CULTIVATING OBATALA ENERGY
Clarity, Peace, and Wisdom

Obatala is the energy of calm wisdom, ethical clarity, and pure consciousness. When balanced, you see clearly, act with integrity, and remain peaceful amid chaos. When weak, you feel confused, impulsive, or directionless. When excessive, you become cold, rigid, or overly detached.

Practical Ways to Strengthen your Obatala Energy

Practice Stillness Daily: Sit quietly each morning or evening for 5–10 minutes. Focus on your breath or a calming word. Let thoughts come and go without attachment. Return to silence again.

Seek Clarity Before Acting: When facing decisions, pause and breathe. List your options and possible outcomes. Reflect before responding. Let wisdom guide rather than impulse.

Reflect on Ethical Choices: Consider how your actions affect others. Journal about what aligns with your integrity. Ask yourself: "Is this fair? Is this kind? Is this true?" Let your conscience be your guide.

Cultivate Patience: Notice moments of frustration. Pause before reacting. Respond with calm words or thoughtful action. Let patience become your default.

Create Flexible Order: Organize your space and schedule. Leave room for spontaneity within structure. Let order support you rather than constrain you. Adjust when rigidity appears.

Wear White: Incorporate white clothing or accessories. Notice how it affects your mental state. Let white remind you of clarity and purity. Use color as a cue for calm awareness.

Spend Time in Silence: Take quiet walks without music or podcasts. Sit in a peaceful room with no distractions. Unplug from noise periodically. Let silence restore your mind.

Make Decisions from Calm: When triggered, pause before responding. Take three deep breaths. Ground yourself in your body. Choose from wisdom, not reaction.

Practice Detached Observation: Notice your thoughts without judging them. Observe your emotions without being controlled by them. Watch life arise and pass like clouds. Rest in the awareness behind it all.

* * *

<u>OYA</u>

CULTIVATING OYA ENERGY
Transformation and Change

Oya is the energy of change, transformation, and healthy endings. When balanced, you flow with life's transitions, release what no longer serves, and welcome the new. When weak, you cling to the past and fear change. When excessive, you create chaos and struggle to find stability.

Practical Ways to Strengthen your Oya Energy

Embrace Change as Growth: When change comes, ask: "What can this teach me?" Reframe challenges as opportunities. Remind yourself: "Every ending is a beginning." Trust that transformation brings strength.

Release What No Longer Serves: Declutter your physical space. Let go of toxic relationships or commitments. Drop habits that drain your energy. Practice letting go daily in small ways.

Welcome Endings: When something ends, acknowledge it consciously. Create a small ritual: write it down, thank it, release it. Open space for what wants to come. Honor endings as sacred.

Stay Flexible: Try new approaches to old problems. Be open to unexpected opportunities. Adapt when plans change. Let flexibility be your strength.

Trust the Process: Release control over outcomes. Trust that growth unfolds in its own time. Surrender to what you cannot control. Let life carry you forward.

Work with Breath: Practice deep, intentional breathing. Use breath to release tension. Let each exhale symbolize letting go. Stay present through the breath.

Allow Grief: When you need to grieve, give yourself permission. Journal, cry, or talk with someone trusted. Let emotions move through you fully. Grief clears space for new life.

Clear Space for the New: Before seeking something new, make room. Clear a drawer, a shelf, a corner. Let physical space reflect inner openness. Invite what's next by preparing for it.

Welcome Storms: When life gets turbulent, don't hide. Stand in the wind and let it move you. Trust that storms clear the air. Emerge renewed on the other side.

* * *

<u>ESHU</u>
CULTIVATING ESHU ENERGY
Communication and Choice

Eshu is the energy of crossroads, communication, opportunity, and conscious choice. When balanced, you communicate clearly, make wise decisions, and remain open to life's possibilities. When weak, you feel stuck, confused, or unable to choose. When excessive, you create chaos, self-sabotage, or manipulate situations.

Practical Ways to Strengthen your Eshu Energy

Remain Open to Learning: Ask questions instead of assuming you know. Explore topics outside your usual interests. Read books that challenge your perspective. Approach situations with curiosity.

Make Conscious Choices: Before acting, pause and reflect. Consider pros and cons. Check your intentions. Choose deliberately rather than reactively.

Communicate Clearly: Speak truthfully, especially in difficult conversations. Listen to understand, not just to respond. Ask for clarification when needed. Let your words match your meaning.

Embrace Unexpected Opportunities: Say yes to invitations you hadn't planned. Try something new on impulse. Let curiosity lead you. Trust that detours have purpose.

Laugh at Paradox: Notice life's ironies and absurdities. Tell jokes, especially at your own expense. Don't take yourself too seriously. Let humor lighten heavy moments.

Honor Crossroads: When facing important decisions, mark them. Light a candle, write your intentions, speak to them aloud. Leave a small offering to acknowledge the choice. Treat decisions as sacred.

Play and Explore: Try unplanned activities. Take a different route home. Explore new hobbies just for fun. Let spontaneity enliven your days.

Consider Multiple Perspectives: Imagine yourself in another's situation. Explore different ways to solve problems. Ask: "How might someone else see this?" Let multiple views enrich your understanding.

Solve Creatively: Do brain teasers or puzzles. Try improvisational exercises. Play games that require flexibility. Keep your mind nimble.

Celebrate Unexpectedly: When something goes well, reward yourself spontaneously. Create small, surprising celebrations. Let joy arise unpredictably. Cultivate delight in the unexpected.

Use Humor to Diffuse: When tension rises, find a funny angle. Share a light moment with others. Let laughter release pressure. Keep energy flowing with playfulness.

Reflect on Choices: Each evening, notice how small decisions rippled outward. Learn from what worked and what didn't. Appreciate the complexity of cause and effect. Navigate life's crossroads with growing wisdom.

* * *

<u>BABALU-AYE</u>
CULTIVATING BABALU-AYE ENERGY
Healing and Acceptance

Babalú-Ayé is the energy of healing, humility, and transformation through suffering. When balanced, you accept human limitations, learn from pain, and cultivate compassion. When weak, you deny pain or avoid vulnerability. When excessive, you identify too strongly with suffering or become resigned.

Practical Ways to Strengthen Babalú-Aye's Healing Energy in your Life

Acknowledge Your Wounds: Honestly notice your physical, emotional, or mental pain. Say to yourself: "It's okay to feel this." Recognize that wounds are part of your journey. Don't hide from what hurts.

Accept Human Limits: Acknowledge that mistakes, fatigue, and imperfection are natural. Treat yourself with understanding when you fall short. Release the demand for perfection. Embrace your shared humanity.

Seek Healing Without Demanding Perfection: Follow treatment, therapy, or self-care routines. Don't pressure yourself to recover instantly. Let healing unfold at its own pace. Celebrate small improvements.

Practice Compassion: Offer kindness to yourself when struggling. Extend compassion to others who suffer. Small gestures matter: a kind word, a moment of presence. Let suffering soften rather than harden you.

Honor Your Body's Wisdom: Listen to signs of fatigue, hunger, stress.

Adjust your activity when your body speaks. Nurture yourself with rest, nutrition, gentle movement. Treat your body as wise, not as an enemy.

Rest Without Guilt: When ill or exhausted, allow yourself to pause. Sleep, rest, recover fully. Understand that rest is part of strength. Let healing happen in stillness.

Learn from Pain: Reflect on difficult experiences. Ask: "What insight does this offer?" Let suffering teach you resilience. Grow without letting pain define you.

Cultivate Humility: Remember that everyone suffers. No one is immune to hardship. Let your own struggles connect you to others. Walk gently with your fellow humans.

Accept What Cannot Be Changed: Identify what is beyond your control. Practice surrendering to reality. Find peace in acceptance. Conserve energy for what you can influence.

* * *

<u>OCHOSI</u>

CULTIVATING OCHOSI ENERGY

Focus and Purpose

Ochosi is the energy of focused intention, precision, and intuitive aim. When balanced, you know what you're pursuing, stay on target, and trust your instincts. When weak, you feel scattered, unfocused, or miss opportunities. When excessive, you become obsessive or unable to adapt.

Practical Ways to Strengthen Ochosi's Energy in your Life

Set Clear Intentions: Each day, write down exactly what you want to achieve. Be specific: not "work on project" but "complete outline by noon." Let your intention guide your actions. Return to it when distracted.

Focus Your Attention: Work on one task at a time. Eliminate distractions: silence phone, close tabs. Give your full presence to what matters. Notice when your mind wanders and gently return.

Pursue with Precision: Break larger goals into specific steps. Complete each step carefully and deliberately. Quality matters more than speed. Let each action be aimed true.

Adapt When Needed: When circumstances change, adjust your aim. Don't cling to a target that no longer serves. Stay flexible within your focus. Let new information guide new direction.

Trust Your Intuition: Notice gut feelings about decisions. Allow inner knowing to guide you. Practice listening to subtle signals. Let instinct complement logic.

Spend Time in Nature: Walk in forests or natural settings. Observe birds, animals, the quiet movement of life. Sharpen your awareness through presence. Let nature teach you patience and attention.

Practice Patience: Pace yourself in pursuit of goals. Wait for the right moment to act. Stay calm even when results are slow. Trust that steady focus yields results.

Aim Before Shooting: Before acting, clarify your target. Ask: "Is this what I really want?" Check alignment with your values. Then move with confidence.

Observe Carefully: Notice details others miss. Pay attention to patterns and signs. Let observation inform your actions. See clearly before you act.

* * *

OLOKUN

CULTIVATING OLOKUN ENERGY
Depth and Mystery

Olokun is the energy of the deep unconscious, ancestral memory, and the mysteries beneath ordinary awareness. When balanced, you access inner wisdom, honor dreams, and remain comfortable with the unknown. When weak, you fear depth or avoid introspection. When excessive, you lose boundaries or become overwhelmed by the unconscious.

Practical Ways to Strengthen Olokun's Energy in your Life

Sit with the Unknown: Each day, spend time with questions that have no answers. Practice being comfortable with not knowing. Let mystery be enough. Cultivate patience with uncertainty.

Honor Your Dreams: Keep a journal by your bed. Write dreams immediately upon waking. Notice patterns, symbols, messages. Let dreams inform your waking life.

Respect Mystery: Accept that not everything can be explained. Allow curiosity without demanding resolution. Let wonder guide your exploration. Trust that some truths reveal themselves slowly.

Go Deep in Reflection: When journaling, don't stay on the surface. Ask yourself: "What's underneath this feeling?" Explore ancestral patterns in your life. Dive into the waters beneath awareness.

Create from the Depths: Paint, write, or make art without planning. Let unconscious material emerge. Don't judge what arises. Honor the deep source of creativity.

Practice Silence and Darkness: Spend time in quiet darkness. Let your eyes adjust to the unseen. Listen to what emerges in stillness. Trust the wisdom of the depths.

Honor Ancestors: Learn about your lineage. Set a small space with photos or mementos. Speak their names, tell their stories. Recognize their presence in your life.

Explore the Collective Unconscious: Study myths, symbols, and archetypes. Notice patterns across cultures and times. Recognize the deep currents we all share. Let this knowledge enrich your understanding.

Trust What Arises: When insights come from deep within, honor them. Don't dismiss intuition as imagination. Let the depths speak. Integrate their wisdom into daily life.

* * *

A Note on Balance

These practices are not about becoming any single energy exclusively. The goal is harmony each Orisha in its proper place, each force available when needed. Ogun helps you act, but Obatala helps you act wisely. Oshun helps you love, but Yemaya helps you love without losing yourself. Oya helps you change, but Babalú-Ayé helps you heal from change.

Notice which energies feel weak in your life and which feel excessive. Choose practices accordingly. Return to balance not once, but continually for life itself is constant movement, and balance is always a fresh choice.

INTEGRATION
The Inner Pantheon

Together, the Orishas form a living inner system a sacred balance of wisdom, strength, love, change, and awareness. When these forces are harmonized, the individual lives with clarity, purpose, and wholeness. No single energy dominates; each has its place and its season.

This inner pantheon is not static but dynamic. Different situations call forth different energies. Times of challenge may require more Ogun energy; times of loss may need more Yemaya's energy; times of opportunity may call for more Eshu's energy. The goal is not to suppress any energy but to allow each to flow freely and appropriately, guided by the wisdom of a clear Orí. When the inner pantheon is balanced, we are said to be in IRE in a traditional sense:

1. *Thought and action align*
2. *Emotion and reason cooperate*
3. *Individual needs and community responsibilities harmonize*

4. *Past, present, and future integrate*

5. *The divine presence shines clearly through one's life*

* * *

MANY VIEWS, ONE SACRED MYSTERY

In conclusion, the Orishas, whether understood as inner archetypal forces or independent divine beings, embody the flow of Olodumare's power through all creation. They govern nature, influence destiny, and connect humanity to the Divine. Existing both within us and beyond us, they are forces to be honored and understood. To walk the path of the Orishas is to seek harmony: within oneself, with nature, and in alignment with the sacred order of the universe. It is the recognition that the same divine energy that moves the stars and stirs the oceans also lives within the human heart. In this awareness, healing the self becomes part of healing the world, and honoring the Orishas becomes an expression of one's deepest truth. In this balance, the One Light reveals itself through many forms, and the Divine becomes knowable both in the world around us and in the depths of our soul.

* * *

CHAPTER 3

ANCESTORS AS GUIDES
THE ENDURING WISDOM OF YORUBA SPIRITUAL LINEAGE

In Yoruba cosmology, ancestors are far more than historical figures or distant memories. Known as *Egun,* they are conscious presences that actively shape the rhythms of the living world. They carry the spiritual DNA of families, communities, and nations, acting as a living memory of the lineage. Honoring them is not simply a ritual; it is a recognition of life's continuity and an acknowledgment that every individual is a thread in a vast tapestry woven across generations.

THE EGUNGUN
Embodied Memory and Masquerade

The *Egungun* are the collective spirits of ancestors, brought into the community through masked figures during ritual performances. When these figures appear in the village square, the spectacle is both theatrical and sacred. Each layer of fabric, each step in the dance, carries ancestral energy. Music, movement, and color transform the festival into a living archive: memory becomes movement, story becomes spirit, and the invisible becomes tangible. The Egungun masquerade reconnects the living with their origins. In a modern world where urbanization, technology, and migration fragment families and communities, these festivals serve as spiritual medicine. They remind participants that their lives are anchored in lineage, and that every joy, struggle, and triumph is part of a rhythm that began long before they were born.

Physically, the dance releases tension and invigorates the body. Psychologically, participation strengthens social bonds, fosters belonging, and encourages mutual support. Spiritually, the ritual creates a charged atmosphere in which ancestral presence is palpable, offering clarity, guidance, and renewal.

ANCESTRAL CONNECTION & SPIRITUAL AWAKENING

Honoring ancestors is not only about respect for the past it is a doorway to our own spiritual consciousness. Each living human carries the DNA of their ancestors, along with inherited spiritual potential. By consciously engaging with *Egun,* individuals awaken aspects of themselves encoded in their lineage, accessing intuition, resilience, wisdom, and guidance cultivated over generations. It is crucial to distinguish *Egun* from *Iwin,* or wandering spirits. While Egun are conscious, familial presences tied to lineage, Iwin are non-ancestral spirits that may be restless or seek attention but lack a direct family connection. Yoruba belief emphasizes honoring Egun because they are guardians of the family's spiritual and moral heritage. Engaging with Egun aligns one with life's continuity, reinforces ethical and spiritual patterns, and strengthens personal and communal identity. This practice serves both protection and empowerment. By recognizing and honoring ancestral lineage, one strengthens one's spiritual framework, attunes to subtle energies, and gains insight into the patterns that govern personal and collective life. It fosters groundedness, clarity, and conscious awareness of purpose and responsibility.

PSYCHOLOGICAL AND SPIRITUAL INTEGRATION

Ancestral veneration mirrors Carl Jung's idea of the collective unconscious. Honoring Egun engages inherited patterns, beliefs, fears, and habits that silently shape our lives. Ritual becomes a sacred form of self-reflection, helping us understand how the past influences the present. By recognizing these influences, we reconcile with history, release intergenerational trauma, and reclaim agency over our choices. Spiritually, connecting with ancestors strengthens continuity and purpose. Humans are participants in a lineage that transcends individual lifetimes. Physically, rituals often involve movement, drumming, chanting, or communal gatherings, which reduce stress, improve health, and foster vitality. Emotionally, the awareness that ancestors are present and protective provides comfort, courage, and resilience in a complex world.

MODERN APPLICATIONS
Why Ancestors Matter Today

In today's fast-paced, digital, and often fragmented world, honoring ancestors is more than cultural preservation; it is transformative wisdom. Ancestral awareness anchors individuals in a broader perspective, reminding us that achievements and struggles are part of an ongoing human narrative. It teaches patience, humility, accountability, and supports ethical decision-making and emotional resilience. Ancestral veneration also fosters creativity and innovation. Just as the Egungun translates memory into dynamic art, modern humans can channel ancestral wisdom into work, community-building, and problem-solving. By bridging past and present, the ancestors inspire insight, strategy, and vision informed by generations of lived experience.

HONORING ANCESTORS IN MODERN LIFE

Connecting with ancestors today is both spiritual and practical. Yoruba belief teaches that our DNA carries ancestral potential, and engaging with Egun awakens latent aspects of consciousness. The following practices make ancestral veneration accessible:

1. CREATE A SACRED SPACE

- Designate a small altar with photographs, heirlooms, candles, incense, or natural elements.
- Include objects symbolizing lineage or personal connection to ancestors.
- Maintain the space as a sign of respect and to invite energy flow.

- **Benefits:** Enhances mindfulness, daily connection, and spiritual focus.

2. DAILY OFFERINGS AND INTENTIONS

- Offer food, water, fruits, grains, or flowers.
- Speak aloud gratitude, challenges, or requests for guidance.
- Even small, consistent offerings build a spiritual dialogue.
- **Benefits:** Strengthens connection, encourages emotional release, and fosters gratitude.

3. MEDITATION AND REFLECTION

- Meditate on your ancestors, imagining their lives, struggles, and wisdom.
- Reflect on family patterns, strengths to emulate, challenges to transform.
- Journal insights to track spiritual growth.
- **Benefits:** Enhances self-awareness, integrates ancestral influence, and unlocks spiritual potential.

4. STORYTELLING AND MEMORY

- Share family stories or genealogical knowledge.
- Record or write them down to reinforce lineage.
- Recognize the lessons and values embedded in ancestral experiences.
- **Benefits:** Preserves cultural memory, strengthens identity, and nurtures intergenerational continuity.

CONCLUSION

Honoring ancestors bridges past and present, awakening hidden dimensions of consciousness, and connecting us to lineage wisdom. Through ritual, meditation, movement, and storytelling, we invite *Egun* into our lives, transforming ancestral memory into living guidance. By actively engaging with ancestors, we heal ourselves, strengthen communities, and consciously participate in the ongoing dance of life.

In doing so, we awaken latent parts of our own consciousness, access wisdom encoded in our bloodlines, and gain spiritual, psychological, and physical vitality. The ancestors remind us that we are never truly alone: we walk forward on paths illuminated by generations past, carrying their lessons, love, and enduring presence in every step.

* * *

CHAPTER 4

SPIRITS OF OPPOSITION
AJOGUN, ELENINI, AND THE HIDDEN LAWS OF BALANCE

Nature and Origin of Ajogun

In the vast cosmology of Yoruba spirituality, the Ajogun are not merely demons or evil spirits they are archetypal forces born from the fractures of cosmic balance. The very word *Ajogun* stems from Ajo (group) and *Igun* (adversary), implying a collective of oppositional energies that exist to challenge, test, and refine the human spirit. They are not creations of malice, but manifestations of imbalance: chaos given form so that harmony may once again be pursued. These entities embodiments of death (*Iku*), disease (Arun), loss (*Ofo*), and misfortune (*Epe*) move invisibly between the spiritual and physical worlds, pressing upon human lives to expose weakness, fear, and pride. Their presence is not random; they serve as mirrors through which we confront the unhealed parts of our being. Yet, their ultimate purpose is paradoxical to destroy illusions so that truth may emerge. To know Ajogun, then, is to acknowledge that disorder, too, is part of divine design.

Moral and Spiritual Alignment

The human soul is the eternal traveler moving through the vast field of cosmic tension forever suspended between harmony and chaos, light and shadow. Unlike the Ajogun, whose nature is fixed and unchanging, the human soul is fluid. It can rise toward divine awareness or fall into confusion, depending on the quality of its moral and spiritual choices. Within every human being lives the sacred breath of Olodumare, the Supreme Source, granting us the ability to reflect divine harmony through iwa pele gentle and noble character. Ajogun, as forces of disorder, vibrate on frequencies of fear, anger, envy, and pride. They are drawn to imbalance just as decay is drawn to neglect. When a person strays from their Orì their inner divine consciousness their energy becomes distorted. Pride replaces humility, greed dulls gratitude, and resentment erodes peace. In this state, the individual begins to resonate with Ajogun vibrations, becoming a vessel through which these disruptive forces may manifest.

Thus, Ajogun are not only external spirits of calamity they are also reflections of inner disharmony made visible in the world. Yet Yoruba philosophy provides a deeper understanding by distinguishing between the forces that confront us from outside and those that rise from within. These two categories Ajogun and Elenini represent the dual challenges that shape a person's spiritual journey through the physical world (Aye). While both are disruptive, they differ in their origin and operation: Ajogun are external adversities such as death (Iku), illness (Arùn), loss (Ofo), curse (Epe), and conflict (Oran). They move through the spiritual and physical worlds to test, challenge, or correct human imbalance. Ajogun often manifest as events, conditions, or spiritual afflictions that arise when a person's energy falls out of harmony through neglect of ritual, poor conduct, or violation of divine order. Elenini, in contrast, are internal adversaries that emerge from the human psyche and spirit. They are born from unresolved emotions jealousy, guilt, fear, resentment, or self-loathing. While Ajogun strike from the outside, Elenini grow quietly within, whispering doubt, distortion, and despair. If Ajogun are the storm that batters the body, Elenini are the tempest that consumes the mind.

The two are deeply interconnected. Inner turmoil invites outer disturbance; Elenini within can attract Ajogun without. Likewise, purification of the heart can repel both. A spirit weighed down by envy, anger, or bitterness becomes an open door for chaotic forces, while a heart anchored in humility, gratitude, and courage radiates a light that wards them off. True spiritual alignment is, therefore, a balance between the inner and outer worlds. It is not achieved by denying the presence of darkness but by mastering it by recognizing the seeds of Elenini before they mature into Ajogun. The goal is not to destroy darkness but to transform it into wisdom and clarity.

INTERACTION WITH HUMANS

Ajogun's influence upon human life is both intimate and impersonal. They enter through cracks unhealed wounds, spiritual negligence, or unbalanced emotions. They are, in essence, teachers of consequence. When ignored or misunderstood, they attach themselves, feeding upon fear and confusion. When recognized with wisdom and expelled through ritual, they dissolve, for their power lies only in the resonance we give them. Yoruba philosophy warns that we must never "feed" these entities with excessive fear or obsession. To fear them is to empower them; to face them in calm awareness is to neutralize their grasp. Hence, before any spiritual work, one must undergo ìwe a cleansing of the inner and outer self to ensure that the Ajogun find no place to dwell. Purity of intention is the greatest protection.

FATE AND FUNCTION

Ajogun serve a divine function in the grand order of existence. They are the guardians of equilibrium through opposition. Where humans see punishment, the cosmos sees correction. They ensure that those who deviate from spiritual order encounter experiences that lead them back toward balance. The wise understand that misfortune is not always condemnation it may be initiation. For the one who endures with humility and reflection, each trial becomes an alchemical fire transforming ignorance into wisdom. Thus, Ajogun are not enemies to be hated, but forces to be understood. Their role in the moral economy of the universe is to sharpen the soul, like friction sharpens the blade.

AFTERLIFE DIFFERENCE

In the continuum of existence, the fates of Ajogun and human souls diverge eternally. Ajogun are static they neither evolve nor devolve.

They remain forces, not persons, eternal instruments of correction within the cosmic mechanism. Human souls, however, are dynamic and aspirational. Yoruba philosophy speaks of various kinds of souls, each reflecting a stage in the soul's journey:

- *Pure Spirits have transcended moral duality, becoming luminous reflections of divine wisdom.*
- *Good Spirits continue to strive upward, shedding imperfections with patience and love.*
- *Impure and Straying Spirits wander in confusion, still attached to material illusions or desires.*
- *Guardian Spirits descend to guide and protect the living, serving as bridges between realms.*
- *Suffering Spirits undergo purification, burning away karmic residue through remorse and atonement.*

Unlike the Ajogun, these souls can evolve, ascend, and even become Orisha, divine intermediaries between God and humanity. A human soul may rise to divinity, but it can never descend to become Ajogun, for divinity's essence cannot be reversed.

PURIFICATION: RETURNING TO HARMONY

The path of purification is the human response to the presence of Ajogun. Cleansing (ìwe ara àti okàn) is not merely a ritual act it is a metaphysical realignment of vibration. It calls for the washing of the body, the clearing of the mind, and the softening of the heart. To purify oneself is to silence the noise within, where Ajogun whisper confusion. It is to reconnect with one's Orì (divine consciousness), invoking clarity through prayer, humility, and disciplined action. Ritual baths, sacred chants, offerings of light, and acts of kindness all function as spiritual disinfectants that restore balance. When we cleanse ourselves, we become uninhabitable to chaos. Ajogun lose their foothold, and the human soul reclaims its rightful rhythm with the divine order.

The struggle between harmony and chaos is eternal, yet not hopeless. Ajogun remind us that even darkness serves the light. Through them, the human soul learns vigilance, compassion, and self-knowledge. To live wisely is not to flee from adversity, but to purify oneself continually to remain a clear vessel for the divine spark within. In doing so, we transcend the reach of Ajogun and approach the radiance of the Orisha the perfected state of being that awaits every soul that dares to know itself fully.

SACRED RHYTHMS & TIMEKEEPING
PART II

CHAPTER 5

THE KOJODA

THE YORUBA FOUR-DAY SACRED WEEK

There comes a moment in every busy person's life when they pause and ask themselves: *Is this all there is?* You check your phone for seventeen notifications. Three back-to-back commitments await: a grocery list, a looming deadline, and a forgotten birthday. The day slips away before it truly begins, swallowed by the machinery of obligation. You collapse into bed, exhausted but unfulfilled, sensing deep down that you've been busy without ever being present. In a world ruled by the relentless tick of the clock and an endless stream of digital alerts, we've lost touch with the deeper meaning of time. We move from one task to the next, measuring our days by productivity rather than purpose. We have become masters of efficiency but novices in meaning. Our ancestors once measured life by purpose; in the modern world, losing this connection has contributed to widespread stress, disconnection, and illness.

TIME THAT BREATHES

The Yoruba people of West Africa have known something for thousands of years that our modern world has largely forgotten: time is alive. They called their calendar the *Kojoda*, meaning "may the day be clearly foreseen." It is one of humanity's oldest systems of sacred timekeeping. Unlike the modern calendar, a neutral grid overlaid with appointments and deadlines, the Yoruba calendar moves with purpose. It flows in harmony with something far deeper: the rhythms of our ancestors. At the heart of this calendar are the Orishas, sacred divinities central to

Yoruba life. The Orishas shape creation and reflect the deepest truths of the universe, as well as each person's purpose within it. They are not only forces in the natural world but also exist within every human being. Central to this wisdom is the Four-Day Sacred Week, a cycle so ancient and fundamental that it mirrors the very process by which things come into being. Each day carries its own energy, its own invitation, and its own type of inner work.

THE FOUR-DAY CYCLE
A Path to Self-Mastery

In the Yoruba calendar, called "Kojoda," each week consisted of four days, unlike the Gregorian calendar that we are familiar with, which has seven days. These four days held deep cultural and spiritual significance for the Yoruba people, with each day dedicated to a specific Orisha and a corresponding theme that guided the rhythm of life.

1. The first day was dedicated to the Orisha Obatala, who is associated with peace, wisdom, and purity. This day was considered a time for tranquility, reflection, and creating harmony both within oneself and the community. People observed this day by engaging in acts that fostered communal peace, such as helping others, volunteering, or contributing to the well-being of their surroundings. At the same time, it was a day to nurture personal peace of mind, whether through quiet reflection, meditation, or simply taking time to rest and restore one's own energy. In this way, the day balanced self-care with service to others, reinforcing the Yoruba principle that personal and communal harmony are deeply interconnected.

2. The second day was dedicated to the Orisha Orunmila, the deity of insight, wisdom, and divination. It was seen as a day for careful planning, thoughtful decision-making, and seeking guidance before taking action. This day encouraged individuals to reflect on their goals, consider possible outcomes, and make informed choices. Activities might include consulting divination, strategizing for personal or community projects, or

simply taking the time to think deeply about the next steps in one's life. In essence, the day was devoted to preparation, ensuring that actions taken on subsequent days would be purposeful and effective.

3. The third day honored the Orisha Ogun, the deity of iron, war, and labor. This day emphasized action, determination, and hard work, encouraging individuals to carry out their plans without delay. It was a time to apply the insight gained on the previous day, tackle challenges decisively, and transform intentions into tangible results. The day celebrated courage, effort, and persistence, reminding people that progress requires both energy and commitment.

4. The fourth day was dedicated to the Orisha Shango, associated with balance, justice, and reflection. This day provided an opportunity to review the accomplishments and lessons of the previous days, restore personal and communal equilibrium, and reflect on successes and setbacks. It was a time to harmonize one's actions, learn from experience, and prepare mindfully for the cycle to begin again, ensuring that the rhythm of the Yoruba week maintained its balance of planning, action, and reflection.

IN SUMMARY

1. The <u>first day</u> was dedicated to <u>Obatala</u> and was regarded as a day of peace, stillness, and inner calm.
2. The <u>second day</u> was dedicated to <u>Orunmila</u> and was seen as a time for insight, wisdom, and thoughtful planning.
3. The <u>third day</u> was dedicated to <u>Ogun</u> and represented action, a day for doing, building, and moving forward without delay.
4. The <u>fourth day</u> was dedicated to <u>Sango</u> and symbolized balance, a time to reflect on the previous three days and restore harmony.

This four-day cycle repeated continuously, forming a spiritual rhythm that harmonized reflection, planning, action, and review. Among the Yoruba, there is a saying: *"It is acceptable to delay something, but only until the third day, then you must act."* This wisdom emphasizes that balance and order are essential in life.

MONTHLY INTEGRATION

The four-day rhythm provides a powerful framework for daily life, but its wisdom extends further. As each month comes to a close, you can use this same cycle for a deeper reflection, a sacred check-in with yourself that honors all dimensions of your being. Find a quiet hour at month's end. Light a candle if it helps. Pour a glass of water. Sit with these questions, letting the energy of each domain guide your reflection.

1. EMOTIONAL & MENTAL WELL-BEING *(GUIDED BY STILLNESS)*

Begin by creating a moment of quiet. Settle into yourself before you begin any analysis. From this place of calm, ask:

- What helped me cope with stress this month? What made things harder?
- When challenges arose, how did I respond and how would I like to respond differently next month?
- What emotions did I avoid? Which ones did I welcome?

Why this matters: You cannot sort through confusion while you are still in the middle of it. True clarity requires a foundation of inner stillness. This section invites you to find that calm before examining your emotional world.

2. PHYSICAL WELL-BEING *(GUIDED BY DISCIPLINE)*

Now turn your attention to your body with honesty and care. This is not about judgment but about clear-eyed assessment. Ask yourself:

- What healthy habits did I consistently keep this month?
- What obstacles got in the way of caring for my body?
- What is one concrete change I can make to better support my physical health in the coming month?

- When did my body feel most alive? Most depleted?

Why this matters: The body responds to action, not just intention. Lasting change comes from small, consistent steps taken with discipline. This section helps you identify what is working and where a gentle adjustment is needed.

3. Social Well-Being (*Guided by Awareness*)

Bring your attention to the people in your life. Approach this reflection with balanced awareness, noticing both the light and the shadow. Ask yourself:

- Which relationships truly supported me this month?
- Where did I notice warning signs, imbalances, or drains on my energy?
- What is one action I can take to strengthen a healthy bond, and what is one boundary I need to set?
- Who am I neglecting? Who is neglecting me?

Why this matters: Healthy relationships require awareness. You cannot strengthen what you do not see clearly, and you cannot protect yourself from what you refuse to acknowledge. This section brings honest attention to your social world.

4. Intellectual Well-Being (*Guided by Curiosity*)

Shift your focus to your mind and its growth. Approach this with genuine curiosity, not pressure. Ask yourself:

- What did I learn this month, formally or informally?
- What topic, skill, or question am I most curious about for next month?
- What is one specific step I can take to feed my mind?
- When did my mind feel most alive? Most stagnant?

Why this matters: Learning is not just about accumulating facts. It is about staying curious, open, and engaged with life. This section honors the mind's need for fresh ideas and new understanding.

5. Environmental Well-Being *(Guided by Clarity)*

Look around at the spaces you inhabit each day. Your surroundings are not neutral; they are either supporting your peace or quietly undermining it. Ask yourself:

- How did my physical environment affect my mood and focus this month?
- What is one small change I can make to my home or workspace to improve my sense of calm?
- What space in my life feels most chaotic? Most peaceful?
- What does my environment say about what I value?

Why this matters: Outer order supports inner peace. When your space is cluttered or chaotic, your mind absorbs that chaos. This section invites you to create an environment that nurtures rather than drains you.

6. Spiritual Well-Being *(Guided by Wholeness)*

Now step back and look at the bigger picture. Spiritual well-being is not about any single practice it is about how you connect to something larger than yourself. Ask yourself:

- How did I nurture my spirit this month? Through prayer? Nature? Stillness? Community? Creativity?
- What spiritual practice do I want to deepen or explore in the month ahead?
- When did I feel most connected? Most disconnected?
- What does my soul long for right now?

Why this matters: You are more than your to-do list. You are more than your worries and ambitions. This section honors the part of you that longs for meaning, connection, and transcendence.

7. Gratitude *(A Practice for Every Day)*

Before moving into goal setting, ground yourself in appreciation. Gratitude is not a platitude it is a practice that reshapes how you see everything. Ask yourself:

- What am I most thankful for right now?
- Who or what brought me unexpected joy, comfort, or support this month?
- What challenge am I grateful for and what did it teach me?
- How can I carry more gratitude into my daily life?

Why this matters: What you appreciate appreciates. Gratitude shifts your focus from what is missing to what is present. It is the soil in which all growth occurs.

8. Monthly Goal Setting *(Guided by Vision and Action)*

Finally, bring together what you have learned and set your intentions for the month ahead. This requires both clarity of vision and commitment to action. Ask yourself:

- Which of my long-term and short-term goals did I make progress on this month?
- What specific steps and what kind of support helped me move forward?
- How did I track my progress and overcome obstacles?
- Based on all my reflections, what is my single most important intention for the new month?
- What one small action can I take on day one to honor this intention?

Why this matters: A goal without a vision is just a wish. A vision without action is just a dream. This section brings together the clarity of your insights and the discipline of your actions to create a path forward.

RETURNING TO THE RHYTHM

The Orisha calendar is not a system of rigid rules but an invitation to a relationship with time, with the divine forces that move through all things, and with yourself. The Yoruba elders say that destiny is not a fixed point you arrive at but a path you walk one day, one cycle, one season at a time. When you align with the rhythm of the days, you align with something larger than yourself. You stop fighting the current and start moving with the river. And in that movement, you discover what you were always meant to find: not more hours, but more *life* in the hours you have.

Ase.

CHAPTER 6

THE 13 ORISHA MOONS
EMBODYING ANCESTRAL
TIME IN THE MODERN WORLD

The *13 Orisha Moon Calendar* is a spiritual reconstruction an interpretation of what may have once been the ancient lunar cycles of the Yoruba people, harmonized with today's twelve-month Gregorian calendar. It bridges past and present, inviting modern practitioners to reconnect with a rhythm of time rooted in nature, spirituality, and cosmic order. In Yoruba cosmology, time was never viewed as a mechanical progression of numbers but as a sacred pulse a living dialogue between the divine, the earth, and human consciousness. The moon's phases marked transitions not only in agriculture and ritual but in the inner life of the soul. Each full moon carried the energy of a specific *Orisha*, offering a season of reflection, transformation, and alignment. This reconstructed calendar honors that tradition by assigning each Gregorian month (and a rare thirteenth moon) to an Orisha whose essence reflects the spiritual themes of that time. Through this rhythm, the moon becomes more than a celestial event it becomes a guide for living with awareness and harmony.

January Moon: Obatala — Purity and Wisdom
Begin the year in clarity and peace. Cleanse your body, home, and mind.
Focus: forgiveness, mental clarity, balance.

February Moon: Sopona (Babalú-Ayé) — Wellness and Protection
Tend to your health and spirit. Seek cleansing and humility.

Focus: healing rituals, protection, purification.

March Moon: Yemoja — Emotional Renewal
The waters of the Mother bring emotional healing and rest.
Focus: fertility, nurturing, spiritual baths.

April Moon: Oshun — Love and Prosperity
Celebrate beauty, pleasure, and abundance.
Focus: attraction, joy, heart healing.

May Moon: Egungun — Ancestral Remembrance
Honor your lineage. The ancestors walk with you.
Focus: remembrance, offerings, dream guidance.

June Moon: Orunmila — Destiny and Insight
Seek the wisdom of destiny. Clarify your purpose.
Focus: divination, reflection, foresight.

July Moon: Eshu — Open Roads and Choices
Doors open for the brave. Speak truth and make your move.
Focus: communication, crossroads, opportunity.

August Moon: Shango — Power and Renewal
Thunder awakens courage and balance.
Focus: justice, confidence, empowerment.

September Moon: Ogun — Work and Victory
Forge ahead with discipline and determination.
Focus: productivity, strength, perseverance.

October Moon: Oya — Change and Ancestral Winds
Embrace transformation and release.
Focus: endings, rebirth, shadow integration.

November Moon: Iyaami / Osoronga — Mystery and Power
The Mothers test your strength. Honor the mysteries.
Focus: intuition, sacred feminine, protection.

<u>**December Moon: Obaluaye — Healing and Completion**</u>
End the year in humility and release.
Focus: healing, forgiveness, closure.

13th Moon: Oṣù Olódùmarè — Divine Source and Unity
A rare moon of transcendence. Enter silence and merge with the Source.
Focus: enlightenment, prayer, unity with Spirit.

* * *

A Living Reconstruction

This reconstructed lunar calendar is not a fixed historical record but a living spiritual framework a way to remember what may have once been a sacred rhythm guiding the Yoruba people. By applying it to the Gregorian year, we honor ancient wisdom in a modern world. To live by the 13 Orisha Moons is to restore time to its original purpose: not a chain of days to endure, but a cycle of divine energy to embody. Each moon becomes a teacher, each season a lesson, and each phase a mirror of the soul's eternal journey toward balance and awakening.

* * *

THE ORISHA PATH TO SELF-MASTERY

PART III

CHAPTER 7

THE HEALING WATERS OF OSHUN
EMOTIONAL RENEWAL AND SELF-LOVE

In the golden light of dawn, where rivers shimmer and groves whisper with life, the spirit of Oshun moves like a gentle song. She is the breath of beauty in all things, the pulse of love that runs beneath creation. Yoruba tradition teaches that when the world was first forming, the other Orishas tried to build without her. They believed that strength and power alone could create life. But the earth remained barren. Rivers ran dry. Harmony withdrew from the world. Only when Oshun poured her sacred waters across the land did life return. Flowers blossomed. Laughter filled the air. Even the gods, who had trusted only in force, remembered the sweetness of compassion. Her story holds a timeless truth: *without love, the universe becomes a machine. Without tenderness, creation loses its rhythm.* Oshun's presence reminds us that true healing begins not with resistance, but with flow. Like water, emotions are meant to move to be felt, honored, and released. When we dam our feelings, pain stagnates. When we let them flow with honesty and care, they become medicine.

THE LEGENDS OF OSHUN

Oshun's myths offer timeless guidance for the human heart. One story tells of the great Orisha Oduduwa, who sought to shape the earth. He sent his children to raise mountains and dig rivers, to plant forests and fill the seas. Yet despite their efforts, nothing thrived. The land remained lifeless. It was Oshun who approached, carrying a pot of honeyed water. She poured it over the barren soil and sang a song of tenderness. Instantly, flowers bloomed. Rivers swelled. Laughter returned to the world. Even the sternest Orishas understood at last: power alone could not create life. Only love could. Another tale speaks of Oshun's river as a healer of hearts. A mortal man, burdened by grief so heavy it bent his spine, came to her waters. Oshun appeared before him, shimmering in gold, and guided him to immerse his hands in the river. As his tears flowed, the water absorbed his sorrow, leaving behind clarity and peace. He learned what Oshun teaches all who come to her: *emotions are not obstacles to strength, but conduits of wisdom. Embracing vulnerability is itself a form of courage.* These stories remind us that tenderness is not weakness. Love and compassion are forces powerful enough to shape life itself.

Honoring Emotion as Sacred Flow

To walk with Oshun is to discover that emotion is not weakness, but wisdom.

- *Tears are sacred libations that cleanse the soul.*
- *Anger, when understood, reveals where our boundaries must stand.*
- *Sadness, when embraced, opens the heart to deeper compassion.*
- *Joy, when shared, multiplies itself and blesses all it touches.*

Oshun invites us to become listeners to the tremor in our chest, to the longing behind our silence, to the quiet voice of our inner river. She teaches that *love begins where judgment ends.* When we stop condemning our own feelings, we begin to nurture the garden of our inner world. Her waters demonstrate a profound truth. They do not fight the stones in their path; they flow around them with grace, polishing them over time, yet never losing their direction toward the sea. This is the nature of true strength, not rigidity, but a softness that endures. By embracing our emotions rather than repressing them, we return to the natural rhythm of the spirit: balanced, flowing, and whole.

Many people grow up believing that sensitivity is weakness, or that loving oneself is selfish. These beliefs dry up the inner river, leaving the soul parched and desperate for validation from others. Oshun restores the original truth: *emotional awareness is strength, and self-love is the foundation upon which all other love is built.* When we acknowledge our pain, we permit it to transform. When we express our feelings without shame, we allow our nervous system to release tension and restore harmony. Modern psychology calls this emotional regulation. Yoruba tradition refers to it as the sacred art of honoring the waters within oneself. On a philosophical level, Oshun's lessons reveal that life is not about control, but about attunement. Rigidity creates suffering. Flexibility and surrender cultivate harmony. Softness and compassion are not passive qualities; they are active forces that sustain life and make transformation possible.

RITUALS AND PRACTICES FOR EMOTIONAL RENEWAL
These simple practices can help you embody Oshun's wisdom and bring emotional healing into your daily life:

WATER RITUAL

Fill a bowl with water. Speak aloud the emotions you wish to release: grief, anger, fear, or anything else you have been holding. Then dip your hands into the water, imagining it carrying away what no longer serves you. Pour the water into the earth as an offering.

SELF-LOVE MIRROR EXERCISE

Stand before a mirror, look into your own eyes, and speak these words aloud: *"I am worthy of love. My feelings are valid. I honor my heart."* Repeat until you feel the truth of them settle in your chest.

Reflect on questions similar to the following:

- *What part of me needs tenderness today?*
- *Where have I been denying my emotions, and what would happen if I let them flow?*
- *What would it feel like to forgive myself for something I still hold against me?*

NATURE CONNECTION

Spend time near a river, stream, or any moving water. If none is available, sit in the rain or run water over your hands. Allow yourself to mirror Oshun's flow, releasing, receiving, and renewing.

A Mantra for Emotional Renewal

Short poems and prayers can reinforce your connection to Oshun's healing energy. Use these words in meditation, as journaling prompts, or as daily invocations:

OSHUN, FLOW THROUGH ME

Oshun, flow through me, golden and bright,
Cleanse my heart in your gentle light.
Wash away sorrow, fear, and despair,

Fill me with courage, tender and fair.
Let your waters guide my way,
Turn my tears to joy each day.

Oshun, river of wisdom and grace,
Mirror the beauty that shines in my face.

* * *

THE STAGES OF RENEWAL

Emotional healing unfolds like a journey along a river. These stages can help you navigate the process:

1. **Recognition** – *Notice which emotions you have been ignoring or suppressing.*
2. **Acceptance** – *Allow all your feelings to exist without judgment or resistance.*
3. **Release** – *Use ritual, journaling, or meditation to let your emotions flow.*
4. **Integration** – *Embrace the wisdom your emotions have revealed. Let them cultivate resilience, self-love, and inner harmony.*

This process transforms reflection into action, creating a spiritual practice that continually renews the heart.

RETURNING TO THE RIVER
A Guided Contemplation

Find a quiet space where you will not be disturbed. Close your eyes and bring your awareness to your breath. In your mind's eye, picture a river at dawn. Its surface shimmers with gold as the first light touches the water. Hear its gentle murmur as it speaks with the stones along its banks. Feel its coolness on your skin. This river is not separate from you. It is Oshun's presence, flowing within your own heart.

ASK YOURSELF SOFTLY

- *What emotions have I been holding back? What would it mean to let them flow?*
- *How can I show myself gentleness today?*
- *Where does a part of me still hurt, and how might love for myself, for others, for life bring healing to that place?*

Breathe deeply. Allow your heart to soften. Let forgiveness and compassion rise naturally, like leaves carried by the current. This is Oshun's river, washing through you, cleansing, renewing, and awakening you to your own profound worth.

* * *

SPIRITUAL ACTIVITY
Oshun's Sunlight Vitality & Energy Bath

- **Purpose:** To renew spiritual energy, awaken vitality, and strengthen the life force within.

INGREDIENTS

1. **Marigold petals (Calendula) or orange peels** – for protection and vitality
2. **Cinnamon sticks** – for warmth and energy
3. **Lemongrass or lemon peels** – for clarity and rejuvenation
4. **Honey** – for nourishment and sweetness
5. **Spring water** – if using water from a natural source, be sure to **boil and purify it** to remove any harmful contaminants, toxins, or bacteria

INSTRUCTIONS

1. Place the herbs and cinnamon in a pot of water and bring to a boil to release their essence.
2. Remove the solid particles, and allow the water to cool to a comfortable temperature for bathing.
3. **Invocation:** Before entering the bath, recite the mantra above " *Oshun, flow through me golden and bright"* While reciting, ask Oshun to bless and infuse the bath water with her energy.
4. **During the Bath:** Immerse yourself or pour the water over your body, focusing on cleansing, renewal, energies flowing into your body
5. **After the Bath:** Gently pat yourself dry and wear all white to preserve the bath's spiritual effects and maintain the purity of the energy.

Oshun teaches that healing is not found in control, but in surrender to love. Her golden waters are a mirror, reflecting the radiant, fluid, and resilient truth of your own being. Every act of self-care is a prayer whispered to Oshun. Every moment of compassion you extend to yourself creates a ripple in her sacred stream. She does not ask for perfection, only for your presence, fully felt and fully alive. When you learn to love yourself as she loves all creation, you transform. You are no longer just someone seeking healing. You become a source of healing in the world. Flow gently. Feel deeply. Love fully. For in the river of your own heart, Oshun is waiting golden, smiling, and endlessly alive.

CHAPTER 8

OBATALA AND ITUTU
THE SACRED POWER OF COOLNESS

THE CONCEPT OF ITUTU
The Sacred Power of Coolness in Yoruba Spirituality

In Yoruba thought, one of the most important qualities a person can possess is *itutu*. The word literally means "coolness," but its meaning goes far beyond temperature. Itutu describes a calm and balanced mind, mastery over one's emotions, and a steady, clear spirit. It is the ability to remain composed in difficult situations, to think carefully before acting, and to respond with thoughtfulness rather than impulse. Those who possess *itutu* are also believed to have greater *ase* a kind of power or influence over life than those who do not. They speak gently, act with purpose, and move through the world with quiet strength. Their presence brings peace, not only to themselves but to everyone around them. In traditional Yoruba society, elders and people in positions of authority are expected to display a high degree of mental calmness and clarity in their interactions. This trait is often cultivated long before a person assumes such a role, forming the foundation of the wise and respected leadership required to guide their communities.

COOLNESS AS SPIRITUAL BALANCE

The Yoruba worldview sees the universe as alive with powerful spiritual energies. These forces can nurture growth and create opportunity, but they can also disrupt and destabilize when approached without care. **Itutu** serves as a stabilizing force, an inner compass that helps a person regulate their emotions and maintain harmony with these energies. When emotions such as anger, jealousy, or pride take control, a person is said to become "hot." This agitation is believed to throw them out of alignment with their destiny. Yet there are moments in life and in social situations when such emotions are necessary to express. The key is to remain in control. A restless, uncontrolled mind leads to poor decisions, unnecessary conflict, and disconnection from deeper purpose. By contrast, a cool mind allows for thoughtful responses, sound judgment, and deliberate action. For this reason, Yoruba culture places great value on patience, humility, and careful speech. Exhibiting coolness is believed to enable a person to remain spiritually in control of a situation and to retain their **Ase**, their spiritual power and influence. The outer state of a person's emotional stability is also thought to reflect the inner state of the **Ori**, or the soul. To clarify, when Yoruba teachings speak of the head being "hot" or "cool," they are referring to a person's emotional state and behavior, not the actual physical temperature of the body.

THE ORISHA OBATALA

In Yoruba cosmology, the head is understood in two distinct aspects. The **Ori-inu**, or "inner head," is the seat of a person's consciousness and the carrier of their destiny, chosen before birth. The **Ori-ode**, or "outer head," is the physical, visible head. Among the Yoruba, the head is considered the most sacred part of the body, housing both spiritual essence and destiny. For this reason, it is regarded as deeply disrespectful and taboo to touch another person's head without permission. This reverence also explains why many Yoruba people wear head coverings, as an act of protection and honor for the sacred Ori within.The Orisha Obatala is intimately connected to the head. As the deity of purity, peace, and calmness, Obatala exemplifies the serenity and clarity that humans are encouraged to cultivate. By following Obatala's example, we learn that a clear and nurtured Ori allows a person to navigate life with integrity, make thoughtful and deliberate decisions, and remain aligned with their spiritual destiny. Maintaining a calm head is therefore both a spiritual necessity and an essential quality for daily life.

When the Ori becomes "hot," disturbed by anger, anxiety, or impulsive behavior, judgment clouds, and confusion rises, and decisions stray from higher purpose. Cooling and calming the head becomes essential.

TRADITIONAL PRACTICES FOR COOLING THE HEAD

Several traditional practices exist to restore coolness to the Ori. Some may be performed individually, while others require the guidance of a trained priest or priestess.

Feeding and Strengthening the Ori

This ritual is performed to honor and support a person's **Ori-inu**, the inner head. Offerings may include cool water, coconut, honey, shea butter, or fish. Because the ritual involves specific spiritual procedures, it should be performed under the guidance of a trained Yoruba priest or priestess. When done improperly, it can create spiritual imbalance rather than restore harmony. In Yoruba diaspora traditions, particularly in *Santería,* a similar ceremony exists called *Rogación de Ori,* meaning "prayer or petition to the head." This ritual is performed to cool or calm the Ori when it becomes "hot," and to strengthen a person's connection to their spiritual destiny so that life decisions remain aligned with divine purpose. The ceremony usually begins with prayers and invocations asking for the blessing of the *Orisha* and the person's Ori. The individual typically sits or kneels while the priest prepares a small ritual space. A white cloth is often placed over the head or shoulders to symbolize purity, peace, and spiritual cooling. During the ritual, sacred substances may be placed on the head, including coconut pieces, cocoa butter (orí), shea butter, *cascarilla* (powdered eggshell), and sometimes cool water or milk.

These materials symbolize cooling, clarity, and spiritual balance. The priest applies them while reciting prayers or traditional chants. In some cases, two halves of a coconut are briefly placed on the head and wrapped with a white cloth. This is believed to calm the Ori and absorb spiritual agitation. After the ritual, the offerings are respectfully removed and later disposed of according to tradition, often in nature.

The person may also receive guidance afterward, such as wearing white clothing for a period of time, resting, and avoiding conflict to preserve the "coolness" of the Ori. The purpose of a *Rogación de Ori* is to restore balance when a person feels emotionally or spiritually unsettled, and to strengthen their connection to their destiny and spiritual guidance.

Spiritual Baths

A spiritual bath may be prescribed to cleanse negativity from the entire body, not just the head. In Yoruba spiritual practice, these baths are used to restore balance, calm the mind, and remove spiritual disturbances that may affect a person's well-being or alignment with their destiny. The baths are typically prepared using water infused with specific plants, herbs, and other natural ingredients. The particular plants used often have symbolic or spiritual associations with a person's **Ori**, with the Orisha *Obatala* who is strongly connected with clarity, purity, and calmness or with guidance received through divination from a trained priest or priestess. Common ingredients may include cooling herbs, leaves, flowers, or other natural substances believed to promote peace, protection, and spiritual clarity.

The bath is usually prepared by steeping the plants in water, allowing their spiritual essence to infuse the mixture. During the bathing process, prayers or intentions may be spoken, asking for purification, protection, and guidance. The person may pour the water over their body or gently wash with it, often focusing on the head and upper body while reflecting on the intention of spiritual cleansing and renewal. Spiritual baths are commonly recommended during times of stress, emotional turmoil, spiritual imbalance, or after negative experiences. They may also be prescribed following divination, when it is believed that a person needs spiritual cleansing or strengthening. The purpose of the bath is to restore inner calm, remove spiritual burdens, and help the individual return to a state of clarity and balance.

Other Personal Practices

In addition to guided rituals, personal practices such as meditation, prayer, reflection, and mindful breathing can help restore balance and allow the **Ori** to regain its natural clarity. In Yoruba thought, the state of the head mirrors the condition of the soul. Maintaining a cool Ori is not merely emotional composure; it is a sacred responsibility. Daily habits that cultivate awareness and self-discipline are also considered essential. Practices such as setting aside quiet time for contemplation, expressing gratitude, journaling one's thoughts, or engaging in acts of service help reinforce inner harmony. Attention to speech and behavior speaking gently, acting intentionally, and avoiding unnecessary conflict further supports the cooling and strengthening of the Ori.

Mastering Inner Energy

Itutu is not about suppressing emotions. It is about mastering them. Emotions carry power. When uncontrolled, they can disrupt relationships, fracture communities, and undermine spiritual work. A person who embodies itutu does not deny what they feel. They pause before responding. They observe their emotions without being consumed by them. They choose actions that preserve harmony rather than disrupt it. In spiritual practice, this calmness is essential. Rituals, prayers, and acts of devotion require focus and composure. A restless mind struggles to connect with the sacred. Coolness creates the internal stillness necessary for genuine awareness, enabling action that is deliberate, compassionate, and effective. Serenity, in this sense, is not detachment from the world but mastery within it, a calm clarity that strengthens the self and aligns it with spiritual purpose.

Coolness in the Modern World

The contemporary usage of the word "cool" may have originated from the Yoruba concept of itutu. When we describe someone as "cool" or "chill" today, we often mean they appear calm, confident, and composed, especially under pressure. This modern concept reflects the Yoruba idea of inner balance and self-possession. True coolness, in both the traditional and modern sense, is not about style or appearance. It is about mastering one's own emotions and having the strength and clarity to face life's difficulties with grace. To be truly "cool" is to embody the wisdom of itutu: emotional stability, grounded presence, and the capacity to act with intention rather than reaction.

LIVING WITH ITUTU
Practices for Daily Life

Cultivating *itutu* is a lifelong practice. It requires mindfulness, patience, and discipline. The following practices are drawn from Yoruba tradition and adapted for modern life. They offer concrete ways to embody the philosophy of coolness.

- **Pausing for a moment**: When stress or anger arises, it is important to take a moment, take a pause. This single moment interrupts the impulse to react and restores clarity. Often a person may take a deep breath or count to five during the pause.
- **Observing Emotions:** When an emotion rises, notice it without judgment. Name it quietly: "This is anger. This is fear." Observe where it lives in your body. By watching the emotion rather than being swept away by it, you create space for deliberate response.
- **Choosing Gentle Speech:** take a moment and think before you speak, you can ask yourself three questions: Is it kind? Is it necessary? Is it true? If the answer to any is no, choose silence or gentler words. Speech carries power; use it with care. Once you put it out there you cannot take it back.
- **Water Practice (Omi Tutu)**: Wash your face or hands with cool water. As you do, set an intention: "I release agitation. I restore clarity to my Ori." Let the water carry away what disturbs you.
- **Creating a Cool Space:** Designate a corner of your home for calm reflection. Keep it simple and uncluttered. A white cloth, a glass of water, a quiet seat. Make it a place free from conflict

and distraction, a physical anchor for inner stillness. You can even dedicate this place to the honor and worship of your Ori.

Practices for Good Character

- **Evening Reflection:** At the end of each day, ask yourself two questions: Where did I keep my cool? Where did I lose it? Observe without harsh judgment. Learn from both successes and struggles.
- **Practicing Humility**: Accept mistakes openly. Listen to others with genuine curiosity. Remain grounded in both success and failure. Humility cools the spirit and reduces unnecessary conflict.

Grounding Practices

- **Barefoot Earth Walk**: Walk slowly on grass, sand, or soil. Feel the textures beneath your feet. Silently repeat: "I release tension. I receive clarity."
- **Nature Sound Focus**: Sit quietly outdoors. Listen deeply to the sounds around you: wind, birds, water, leaves. Let each sound anchor your attention and calm your mind.

Daily Anchors

- **Morning Stillness:** Before looking at your phone, before speaking, before planning, sit in silence for five minutes. Let this be the first taste of your day: not noise, but stillness.
- **White Cloth Reminder**: Carry a small white cloth or stone in your pocket. When you feel heat rising, touch it. Let it remind you: "I can return to coolness. I can return to stillness."
- **Evening Release**: At day's end, visualize placing your anxieties on a white cloth. Fold it closed. Whisper: "I have carried this enough. Now I release it." Return your mind to stillness before sleep.

Returning to Stillness with Obatala

Obatala, the Orisha of clarity, purity, and patience, teaches that peace is not something we achieve. It is something we remember. By sitting quietly, allowing thoughts to settle like sediment in clear water, the mind regains its natural calm. The mountain does not argue with the storm. It simply remains. When anxiety returns, and it will, do not see it as failure. Pause. Breathe. Touch the earth. Visualize stillness. The anxious mind is not an enemy; it is a teacher, showing you exactly where you need more patience, more stillness, more of the sacred coolness that has always been your birthright. Peace is not the absence of motion but harmony within it. Master the mind, and you master life itself, embodying purity of thought, gentleness of heart, and the power to act wisely. The mountain of stillness has never left you. It has only been waiting, patient as Obatala himself, for you to remember the way home.

* * *

CHAPTER 9

OYA AND THE WINDS OF TRANSFORMATION
THE PAUSE BEFORE THE STORM

Among the Orishas, Oya is the one who brings the lessons our hearts often resist the most. Her teachings arrive through change, sometimes sudden, sometimes unsettling, but always necessary. She sweeps away what has grown stagnant, making room for something new to emerge. Through disruption, Oya teaches us to let go of control, find courage in uncertainty, and trust life to move forward instead of clinging to what has already passed. In Yoruba tradition, Oya is also called *Yansa*, "mother of nine," a name that points to her rule over the nine mouths of the Niger River. Spiritually, it reminds us that transformation can enter our lives through many channels, often when we least expect it. Oya's influence is everywhere.

She governs the marketplace not only the place where goods are exchanged, but the symbolic space where identities, values, and circumstances constantly shift. What was important yesterday might not hold the same weight today. Spiritually, her marketplace represents the exchanges we make within ourselves. When we go through change, we trade old parts of ourselves, our certainty, familiar identities, or relationships, for something we could not have gained in any other way. Transformation is not just loss; it's an exchange. She is also the guardian of the cemetery gates and has a close connection with *Egungun*, the ancestral dead. Here, her work becomes most profound: overseeing the movement from one state of being to another. Her role is not to block passage but to make sure transitions are complete and authentic. If someone cannot fully grieve an ending, they remain at Oya's gate, caught between the past and the future. Her guidance ensures that endings are real so new beginnings can take root. Her influence in the Odu Ifa is extensive, particularly in *Osa Meji*, the Odu that governs sudden and unexpected change. Here, transformation often comes like lightning fast, decisive, demanding an immediate response.

One story tells of a prosperous town that resisted Oya's winds, determined to preserve what they had built. But the valley they inhabited soon flooded. Those who followed the wind, letting it guide them, found themselves on higher ground and safe. Transformation rarely announces itself in advance; it asks us to trust the unseen currents of life. Oya's work is intimately linked with *Shango,* one of the most revered Orishas. Often considered her husband and spiritual partner, Shango governs thunder, fire, authority, and power, while Oya rules winds, storms, and transformation. Together, they bring renewal and purification. Oya clears away the debris of what no longer serves, while Shango revitalizes stagnant energy and ensures change is purposeful. Invoking both teaches that true transformation requires both release and grounded power, Oya ending what must end, and Shango guiding the new beginnings.

One of Oya's most difficult lessons is learning to let go. Her winds sweep away only what has served its purpose, old relationships, jobs, or beliefs, making space for new opportunities and growth. These endings can feel sudden or unsettling, but they are not punishments; they are openings. By clearing away what is finished, Oya creates room for what is waiting to emerge, often in ways we cannot yet imagine. Learning to trust this process means accepting uncertainty and trusting your spirit guides will help you through even when it challenges your sense of comfort or control. Oya teaches us how to transform and survive. Oya's Transformation often unfolds in four stages:

1. **Observation:** Paying attention to the warnings of approaching change.
2. **Destabilization:** Allowing the wind to shake loose what was never meant to stay.

3. **Void:** Navigating the space between your past self and your future self.
4. **Reconstruction:** Finding your footing and creating a new way forward in the aftermath.

The most confusing stage is often the third stage, when the old situation, life, or circumstances have ended, but the new situation has not yet taken a definitive form. At the center of Oya's influence is the work of release. Those who move consciously through Oya's transformations often discover something powerful: what they truly are cannot be destroyed by circumstance. In the process of change, they discover their inner strength.

ACTIVITY ONE

Letting Go and Inviting Growth

Take a journal and make two columns. In the first, write what you're holding onto that no longer serves you: grudges, fears, unhealthy habits, or relationships. In the second, write what you want to invite into your life: courage, honesty, freedom, and self-compassion. Reflecting on these daily helps release what no longer serves you and makes space for what does.

ACTIVITY TWO

Guided Visualization

Close your eyes and imagine a gentle wind moving through your heart and mind. Ask yourself, "What am I holding onto that I need to release?" Picture the wind carrying away these burdens. Feel yourself becoming lighter. As the storm settles, ask, "What will I place in this new space?" Visualize clarity, renewal, and openness. Stand renewed, free, and ready for what comes next.

Purpose: An offering to Oya to facilitate the release of the old and invite transformative spiritual growth.

Materials

- **9 Incense Sticks or Cones:** Oya's sacred number is nine; ensure you have exactly nine to align with her energy.
- **Lighting Tool:** Matches or a lighter.
- **Safety Vessel:** A fireproof holder, a bowl of sand, or a cleared patch of bare earth.
- **Optional Libation:** A small offering of water, rum, or cornmeal.

Choosing Your Incense

Select your nine sticks based on your specific needs. You can mix and match these to reach a total of nine:

- **For Transformation & Change:** Dragon's Blood, Cinnamon, or Patchouli.
- **For Ancestral Connection:** Myrrh, Copal, or Frankincense.
- **For Protection & Clarity:** Sandalwood, Frankincense, Juniper, or Pine.
- **For Courage & Vitality:** Cinnamon, Clove, or Patchouli.
- **For Communication & Divination:** Frankincense, Benzoin, or Bay Leaves.

The Ritual Steps

1. Prepare the Space: Go outside where the wind can move freely. Clear a small "altar" area on the ground. Ensure the spot is completely free of dried leaves, grass, or debris. Oya rules the storm and the winds, so while we invite her breath, we must keep the physical fire contained and safe.

2. Set Your Intention: Take several deep breaths to ground yourself. Focus on what you are ready to let go of and the growth you wish to invite in. Recite the following prayer (or use your own words):

"Oya, Lady of the Storm and the Marketplace, I honor your winds. I release what no longer serves me and welcome your gift of transformation. With these nine sparks, I ask for your protection, courage, and guidance. I offer this smoke to you."

3. Feed the Wind: Light your nine incense sticks or cones. As the smoke begins to rise, visualize the wind catching it and carrying your prayers directly to Oya. See the "old" energy being swept away by her gusts, leaving your spirit clean and ready for the new.

4. Closing the Ritual: Stand in silence for a moment, feeling the air around you. Give thanks. If you brought a libation (water, rum, or corn-meal), pour it onto the earth now. Allow the incense to burn out completely on its own, or extinguish it safely if you cannot stay. Oya is known for her swiftness and her role as the "Queen of the Gates." By offering nine scents to the wind, you are effectively asking for her guid-ance and help.

* * *

CHAPTER 10

THE WARRIOR WITHIN
OGUN AND THE DISCIPLINE OF ACTION

Before the first path was ever made through the forests of existence, there was only thick wilderness, dense, tangled, and impossible to cross. Long ago, the Orishas looked at this wild place and hesitated. No one knew how to create a path through such strong resistance. The way forward was hidden by confusion and doubt. Then Ogun appeared. He was strong, determined, and skilled with tools and fire. Holding his machete, he stepped forward where no one else dared to go. With each swing, he cut through the thick forest. But he was not only cutting trees, but he was also breaking through fear, hesitation, and the unknown. Through Ogun's hard work and sacrifice, humanity learned the power of progress: the courage to act, to shape the world, and to turn raw life into something meaningful. His iron represents determination made solid. His fire represents the strong will that brings order out of chaos. Ogun's path is not easy. It requires endurance and effort. Through struggle, raw potential becomes skill and mastery. This chapter explores Ogun not as a force of violence, but as a symbol of focused action and discipline, the power that helps us clear a path through the challenges of our own lives.

THE IRON HEART OF PROGRESS
The Sacred Art of Cutting Through

Ogun is known as the Orisha of iron, war, and labor. But his meaning goes deeper than this. In Yoruba spiritual tradition, iron represents transformation. Before iron tools existed, people used softer materials that could not easily clear land, build cities, or protect communities. The discovery of iron allowed humans to shape their environment instead of simply adapting to it. Ogun represents this power. He gives people the strength to say, "I will overcome this challenge. I will not give up." His machete is not meant for aggression but for freedom. It cuts through procrastination, self-doubt, and distraction. It helps people move forward when they feel stuck. Ogun is also the protector of warriors, hunters, and all who work with metal, from blacksmiths to drivers. His influence is present whenever effort meets resistance. Every time you choose discipline over comfort, keep going when you want to quit, or face a difficult task, you walk the path of Ogun.

THE MACHETE LIST

1. *Take a journal and draw a line down the middle of a page.*
2. *On the left side, write "The Tangled Forest." List problems or challenges in your life that feel overwhelming or unclear. This could be a delayed project, a difficult conversation, or a habit you want to change.*
3. *On the right side, write "One Swing at a Time." For each problem, list one small action you can take today or this week to improve it.*
4. *You do not need to solve everything at once. Ogun teaches that progress happens one step at a time. Choose one action and commit to it today.*

* * *

STRENGTH COMES FROM STRUGGLE

Ogun teaches that struggle is not punishment; it is growth. Although people often seek comfort and avoid difficulty, true strength develops through challenge. Every piece of iron is shaped by fire and pressure. The human spirit grows in the same way. Each challenge you face is like a forge shaping you. Pressure and difficulty are not barriers to growth; they create it. Without resistance, strength cannot exist. Without testing, purpose cannot be revealed. Ogun represents discipline and focused effort. He is both a warrior and a builder. His tools can destroy, but they can also create and protect. Like a surgeon's tool, his power can heal when used wisely. He teaches that real power is guided by purpose. Strength must be used carefully and wisely. Sometimes we must act, and sometimes we must wait. True mastery comes from knowing the difference. Ogun does not fight without reason; he acts to clear a path, protect others, and build a better future.

THE IRON PLEDGE

Find a small piece of metal, such as a key, nail, or coin. Hold it in your hand and notice its weight and strength. Remember that it was once raw material shaped by heat and pressure.

Say aloud: *"I am being shaped by my struggles. I will face challenges with strength and patience. I am not being broken, I am being strengthened."* Keep this object with you as a reminder that difficulty helps you grow.

PSYCHOLOGICAL INSIGHT
Turning Hardship into Discipline

Psychologically, Ogun represents the inner strength that turns hardship into self-discipline. Modern life often encourages people to avoid discomfort, but growth requires effort. Each time you complete a difficult task, keep your promises, or push through challenges, you strengthen yourself. Discipline is not punishment; it is commitment to becoming your best self. It helps turn goals into reality. For people who feel stuck or powerless, Ogun's energy can be especially helpful. Anxiety and depression often create feelings of helplessness. Ogun teaches that strength is built through small actions. By setting goals, staying consistent, and facing challenges, people develop confidence and control over their lives. From this view, difficulties become teachers. Each challenge reveals hidden strength and builds endurance.

JOURNAL PROMPT: THE FORGED SELF

1. Think about a difficult experience that helped you grow.

2. What pressure or stress did you face?
3. How did it shape you?
4. What strength or wisdom did you gain?
5. Then write a letter from your future self, the stronger version of you, to your present self. What advice or encouragement would they give?

* * *

THE TWO SIDES OF POWER
Destruction and Creation

Ogun carries a machete, but he is also a blacksmith. This shows his dual nature. Iron can destroy, but it can also build. Fire can burn, but it can also create tools. The result depends on how the power is used. This is an important lesson. Anger, determination, and strong action are not automatically bad. They can be used for harm or for growth. Your focus can become an obsession or mastery. Your strength can protect or control others. Ogun asks you to think about your intention. Why are you acting? What are you building? Are your actions helping or harming?

ACTIVITY: THE INTENTION CHECK

- ***Before making an important decision, ask yourself:***
- *Is this action necessary, or am I reacting emotionally?*
- *Who will benefit from this action?*
- *Will this action create clarity or confusion?*
- *You can write your answers in your journal if you choose to do so for future reference.*

* * *

THE PATH THROUGH THE FOREST

Ogun encourages action, not passivity. He calls you to face your challenges directly. Close your eyes and imagine standing before a thick forest. This forest represents your fears and problems. You cannot see a path. Now imagine holding Ogun's iron blade. It represents your discipline and commitment. With each breath, imagine cutting through the forest. The path opens slowly, one step at a time.

- ***Ask yourself the following:***
- *What am I avoiding that needs to be done?*
- *What habit or skill do I need to strengthen?*
- *How can this challenge help me grow?*

* * *

WALKING MEDITATION

If possible, walk slowly in a quiet place. With each step, imagine moving forward on a newly cleared path. Repeat quietly: "I act. I'm clear. I move forward."

LIVING WITH OGUN'S ENERGY
You can practice Ogun's discipline every day.

- **Daily Task:** Each morning, complete the task you most want to avoid.
- **Focused Work Time:** Set aside time each day for uninterrupted work on your goals.
- **Action Space:** Create a small space with objects that represent strength and effort.
- **Affirmation:** "I create my own path through action."
- **Physical Practice:** Make slow, strong arm movements as if cutting through obstacles.
- **Mindful Awareness:** When touching metal objects during the day, remember your strength and commitment.

THE PATH YOU LEAVE FOR OTHERS

Ogun's greatest gift is not just clearing the path, but creating a way for others to follow. Every act of discipline and persistence helps not only you, but also those who come after you. When you accept challenges instead of resisting them, you begin to see life as a place of growth. Difficulties build strength. Failures teach lessons. Struggles shape your character. Ogun's message is simple: keep moving forward, even when the path is unclear. Each step clears the way ahead. The challenges you face are not your enemies; they are teachers helping you become stronger. The path is before you. The tool is in your hand. The question is simple: will you take the first step?

* * *

CHAPTER II

THE MESSENGER AT THE CROSSROADS

Any serious discussion of *Esu* sometimes also spelled *Eshu,* must begin by correcting a widespread misunderstanding that has persisted for centuries. During the colonial period, particularly in the 1800s, Christian missionaries deliberately equated Eshu with the devil. This was not merely an innocent error of translation or interpretation, it was a calculated strategy. By labeling Eshu as "Satan," missionaries aimed to undermine the Yoruba religious system, discredit its priests, and discourage the local population from maintaining their spiritual practices. This tactic served both to convert people to Christianity and to erode the social and moral structures embedded in Yoruba society. The effect of this colonial distortion has been long-lasting.

Over time, the idea that Eshu is malevolent spread far beyond the missionary texts and even permeated popular understanding, leading some practitioners and observers to approach him with fear, suspicion, or outright avoidance. Yet, a careful study of *Ifa* and the broader Yoruba corpus reveals a completely different reality: Eshu is not evil, he is not a tempter, and he is not the antagonist of moral goodness. In Yoruba cosmology, *Eshu is the indispensable messenger of the spiritual world.* He mediates between humans and the *Òrisa,* carrying prayers, offerings, and messages in both directions. Every ritual, every divination, and every act of spiritual communication passes through Eshu. Without him, the flow of *Ase,* (spiritual power), would be blocked. In essence, he ensures that the intentions of humans reach the divine and that divine guidance can reach the human realm.

His roles are complex and multidimensional. He is the guardian of crossroads and thresholds, the enforcer of divine order, and the teacher of wisdom through paradox, challenge, and discernment. His actions often appear unpredictable or mischievous, but in the Yoruba understanding, this is not malevolence, it is a reflection of the intelligence and balance of the universe. He tests humans, highlights choices, and ensures that destiny unfolds according to divine law. Because of his crucial role, Eshu is known by many titles and descriptors that reflect his functions and attributes, including the following:

1. **Alaaaro** – the one who carries messages
2. **Ojise Orun** – the messenger of heaven
3. **Atoka** – "The One Who Opens the Way."
4. **Jagunlabi** – "Born to Fight," pointing to his role in testing humans and enforcing justice.
5. **Oroboke** – "The Enforcer of Rules and Morality" in some oral traditions.

These names emphasize Eshu's role in *movement, communication, and connection.* Crucially, Eshu is neutral. He does not favor "good" or "bad" people, his responsibility is simply to deliver messages exactly as they are given. A messenger who alters the message loses trust and effectiveness. This neutrality carries an important lesson: in *Ifa,* the universe does not rely on a deity who constantly judges human behavior. Instead, it functions through *natural consequences.* Actions produce results, and Eshu, along with the other **Orishas**, ensure that the flow between cause and effect is preserved, maintaining balance and harmony in the world.

* * *

1. **Pay Attention** – Eshu often interrupts routines or habits to make people notice what they might be ignoring. These interruptions are not punishments, they are reminders that awareness cannot be avoided. As Ifa says: *"Whoever tries to forget Eshu will find that Eshu has not forgotten them."*

2. **Actions Have Consequences** – Eshu does not reward or punish anyone on his own. Instead, he makes sure that every choice naturally leads to its result. Honest actions bring good outcomes, and careless or harmful actions bring problems.

3. **Prepare Before Moving Forward** – Life does not open paths on its own. Success, growth, or insight requires preparation, thought, and clear intention before starting a new project, journey, or spiritual work.

4. **Communication Works Both Ways** – Eshu carries messages to the gods and brings guidance back to humans. A message only works if the person is ready to receive it.

5. **Life Can Be Complicated** – Many situations have more than one possible outcome. This is reality, not trickery. A wise person accepts complexity instead of oversimplifying problems.

6. **Respect and Authority Must Be Earned** – Eshu is honored first in rituals not because he demands it, but because his role is essential. True authority comes from skill, knowledge, and action, not titles or status.

7. **Be Sincere in Rituals** – Offerings and ceremonies only work when they are genuine. Empty gestures have no effect. Your character and honesty form the foundation of spiritual work.

8. **Face Your Own Challenges** – Spiritual guides help others, but they must also face their own problems honestly. Ignoring personal lessons can create issues in the guidance they give to others.

* * *

Proverb: "Corn cannot be cooked without water. Sacrifice cannot be completed without Eshu." **Meaning:** *Any spiritual work requires offerings to Eshu; without him, the work is incomplete or may not succeed.*

Proverb: "Eshu does not chase the lazy; he waits at the threshold." **Meaning**: *Opportunities come to those who prepare and act; Eshu opens the way, but effort is required.*

Proverb: "You cannot carry a message past Eshu without truth." **Meaning:** *Honesty and sincerity are essential in spiritual practice and daily life.*

Proverb: "Where Eshu walks, the world tests you." **Meaning:** Challenges are part of the natural flow of life; Eshu's presence highlights them to teach awareness.

Proverb: "Eshu opens the door, but you must walk through it." **Meaning:** Guidance is offered, but effort and choice are yours.

Proverb: "A gift to Eshu is the seed that makes your work grow." **Meaning:** Offering respect and attention to Eshu strengthens the success of any endeavor.

The Many Faces of Esu

Studying Eshu changes the person who practices Ifa. It teaches people to become more comfortable with life's complexity and encourages them to look honestly at their own thoughts and actions. Over time, this study deepens a person's relationship with the Orisha and helps develop humility. In Ifa, true authority does not come from titles or status. It grows from service, knowledge, and understanding. Part of this understanding comes from recognizing that Eshu has many different forms, often called *paths* or *caminos*. Each path reflects a different side of his personality and his role in the world. Some paths of Eshu are playful and lighthearted, while others appear as wise teachers, fierce protectors, or guardians who maintain spiritual balance. In the Yoruba tradition, it is often said that Eshu has *201 paths*. This number symbolizes that Eshu can appear in many situations and guide people through many kinds of challenges throughout life. Some of the commonly known paths of Eshu include:

Eshu Ananki – A female path of Eshu who lives in the forest and works closely with the Orisha Oya. She is known for healing with *ewe,* or sacred herbs.

Eshu Agbanuke – Known as the Eshu of clairvoyance. He protects Babalawos from people who come with harmful intentions and works closely with the Orisha Orunmila.

Eshu Ala Lu Ban – The opener of roads who helps people move forward in life and find better opportunities.

Eshu Abaile – A path of Esu who receives *ebbo* (spiritual offerings), understands their purpose, and helps deliver them to the correct spiritual destination.

Eshu Aye – This path walks along the seashore and is closely connected to the Orisha Yemaya, the mother of the ocean. He is associated with the conch shell and is said to know the desires of the entire world.

Eshu Afra – A path that comes from the Arará people of Dahomey. He works closely with the Orisha Asojano, who is connected to illness and healing. Esu Afra helps open the roads to remove sickness and epidemics.

Eshu Bi – A path connected to crossroads and difficult lessons. He is known for delivering harsh but necessary teachings when people refuse to listen or learn.

Eshu Odara – His name means "the one who brings goodness." He works with Babalawos and Orunmila to make sure offerings are properly delivered and turned into blessings.

Eshu Alaguana – A strong warrior path of Esu known for quick action and sharp judgment.

Eshu Elegba (Eleguá) – The well-known guardian of crossroads who opens and closes spiritual paths and carries messages between humans and the Orisha.

Eshu Aje – The path connected with wealth, prosperity, and success in business.

Eshu Laroye – A playful and joyful path of Esu who teaches through humor, laughter, and clever tricks.

Eshu Onibara – The trader and negotiator who rules over speech, bargaining, and exchange.

These many paths show that Eshu is not limited to one role or personality. Instead, he reflects the many ways life moves, changes, and communicates.

CONCLUSION

Honoring Eshu is more than performing a ritual. It is understanding his role in the structure of reality. Eshu represents communication, awareness, and the link between action and consequence. A practitioner who truly understands these principles becomes better at guiding others and examining their own life. The road is always open for those who prepare it.

* * *

CHAPTER 12

SACRED STORIES OF THE ORISHAS

SACRED STORIES OF OBATALA

OBATALA'S PEACEFUL VICTORY

In a kingdom ruled by fear, people lived in silence. The king was powerful but harsh. His anger controlled everything, and even small mistakes could lead to punishment. Because of this, people stayed quiet and avoided attention. One day, a stranger wearing white came to the marketplace. He was calm, gentle, and kind. He listened to people when they spoke and treated them with respect. Being around him made people feel less afraid. Slowly, they began to talk again and feel some peace returning to their lives. The king heard about the stranger and became angry. He thought this man was weakening his control over the kingdom. So he ordered him brought to the palace. The stranger stood before the king calmly and did not argue or resist. The king saw this as disrespect and had him imprisoned. After this, the kingdom began to fall apart. Fear returned even stronger, now joined by confusion and misfortune. Crops failed, problems spread, and the people suffered. Soon after, the king became seriously ill. No healer could cure him, and his condition grew worse each day. In desperation, he called for a diviner. The diviner listened and said, "Your sickness is connected to your actions. The only person who can heal you is the man you imprisoned." The king realized he had made a serious mistake. Weak and humbled, he ordered the stranger to be released and brought to him. When the man in white returned, he showed no anger or revenge.

He remained calm, just as before. The king asked for forgiveness and begged to be healed. The stranger responded with compassion, and the king slowly recovered. After this, the king changed how he ruled. He made the man his chief spiritual advisor. The stranger helped guide the kingdom with wisdom, peace, and balance instead of fear. Over time, the kingdom became peaceful and extremely prosperous, more so than before.

Spiritual Insight: *Fear may control people for a time, but it ultimately destroys both the ruler and the kingdom. Compassion, humility, and the willingness to admit mistakes restore balance and bring true strength. Peace and wisdom create lasting prosperity where force and anger cannot.*

* * *

The Burden of Perfection

Obatala once decided that the world should be perfect. He walked through towns, correcting everything he saw. He straightened crooked paths, reshaped uneven land, corrected speech, and disciplined behavior. At first, people were grateful. But soon, something changed. The laughter disappeared. The unpredictability of life faded. Everything became orderly, but lifeless. Children stopped playing freely. Artists stopped creating boldly. Even the wind seemed hesitant. Obatala stood in the center of a silent town and realized something important. Perfection had removed life. So he stepped back. He allowed crooked paths to remain. He allowed people to stumble, to learn, to grow. And slowly, life returned, messy, vibrant, real as it was originally.

Spiritual Insight: *Life is sacred not because it is perfect, but because it is alive, changing, and imperfect.*

* * *

The White Cloth That Covered All

During a time of conflict, villages turned against each other. Disputes grew into violence. Obàtálá descended quietly, carrying a large white cloth. He walked into the center of the battlefield and spread the cloth across the ground. "Step onto it," he said. One by one, warriors from both sides stepped forward. On the cloth, they removed their weapons. On the cloth, they spoke rather than fought. The whiteness beneath their feet reminded them of something deeper than conflict, something shared. When the cloth was lifted, the fighting had ended. Peace, like the cloth, had covered them all.

Spiritual Insight: *When people remember what they share, conflict dissolves; peace begins where separation ends.*

* * *

SACRED STORIES OF ESHU

THE TWO FRIENDS AND THE HAT THAT CHANGED EVERYTHING

Two close friends lived in neighboring villages. They shared food, stories, and trade. Nothing could divide them. One day, Eshu walked between their villages. He wore a hat that was red on one side and black on the other. As he passed the first friend, the man said, "Did you see that stranger? His hat was red!" Later, Eshu passed the second friend, who said, "No, his hat was black." Confused, the second friend confronted the first. "You are lying," he said. "It was black." "No," the first insisted, "it was red." The argument grew. Words became accusations. Accusations became anger. Soon, the friendship broke. Later, Eshu returned. He walked between them again. "This hat," he said, turning it slowly, "is both red and black." The two friends stood frozen. They realized too late: Truth depends on where you stand, and what you assume, but Eshu did not fix the damage. He only revealed how it happened.

Spiritual Insight: *Partial truth, when held without humility, becomes a source of division.*

* * *

THE OFFERING THAT WAS PLACED LAST

A man once prayed to the Orìshas, asking for success in his life. He prepared offerings for many spirits, but he placed Eshu's offering last. He thought it did not matter. "I will honor him too," he said, "after the others." He completed the ritual and waited for blessings. But nothing in his life moved forward. Confused, he returned to the diviner. The diviner listened carefully and said, "You fed the spirits of many houses, but ignored the door." The man did not understand. So the diviner explained: "No path opens unless Eshu allows it." The man returned and corrected his offering. This time, he placed Eshu first. And slowly, everything that had been blocked began to move. Not because Eshu changed, but because the path finally opened.

Spiritual Insight: *Before anything can grow, flow, or succeed, the path to it must first be open.*

* * *

THE MARKET OF MISUNDERSTOOD WORDS

There was once a busy marketplace where people traded more than just goods. They also traded words, promises, agreements, and deals were made every day. In this marketplace, there was a spirit named Eshu who often walked through the crowd. He didn't change what people said, but sometimes he influenced how their words were understood. One day, a merchant told a buyer, "I will deliver tomorrow." The merchant said it quickly, without much certainty. He wasn't completely sure he could keep the promise. As Eshu passed by, something subtle shifted in how the words were heard. The buyer heard strong confidence, as if the promise was guaranteed. But the merchant had only meant, "I will try." The next day, the goods did not arrive on time. The buyer felt betrayed and became angry. "You lied to me," he said. The merchant defended himself. "I didn't lie. I only said I would deliver tomorrow. I never promised for sure." Soon, the disagreement grew into a serious conflict. Neither side could understand the other. Eshu stood nearby and watched everything quietly. Finally, he stepped forward. "You both heard the same words," he said, "but you did not hear them the same way." The marketplace went completely silent. After that day, people in the market began to speak more carefully. They learned to choose their words better and to make sure they were truly understood. Because

they realized something important: Meaning is not only in what is said,
but also in how it is understood.

Spiritual Insight: *Words do not carry meaning on their own, people assign meaning based on what they expect to hear.*

* * *

THE CHILD AT THE CROSSROADS

A child once stood at a dirt crossroads where two paths split in different directions. One path was wide, smooth, and familiar. It led toward a nearby village where life felt safe and predictable. People there worked steady jobs, followed routines, and avoided risk. It was a place where nothing surprising usually happened. The other path was narrower and uneven. It disappeared into the hills and forest. No one could see far down it. People said it led to uncertainty, but also to new places, new skills, and new experiences. It was harder, and there were no guarantees. The child stood between the two, unable to decide. After a while, a traveler appeared beside them. It was Eshu, though he looked like an ordinary wanderer resting on the road. "Why do you hesitate?" he asked. "I don't know which path is right," the child said. "One feels safe. The other feels scary." Eshu nodded as if he understood perfectly. "Both are right," he said. The child looked confused. "How can both be right if they go in different directions?" Eshu walked to the first path. "This one gives comfort. You will be protected, and life will be steady. But you may stay the same for a long time." Then he walked to the second path. "This one gives a challenge. You may struggle. You may fail. But you will change. You will grow." The child felt torn. "I still don't know what to do." Eshu stepped back. "That is not my decision." The child looked at the two paths again. They thought about their life so far, how everything had been predictable, how they often wondered what else the world had to offer, and how part of them felt tired of staying in the same place. The safe road felt comforting, but also small. The unknown road felt frightening, but also full of possibilities. After a long silence, the child finally spoke. "I don't want to stay the same forever." Then they took a breath... and stepped onto the narrow path. It was not an easy choice. The ground was uneven, and the forest ahead looked dark. But as they walked, they felt something new: fear mixed with excitement, and uncertainty mixed with freedom. Eshu watched quietly from the crossroads. He said nothing, but he smiled. The child continued forward on the harder path not because it was guaranteed to be better... but because they chose growth over comfort, and discovery over certainty.

Spiritual Insight: *Life does not give certainty before choice; clarity comes after commitment.*

* * *

SACRED STORIES OF OGUN

The Path That Did Not Exist

In the beginning, when the world was still wild and unshaped, there was no clear path between the heavens and the earth. The orisas looked down at the land below. It was beautiful, but impossible to reach. The thick forest stretched endlessly. Vines twisted like living walls. No road could be seen, no passage made. One by one, the orisas tried to descend. But each time, they failed. Finally, they turned to Ogun. He did not speak much. He simply stood, holding his iron tools, machete, blade, and fire-forged strength. Without ceremony, he descended. The forest resisted him. Branches grabbed at him. Roots tangled beneath his feet. But Ogun did not stop. He cut, He cleared, He carved a path where none existed before. Blood mixed with sweat, and sweat mixed with soil, and where he walked, the world opened. When he reached the earth, the others followed the path he created. They called him the opener of the path, but Ogun did not celebrate. He simply looked at the trail behind him and understood something: Every path forward requires something to be cut away.

Spiritual Insight: *Nothing meaningful becomes accessible without something being cut, released, or overcome.*

* * *

There came a time when Ogun was called to war. Not for conquest, but for protection. He fought with unmatched strength. His Iron tools obeyed him like a living extension of his will. Where others hesitated, he advanced. Where others retreated, he struck forward. The war ended, but Ogun did not return the same. The battlefield had entered him. The silence of peace felt foreign now. When he tried to return to his home, people stepped back. Not out of hatred, but fear. They saw him not as a protector, but as something too powerful to hold. Ogun realized something painful: The closer one comes to destruction, the harder it is to return to softness. So he turned away and walked into the forest alone. There, he became both guardian and exile. A protector who could no longer fully belong to what he protected.

Spiritual Insight: *What you fight to protect can change you so deeply that returning to "before" is no longer possible.*

* * *

The Iron That Learned Hunger

In a distant village, people once depended on Ogun's tools; his iron gave them farming, hunting, and building, but over time, they forgot the source. They began to believe the tools belonged to them alone. They used iron without respect. Without ritual. Without gratitude. At first, nothing changed. But slowly, iron began to fail them. The tools broke. Weapons dulled. Machines collapsed, and confusion spread. A wise elder said, "You have taken the gift, but forgotten the giver." So they went to the forest and called Ogun's name. No answer. They brought offerings, but still no response. Only when they returned humility, acknowledging what they had forgotten, did the forest shift. Ogun appeared, not angry, just distant. "You used my body," he said, "but ignored my spirit." Then he turned and disappeared into the trees again. From that day, the people never used iron without remembrance.

Spiritual Insight: *When people separate a gift from its source, the stability of that gift eventually breaks down.*

* * *

THE BLADE THAT TAUGHT ITS OWNER

A young warrior once came to Ogun seeking power, "I want to be strong," he said. "I want no one to defeat me." Ogun studied him. "Strength is not what you think it is," he said. But the young man insisted, so Ogun gave him a blade. A perfect blade, sharp, balanced, and obedient. "At first," Ògún said, "it will obey you. But later, it will teach you." The young man laughed and left. At first, everything was easy. He won battles quickly. He became feared. But over time, something changed. The blade no longer felt like a tool; it felt like a demand. It required discipline. Control. Awareness. When the young man grew careless, the blade became unstable in his hands. Eventually, in a moment of arrogance, he swung without thought, and the blade turned the lesson back onto him. When he returned to Ogun, injured and humbled, the orisha said only: "You asked for strength, but refused responsibility."

Spiritual Insight: *You do not simply wield power, power also shapes how you must live in order to hold it safely.*

* * *

THE IRON THAT REFUSED TO STAY SILENT

There was a time when a kingdom became corrupt. Leaders lied. Justice was ignored. The weak were crushed. The people prayed for change, but nothing moved. Deep in the earth, iron began to stir. Tools became heavy in the hands of craftsmen. Weapons refused to function for unjust purposes. The Smiths were confused. One night, Ogun appeared at the forge. He placed his hand on the iron. "This land is unbalanced," he said. "What will you do?" they asked. Ogun did not answer directly. Instead, every unjust blade dulled. Every corrupt tool was cracked. Every weapon that served oppression fell apart. But tools used for protection remained strong. The message was clear: Iron remembers intent, and Ogun does not serve cruelty.

Spiritual Insight: *What is used for harm eventually loses its strength; what is used for protection retains it.*

* * *

SACRED STORIES OF SHANGO

THE DRUMS THAT SUMMONED THE STORM

In a distant town, a terrible drought had lasted so long that people were starting to forget what rain even felt like. The rivers had dried up, the fields were cracked and empty, and even the air felt heavy and exhausted. The people prayed for rain, but nothing changed. Only one man still remembered the name of Shango, the thunder king. He was a drummer. Every night, he sat alone and played rhythms as a prayer, dedicating each beat to Shango. His drumming echoed through the dry town, steady and strong. At first, nothing happened. The sky stayed clear and empty. But still, he continued. Night after night, beat after beat, refusing to stop. Some mocked him. "Your drums cannot call rain," they said. Still, he played. On the seventh night, the wind shifted. On the eighth, clouds gathered. On the ninth, lightning flickered far away. The drummer did not stop. Then, as he struck the final rhythm of that night, the sky broke open. Rain fell, not gently, but fully, as if the heavens had been holding it back for too long. The town rejoiced. And from that day forward, they understood: Shango does respond to those who call his name.

Spiritual Insight: *Spiritual alignment is often proven not in instant results, but in sustained faith through silence.*

* * *

THE KING WHO LOVED FIRE TOO MUCH

Before he became thunder in the sky, Shango was a king on earth. His court was loud, his presence larger than life. He spoke like rolling thunder even when the skies were clear. People admired him, but also feared him. Shango was not only a ruler; he was a force. He loved power, music, and the crackle of energy that came when he was at his peak. But he had a flaw: he did not always measure the weight of his own strength. One day, in a moment of pride and anger, he called upon his spiritual power to demonstrate his greatness. The sky responded, and lightning split the horizon. The people fell silent, but the demonstration did not stop when he wanted it to stop. Fire spread farther than intended. Fear replaced admiration. For the first time, Shango realized something unsettling: Power does not always obey the one who wields it. Shamed by what had happened, he left the throne, not defeated, but transformed, and in time, the sky itself became his throne. Now, when thunder rolls, it is not only power being shown. It is memory.

Spiritual Insight: *True power is not measured by how strongly it can be unleashed, but by how responsibly it is carried and contained.*

* * *

THE MAN WHO BORROWED LIGHTNING

There was once a man who desired greatness. He prayed to Shango constantly, asking for power, influence, and fearlessness. One night, Shango appeared. "I will give you a fragment of my fire," he said. "But you must respect it." The man accepted eagerly. At first, everything changed. His voice carried authority. His presence demanded attention. People obeyed him. But soon, he stopped respecting what had been given. He used the power to dominate rather than to balance. To control rather than to build. The fire inside him grew unstable. One evening, in anger, he called upon it recklessly. The lightning did not respond as he expected. It turned inward. The man lost everything he had built. When he returned to the place where he first prayed, Shango spoke: "You wanted fire, but not responsibility." The lesson was clear: *Lightning does not belong to those who cannot carry its consequences.*

* * *

SACRED STORIES OF YEMAYA

Yemaya and the Seven Broken Boats

Seven fishermen lost their boats in different storms and came together in anger, blaming the sea. They planned to curse Yemayá and abandon her worship. That night, a great wave formed, but did not strike. Instead, it showed them visions of their own mistakes: greed, ignoring warnings, overfishing, disrespecting rituals. Yemayá spoke through the wave: "The sea does not destroy without reflection." The fishermen rebuilt their boats and began offering thanks before each journey. Only then did their waters become calm again.

Spiritual Insight: *Your actions shape the waters that return to you.*

* * *

Yemayá and the Man Who Tried to Empty the Sea

There was once a man who believed his suffering was greater than anyone else's. He carried his pain loudly, speaking of it in every place, comparing it, measuring it, insisting that no one could understand. One day, in frustration, he stood before the ocean of Yemayá and shouted: "If you are truly the mother of all, then take this pain from me!" The sea remained calm. Enraged, he began to scoop water with his hands, throwing it onto the shore. "I will empty you," he said, "so you can feel what I feel, emptiness." He worked for hours, then days. His hands blistered. His body weakened. Still, the ocean did not change. Finally, exhausted, he collapsed at the water's edge. That night, Yemayá came to him in a dream, not as a force, but as a vast presence that filled everything. "Why do you try to empty what cannot be emptied?" she asked. "So you can understand me," he replied. Yemayá's voice was steady: "I already do. But you do not understand yourself. You are trying to remove your pain instead of learning its depth." She placed his hand into the water. "Feel this," she said. The man expected coldness, but instead he felt movement, layers beneath layers, currents flowing in different directions, life hidden within what seemed like a single surface. "This is how your pain exists," Yemayá said. "Not as one thing, but as many things you refuse to explore." When he woke, he did not try to empty the sea again. He sat beside it. And for the first time, he listened.

Spiritual Insight: *Pain cannot be removed by force. It must be understood in its depth before it can transform.*

* * *

Yemaya and the Woman Who Collected Tears

A woman lost her family and began collecting her own tears in jars, believing grief should be preserved. Her house was filled with jars until there was no space left for light. Yemaya visited her, disguised as a traveler, and asked, "Why do you imprison the water of your sorrow?" The woman said, "If I release it, I will lose them completely." Yemayá tipped one jar into the earth. Flowers grew instantly. "Grief is not meant to be stored. It is meant to transform." The woman slowly released each jar into the soil. Her pain did not vanish, but became life again.

Spiritual Insight: *Emotional energy must flow to transform. Holding grief too tightly prevents healing.*

* * *

Yemayá and the Broken Boat

A fisherman's boat cracked during a storm. Though it still floated, it took on water slowly. Instead of repairing it, the fisherman ignored the damage. "It still works," he said. Over time, the boat became harder to manage. Fishing became more exhausting. Still, he refused to fix it. One day, far from shore, the boat began to sink. In desperation, he called out to Yemayá. The sea grew calm. "You have been sinking for a long time," Yemayá said. "Today is only the moment you noticed." She guided him safely back, but the boat did not survive. On the shore, she spoke again: "What you ignore does not stay small. It deepens quietly until it demands your attention." The fisherman rebuilt, not just his boat, but his awareness.

Spiritual Insight: *Small neglect becomes great crisis when left unattended.*

* * *

Yemaya and the River That Wanted to Become the Ocean

A river once grew proud and became impatient with its winding path. It declared it would become the ocean immediately and refused to follow its natural course. In its force, it swelled beyond its banks, flooding villages and destroying everything in its way. Yemaya appeared and stopped the chaos with calm authority. She said, "Becoming is not rushing. It is arriving." She showed the river the lands it was meant to pass through, the valleys it needed to nourish, the places it was destined to sustain before reaching the sea. The river understood its mistake and softened its flow, returning to its rightful path. When it finally reached the ocean, Yemaya welcomed it gently, like a mother receiving a child who had learned patience.

Spiritual Insight: *Destiny unfolds in stages. Forced transformation leads to destruction.*

* * *

Yemayá and the Silent Fisherman

A fisherman stopped speaking after losing his family to the sea. He never prayed again, only fished in silence. Yemayá visited him repeatedly in waves, but he ignored her. One night, she appeared in human form and sat beside him. She said nothing, only waited. After hours, he finally whispered his grief. The ocean responded with gentle waves instead of storms. Yemayá said, "Even silence becomes prayer when it is honest."

Spiritual Insight: *Spiritual connection does not require perfection, only sincerity.*

* * *

SACRED STORIES OF OYA

Oya and the Door of Sudden Winds

In a village afraid of change, people built tall walls to keep life predictable. Nothing new was allowed, no strangers, no ideas, no departures. One day, Oya arrived as a wind without warning. She did not ask permission. She simply touched the walls, and they began to tremble. The villagers begged her to stop. Oya said, "You are not afraid of destruction. You are afraid of movement." She opened a single crack in the wall, and through it came rain, seeds, and voices from distant lands. The village never stayed the same again; it came alive.

Spiritual Insight: *What feels like disruption may actually be the beginning of growth.*

* * *

Oya and the Marketplace of False Stability

A prosperous city once prided itself on order and predictability. In its center stood a grand marketplace where nothing ever changed; each stall remained in the same place, each merchant sold the same goods, and every rule was fixed so tightly that even new ideas were discouraged. The people believed this stability was the source of their success. Over time, however, the city grew rigid. Creativity faded, trade slowed, and outsiders stopped visiting because nothing new could be found within its walls. Still, the leaders insisted that change would bring chaos, so they tightened control even further. One night, as the air grew heavy and still, Oya arrived as an unseen wind. She moved through the marketplace silently at first, loosening what had been made too rigid. By morning, the stalls had shifted, goods were scattered, signs were overturned, and the once-perfect order had been broken apart. The people awoke in panic, believing destruction had come.

They cried out against the wind, demanding to restore things exactly as they were. Then Oya revealed herself in the moving air and said: "Nothing that refuses change survives life." She showed them how their fixed ways had slowly strangled their own growth, and how life itself is meant to move, shift, and renew. What seemed like disorder was actually release. In time, the people rebuilt the marketplace differently, not with rigid sameness, but with flow, movement, and space for new things to emerge. Traders returned, ideas flourished, and the city prospered again, not because it stayed the same, but because it learned to change with the wind.

Spiritual Insight: *True stability is not rigidity; it is the ability to adapt when life shifts.*

* * *

<u>SACRED STORIES OF OSHUN</u>

Oshún and the Forbidden River

A town declared Oshún's river "unnecessary" and redirected it for profit. Soon, nothing grew in the land. A young girl went to the dried riverbed and poured honey into the cracked earth, saying: "Even sweetness must be remembered." Oshún appeared and touched the ground. Water slowly returned. She said, "You cannot replace flow with greed."

Spiritual Insight: *Love, harmony, and beauty are not luxuries; they are essential forces of life.*

* * *

Oshún and the Warrior Who Lost His Name

A warrior who had spent his life in violence eventually forgot his name. Without it, he felt unanchored, no longer fully human, no longer fully lost, just empty. He wandered until he reached the river of Oshun. Exhausted, he tried to drink, but the water receded from his hands. A voice rose from the river: "You cannot take what is pure while you still carry what is unhealed." So he stayed. Days passed. Hunger turned into stillness. Stillness turned into grief. And grief finally broke him open. He wept, not only for himself, but for every life he had taken and every moment he had erased from himself in battle. When his tears fell into the river, the water stopped pulling away. Oshún spoke again: "Now you are ready to remember." She leaned into the current and whispered his true name into the water. It returned to him like something he had always known but forgotten how to hear. When he spoke, he was no longer just a warrior. He was whole enough to begin again.

Spiritual Insight: *Identity returns when grief is faced, and the heart is made clean enough to receive it.*

* * *

OSHÚN AND THE RIVER OF BROKEN MARRIAGES

A village blamed Oshún for failed marriages. They stopped honoring her. Oshún withdrew love from the village. Couples lived together but felt no connection. A priest advised offerings of humility instead of blame. When they returned with honesty and respect, Oshún restored sweetness to their relationships.

Spiritual Insight: *Love requires reciprocity, respect, and emotional truth.*

* * *

OSHÚN AND THE GOLDEN MIRROR

Oshún placed a golden mirror in the river. Whoever looked into it saw not their appearance, but their heart. Many broke the mirror in fear. One woman accepted what she saw within herself: both kindness and jealousy. Oshún crowned her: "You are now whole."

Spiritual Insight: *Self-awareness is the path to spiritual maturity.*

* * *

OSHÚN AND THE MAN WHO WANTED EVERYTHING

A man came to Oshún asking for wealth, love, success, everything at once. "I am ready," he insisted. Oshún handed him a small bowl filled to the brim with honey. "Carry this across the village without spilling a drop," she said. The man laughed. "That is easy." But as he walked, people called to him. Distractions pulled at his attention. His hands shook. By the time he reached the other side, half the honey was gone. Oshún met him there. "You want everything," she said, "but you cannot hold even one thing with care." The man lowered his head. He returned again and again, practicing until he could carry the bowl steadily. Only then did Oshún begin to grant his requests, one at a time.

Spiritual Insight: *Desire without discipline leads to loss.*

* * *

<u>SACRED STORIES OF OCHOSI</u>

OCHOSI AND THE ARROW THAT WAITED

There was once a hunter who believed speed made him great. He moved quickly, shot quickly, and decided quickly. Many admired his confidence. But one season, his arrows stopped finding their mark. Frustrated, he went into the forest and called upon Ochosi, master of the hunt and guardian of precision. That night, Ochosi came, not as a man, but as a presence that sharpened the air itself. "Why do my arrows fail me?" the hunter asked. Ochosi responded, "Because you no longer wait." The hunter frowned. "If I wait, I lose the moment." Ochosi replied, "If you rush, you lose the truth of the moment." The next day, the hunter entered the forest but did not shoot. He followed tracks slowly. He listened to the silence between sounds. Hours passed before he even lifted his bow. When he finally released the arrow, it struck cleanly. He realized then, the arrow had not needed more force. It had needed more patience.

Spiritual Insight: *Precision is not speed. It is alignment with the right moment.*

* * *

OCHOSI AND THE INVISIBLE TARGET

A skilled hunter found himself unable to aim. There was no prey, no clear goal, only restlessness. He asked Ochosi, "What do I aim at when nothing is in front of me?" Ochosi responded, "Then your target is not outside." He handed the hunter an arrow. "Sit. Do not shoot." The hunter waited for hours, confused. Slowly, his thoughts became clearer. His restlessness faded. He realized he had been chasing movement without purpose. When he finally stood, he knew exactly where to go.

Spiritual Insight: *When direction is unclear, the first target is clarity within.*

* * *

DIVINATION AND THE SACRED TECHNOLOGY OF IFA
PART IV

CHAPTER 13

DIVINATION AND THE SACRED WISDOM OF IFA

REMEMBERING YOUR SOUL'S CONTRACT

According to Yoruba cosmology, your life did not begin at birth. Before you entered the physical realm, which is called Ayé, your soul stood before Olódùmarè, the Supreme Being, and chose its destiny. This pre-birth contract, known as Àyànmọ, was a deliberate selection of your parents, your talents, your struggles, and your ultimate purpose. You saw the entire map of your potential life and you agreed to it. However, a crucial part of this journey involves what we might call a sacred forgetting. Most souls choose to enter the world with a blank slate, ensuring that growth is earned through experience rather than through mere rote memory. We walk through life sensing the pull of our destiny but rarely seeing its full contours. We feel that certain paths are right for us without knowing exactly why. We encounter obstacles that seem to come from nowhere, not realizing they are the very challenges we chose to face. We receive blessings we cannot explain, not understanding they are the fulfillment of purposes we set for ourselves before birth.

Yet this forgetting is not absolute. Some souls choose to remember. These are the prophets, the seers, the ones born with clear knowledge of their purpose. Some remember in fragments, through dreams that carry meaning they cannot fully explain, through intuitions that guide them unerringly, through feelings of recognition when they encounter people or places tied to their destiny. Some choose to forget completely, wanting the full experience of discovery without any prior knowledge. Divination, therefore, is not about predicting a fixed future.

It is often utilized for remembering. When you consult Ifá, you are asking Ọrunmila to help you recall the contract you signed before you were born. You are seeking to understand which part of your chosen destiny is currently active, what lessons must be learned at this moment, what offerings must be made to remove obstacles, what behaviors must be adjusted to align with your path and what part of your destiny can you change and what part you cannot change.

ORUNMILA
The Orisha Who Witness all of Destiny

Orunmila was present at creation. He witnessed every soul choose its destiny, heard every promise made, observed every agreement between spirits. He holds the complete record of every destiny ever chosen, including what each soul chose to forget and remember. This is why Ọrunmila is consulted, not prayed to for favors. He does not change destiny. He reveals what is already true and if you can change your own destiny depending on what you agreed to prior to arriving on Earth. The babalawo are considered priests of Orunmila and it is through them that orunmila reveals the answers given by Ifa on these things.

ASE
The Power That Makes Things Happen

Divination operates within ase, the spiritual power that underlies all existence. Ase turns words into reality, empowers rituals, gives life to prayers. Everything contains ase in different measures. When a Babalawo performs divination, they work with ase. The tools are consecrated to hold it. Prayers direct it. Offerings increase it. The process aligns the seeker's own ase with their destiny, helps to remove blockages, and restores balance within the seekers life. This is why ebo (sacrifice or offering) is often inseparable from divination. When an Odu (A Sacred Sign) reveals blockage, (osogbo) a prescribed offering is often given to the spirits to help clear it from the persons life as long as their chosen destiny permits it. Sometimes no blockage is revealed and the person is in total alignment an offering or ebo should be still given in order to maintain that flow or ire, blessing where no spiritual blockage exists

Esu

The Messenger

Esu is the Orisha of communication and crossroads. He carries sacrifices and offerings (ebo) to the Orishas, guards the crossroads where destinies are chosen, ensures actions have consequences. In Ifá, Esu is always present. His face is carved on the divination tray. His permission must be sought before any reading. He "opens the door" between human and divine realms. Without Esu, prayers go nowhere, offerings go unclaimed, words fall on deaf ears. This is not because Esu is capricious. He is the principle of exchange, the force that ensures reciprocity. Spiritual interaction requires Èṣù to complete the circuit between humans and Orishas. Honoring him is not optional. It is structural.

Odu Ifa

The Sacred Signs

When Ọrunmila speaks through divination, he speaks through the Odu -256 sacred signs, each with its own name, personality, stories, proverbs, prescriptions, and prohibitions. Sixteen are major; 240 are minor combinations. The Odu are not merely symbols. They are living energies, archetypal forces, the fundamental patterns of existence itself. Think of them as the basic frequencies from which all reality is composed. Every human situation corresponds to one or more Odu. To know the Odu is to understand the underlying structure of any situation. The Odu are generated through a binary system, single and double lines that mirrors the structure of creation. The Babalawo is not guessing. They are reading patterns generated by a system too complex for human manipulation. The randomness of the cast is the universe expressing its current state through mathematical language.

Every Odu contains both blessing and challenge, expressed through Ire and Osogbo. Irè represents alignment harmony with destiny. When in Ire, blessings flow freely: wealth, children, longevity, victory, spiritual growth. Irè is the natural consequence of alignment. Osogbo represents misalignment straying from the path. When in Osogbo, obstacles arise: death, sickness, loss, conflict, stagnation. Osogbo is the natural consequence of misalignment, not punishment.

When an Odu appears, it contains both possibilities simultaneously. The Babalawo explains what blessings are available if the seeker walks a certain path, and what challenges await if they walk another. They describe offerings required to secure blessings and avert dangers. Divination is not a verdict. It is a map. It shows where roads lead, but the seeker must choose which to travel. The future is shaped by choices, character, alignment. Problems are signals. They indicate where alignment has been lost, where offerings are needed, where character must be refined. Divination reveals these signals to guide, not to frighten. In the next chapter we will discuss the sixteen major Odu of Ifa.

* * *

THE 16 MAJOR ODU

EXPLORING THE INTERPRETATION OF THE 16 MAJOR SIGNS

There are sixteen principal Odù, known as the *Olódù,* which serve as the primary framework for understanding the patterns of existence. Each Odù offers a unique roadmap, carrying its own specific teachings, blessings, and requirements. This chapter explores the essence of the sixteen major Odù, presenting their meanings and practical applications. It provides a foundational understanding of these sacred signs, serving as the essential starting point for further study of the Ifá corpus.

THE MAJOR SIXTEEN ODU IFA

1. EJI-OGBE

Eji Ogbe is the light so bright,
From it, all creation takes flight.
A spark of pure potential and might,
It shines with no darkness in sight.

Ejì Ogbe speaks of primordial light, embodying pure illumination and clarity. In Ifá cosmology, light is not merely the absence of darkness; it is the active force of existence itself. Èjì Ogbè represents this original light, present before the stars, moon, or sun. It is the radiance that Olódùmarè (the Supreme Being) used to illuminate the consciousness of the Irúnmolẹ (primordial divinities), guiding them in the creation of the world. To say it "embodies pure light" means its essence is truth and revelation; nothing can hide in its presence. When Èjì Ogbè appears, it brings clarity, cutting through confusion and uncertainty.

This Odu governs the power of spoken words. What is spoken under its influence manifests reality, making integrity essential. Promises, prayers, and affirmations are magnified, as words are spiritual containers capable of creating or destroying, blessing or cursing. Èjì Ogbè emphasizes the care and honor of the Ori (consciousness) through the use of cool water, prayers, and positive thoughts. A cluttered or ego-driven Ori cannot receive its light. When the Ori is honored, it aligns all aspects of life, bringing order and harmony to everything. Great light carries great responsibility.

Those guided by Èjì Ogbè are visible to both community and cosmos. This visibility exposes everything, including flaws, hypocrisy, and bad character, which could be damaging. One cannot claim light while hiding in darkness. The radiance of Èjì Ogbè reveals truth, which can feel overwhelming if one's character is not in alignment with goodness or if one does not want to face the truth in their life. Lastly, this Odu often brings limitless potential and clarity of vision. It restores the ability to see possibilities clearly, illuminating the path ahead and helping one recognize opportunities aligned with destiny. Eji- Ogbe reminds us that with integrity, mindfulness, and alignment with the Ori, we can navigate life with clarity, purpose, and profound spiritual insight.

When Èjì Ogbè is in **Ire (alignment)**, people experience tangible blessings: financial stability, supportive relationships, and clear direction in their work and life. Decisions are wise and well-timed, and spiritual growth unfolds naturally, with opportunities appearing at the right moments.

In **Osogbo (misalignment)**, the opposite occurs: pride, arrogance, or impulsive actions cause missed opportunities, conflicts, and setbacks. Poor decisions create confusion, wasted effort, and obstacles in career, health, or personal life. A neglected Ori blocks insight and guidance, making progress difficult and challenges more pronounced.

* * *

2. Oyeku-Meji

Oyeku Meji, Darkness surrounds the light
so bright, End of day, beginning of night.
A time to pause, reflect on all,
To understand life's rise and fall.

Oyeku Meji represents the original darkness, endings, and transitions. It is the only major Odu without light, symbolizing complete darkness and the absence of creation's spark. In Ifá cosmology, Oyeku is the counterpart to Èjì Ogbè. Where Ogbe represents pure light and creation, Oyeku represents pure darkness and completion. This darkness is not evil or negative. It is the sacred darkness that existed before creation began, the womb from which all things are born, and the tomb to which all things return. It is like the silence between thoughts, the pause between breaths, or a field resting before it is planted again. Oyeku governs the mysteries of the night, the realm of the ancestors, and the wisdom that can only be found in stillness. While Èjì Ogbè shines light on new beginnings, Oyeku teaches us to honor endings and trust the natural cycles of death and rebirth.

Oyeku is unique because it contains no light at its core. Other Odus hold at least a small spark of illumination, but Oyeku is in complete darkness. Yet this darkness has power. It is in Oyeku that we may sense the presence of ancestors, receive spiritual insight, and hear inner guidance more clearly. This darkness is not empty. It is full of potential and wisdom. It is like the darkness of the womb, where new life forms quietly. It is like the darkness of the grave, where the body returns to the earth and supports new growth. In Oyeku, the creative fire of Èjì Ogbè is withdrawn. This teaches an important lesson: creation cannot happen constantly. There must be rest, pauses, and endings. The power of creation (Ashe) must step back so that what has been created can settle, be understood, and eventually be released. Oyeku governs these sacred pauses when life feels quiet or uncertain. Because of this, Oyeku is connected with death (Iku), the end of cycles (Oku), and the idea of returning home. Just as the sun must set and the year must end, every life and every phase must come to completion. Light returns to its source, and we are left in darkness to reflect and prepare for what comes next.

When Oyeku appears in a reading, it often signals that the ancestors are near. It represents the thin veil between the living and the dead. Messages may come through dreams, sudden realizations, elders, or spiritual rituals. The ancestors do not always speak with clear words; they communicate through symbols, feelings, and quiet inner knowing. Oyeku teaches us to become still enough to listen. One of Oyeku's main lessons is the importance of letting go. In a world that encourages us to hold on to possessions, relationships, titles, and even identities, Oyeku reminds us that growth requires release. A seed must break open to grow. Trees must lose their leaves in winter. The soul must leave the body when life ends. Letting go makes space for renewal. During uncertain times, when the future feels unclear, Oyeku calls us inward. Introspection means honestly looking within, sitting with our thoughts and emotions, and learning from them. In darkness, we cannot depend on outside signs; we must trust our intuition and spiritual connection. Oyeku teaches patience and faith. The darkness is not empty; it holds wisdom for those willing to wait and listen.

In **Ire** (Alignment)**,** Oyeku brings protection during times of transition. Sometimes darkness protects us by hiding us from harm. It offers guidance through difficult endings and provides peace when facing what cannot be changed. These blessings may not look dramatic or joyful, but they are powerful. Oyeku's blessings often come as quiet strength, emotional maturity, and spiritual understanding. It protects those moving from one stage of life to another, whether that is a career change, personal transformation, or even the transition from life to death.

In **Osogbo** (Misalignment), fear and resistance often take over. A person may cling to the past, deny that something is ending, or feel overwhelmed by emotional turmoil. Resistance can show up as anger, bargaining, depression, or stubborn refusal to accept change. This creates stagnation and prolongs suffering. Oyeku teaches a simple but difficult truth: everything ends. Our power lies not in stopping endings, but in choosing how we respond to them. When we resist, we suffer. When we accept and release, we grow.

* * *

<u>3. Iwori-Meji</u>

Iwori Meji, a force so strong,
Guides us through change all along.
From light to dark, we grow each day,
Like a butterfly finding its way.

Iwori Meji is the Odu of revelation, awakening, and uncovering hidden truths. It guides us through transitions, moving us from one stage of life to another and helping us transform internally. Like a caterpillar becoming a butterfly, change under Iwori can feel uncomfortable, confusing, or even chaotic, but it is necessary for growth. Its energy pushes us to evolve, uncover deeper truths about ourselves, others, and the world, and prepare for the next stage of life. In Ifá, Iwori exists between the full light of Èjì Ogbè and the deep darkness of Oyeku. It is the moment of dawn, when light begins to break, or dusk, when darkness starts to settle. Neither fully light nor fully dark, Iwori holds the space between opposites. This liminal position gives it unique power: it can perceive both what is visible and what is hidden. True wisdom, Iwori teaches, comes from holding light and shadow together, from balancing clarity and mystery.

Iwori is the force that cracks open the seed, splits the cocoon, and breaks the waters of the womb. It disrupts comfort so that new forms of life, insight, or understanding can emerge. Its energy can feel unsettling because it calls us to leave old habits, identities, and outdated beliefs behind. Yet it also carries enormous potential: each transformation, each revelation, prepares us for the next stage of growth. Life under Iwori is never static; its energy keeps us moving, whether we feel ready or not.

The primary role of Iwori is revelation. It exposes hidden truths, resolves confusion, and brings clarity. These revelations can be liberating, offering insight and direction, or challenging, confronting us with truths we might prefer to ignore. Iwori is direct; it does not ask permission to reveal what must be seen. Once revealed, the truth cannot be unseen. It is the "aha" moment, the sudden insight that changes everything. Iwori also represents ongoing transformation. Growth is not a single event but a continuous process. From childhood to adulthood, from student to teacher, from seeker to finder, we move through many cycles of change. Even when we think we have arrived, another transformation awaits. Iwori's unpredictability keeps us humble, flexible, and open. We do not control its process; we participate in it, surrendering to its flow and trusting that each stage prepares us for what comes next.

Most of Iwori's work happens inwardly. Like a caterpillar inside a cocoon, transformation begins quietly. Others may not notice at first, but eventually, our inner growth manifests outwardly: the butterfly emerges, the truth is spoken, the new self is lived. Iwori teaches patience, reminding us that growth cannot be rushed; what is forming in secret will eventually reveal its full strength and beauty. Ultimately, Iwori is the Odu of awakening (**jii**), transformation (**yipada**), and movement. It shows us that change is inevitable, discomfort often signals growth, and wisdom comes from balancing opposites. Those guided by Iwori learn to trust life's process, embrace the unknown, and remain open to the many ways the universe moves them toward their next stage of being. **Ire (Alignment):** With Iwori in alignment, thoughtful decisions, clear thinking, and spiritual insight allow problems to be solved effectively. Intuition guides both personal and professional success, helping opportunities unfold smoothly.

Osogbo (Challenges): Ignoring inner guidance, acting on impulse, or letting emotions override reason can lead to mistakes, conflicts, and missed opportunities. While great potential exists, flaws in character or judgment can prevent it from being realized.

* * *

<u>**4. O**DI**-M**EJI</u>

Odi Meji's energy, strong and bright,
Speaks of birth and new life's light.
Male and female, working together,
Bringing new life that lasts forever.

Odi Meji is an Odu that embodies fertility, protection, and maternal guidance. It represents the sacred energy that supports life, creation, and growth, providing the structure and stability necessary for new beginnings to thrive. Odi teaches that all creation, whether a child, a project, or a spiritual idea, requires nurturing, containment, and care. Like the womb, it holds life safely until it is ready to emerge into the world. This is not restriction but the proper environment for growth; without it, potential dissipates, and creation cannot be sustained. Fertility under Odi is both literal and symbolic. It includes the ability to bring forth new life, generate creative work, cultivate relationships, and develop spiritual and material abundance. But fertility is effective only when the conditions for growth are secure, and Odi provides those conditions through structure, protection, and steady guidance.

Protection is central to Odi. It mirrors the vigilance of a mother caring for her child, the strength of a home shielding its family, or the stability of a community keeping its members safe. Odi emphasizes the importance of boundaries, deciding what to welcome in and what to keep out. These boundaries create stability, allow energy to focus, and prevent chaos from overwhelming life. True protection is not rigid; it adapts to circumstances while maintaining a safe space for growth. Odi teaches the balance between sheltering and empowering, preparing what is nurtured to eventually stand and act independently. Maternal guidance is another defining aspect of Odi. This guidance is practical, consistent, and patient. It encourages responsibility, discipline, and steady progress, highlighting that meaningful growth cannot be rushed. Under Odi, lessons are taught gently but firmly, emphasizing care, wisdom, and attentiveness. It also emphasizes connections to family, community, tradition, and the divine because strong relationships provide the foundation from which life can flourish. Odi shows that nurturing energy, combined with responsible boundaries, is essential to growth in all forms. When in **Ire**, Odi brings stability, security, safe environments, and successful management of resources. It strengthens connections, supports creativity and productivity, and sustains the transformations and insights gained from other Odu.

In **Osogbo**, Odi manifests as rigidity, inflexibility, or clinging to past successes. Boundaries can become walls, protection can turn into control, and stability can turn into stagnation. Growth is blocked, relationships strained, and opportunities lost.

* * *

5. Irosun-Meji

The past returns to show the way,
Its lessons guide both night and day.
Ancestors whisper, guiding true,
Their wisdom flows in all we do.
Through lineage deep, their voices call,
Shaping destiny, protecting all.

Irosun Meji, the fifth Odu of Ifá, teaches that our past actions shape our present and future. Every choice, word, and deed leaves an imprint, influencing the opportunities, challenges, and blessings we experience. Life is a chain of cause and effect, and understanding our past is essential for navigating the present with wisdom. When Irosun appears, it signals the guidance of ancestral wisdom and the influence of our inheritance. It shows that something from the past, a choice, mistake, recurring pattern, or overlooked lesson, needs to be acknowledged. Ignoring these influences can trap us in repeating cycles or carry hidden burdens into the future. True growth requires not only reflection but also deliberate action, guided by patience, persistence, honesty, humility, and integrity. These qualities help us see truth from illusion and understand our experiences clearly. This Odu emphasizes hard work, sacrifice, and the cultivation of good character. Success rarely comes easily; diligence aligned with virtue brings fulfillment. Irosun reminds us to live for our own destiny rather than someone else's and to give thanks for what we have rather than longing for what we do not. Honoring the ancestors is central to this Odu, as their guidance and wisdom continue to support us through rituals, prayers, offerings, or remembrance. Strengthening this connection illuminates our path, helps us avoid repeating mistakes, and aligns us with our true destiny. In Irosun, the bird Osun serves as the guardian of the head (ori), protecting memory, intellect, and mental clarity, while also acting as a divine messenger to the Orishas and Olodumare. Honoring Osun safeguards our mental faculties and helps carry prayers to the heavens. When Irosun comes in **Ire**, it brings wisdom, ancestral guidance and support, allowing us to have a clear head and grow spiritually, emotionally, and materially.

When Irosun comes in **Osogbo**, it warns against ignoring past lessons or ancestral guidance, which can lead to repeated mistakes, mental confusion, stagnation, or misaligned decisions. By acknowledging and learning from the past while working diligently in the present, Irosun empowers us to create a future of greater clarity, success, and fulfillment.

* * *

6. Owonrin-Meji

At the crossroads, paths divide,
Where choices test the heart and guide.
Some are clear, some hidden, slight,
Their weight reveals in time's own light.

Owonrin Meji, the sixth Odu of the Ifá corpus, revolves around the crossroads, the place where paths diverge, where choices carry weight, and where a single decision can shape countless possibilities. Life under Owonrin is a continuous encounter with such intersections: some obvious, some subtle, often unnoticed until much later. This Odu teaches that awareness of these moments shapes our destiny. The crossroads is not a place to fear, but to honor, for it is here that character is tested, choices bear fruit, and the seeds we have sown reveal their harvest.

Owonrin often appears when unpredictable events enter our lives or when decisive action is required for survival and progress. This Odu emphasizes adaptability in the face of uncertainty. Just when life seems predictable, an unforeseen turn emerges not as a flaw, but as a natural principle of existence. Those who resist this flux exhaust themselves; those who embrace it discover freedom in surrender, peace in uncertainty, and opportunity in the unexpected. Owonrin humbles us, sharpens our awareness, and challenges us to rise beyond comfort zones. Adaptability is Owonrin's central teaching. Crossroads arrive without warning, and the winds of change blow regardless of our desires. Adaptability is not weakness; it is wisdom, the ability to adjust plans to reality, yield preferences to necessity, and bend expectations to life as it is. Like water, the adaptable person flows around obstacles, fills the space life allows, and wears down barriers through steady effort. Those who cultivate this skill thrive where the rigid falter, transforming challenges into growth.

Change is constant under Owonrin. Nothing remains static: relationships, circumstances, bodies, minds, and the world itself are always in motion. Resistance to change is the root of suffering, the futile grasping at what has passed. Acceptance, however, allows life to carry us toward new opportunities. Endings become beginnings, losses clear space for gains, and one form of life always precedes another. Change under Owonrin is not endured, it is danced with, a conscious participation in the flow of existence. These themes converge into Owonrin's core teaching: at life's crossroads, unpredictability keeps us vigilant, adaptability guides us through challenges, and change moves us forward. Together, they form a path of trust in our ability to meet life's tests, in the emergence of the right direction, and in the unfolding of our deeper purpose. Owonrin calls us to stand at these intersections with open eyes and open hands: ready to adapt, willing to change, unafraid of the unpredictable, and confident that the path we need will appear when we are ready to walk it.

When Owonrin appears in **Ire** (alignment), Life flows with successful adaptation, resilience, and growth through transitions. Opportunities arise when one responds mindfully, ethically, and creatively to challenges. When in **Osogbo**(out of alignment), Restlessness, scattered focus, and resistance to change create obstacles. Poor adjustment leads to missed opportunities, confusion, and losses.

* * *

7. Obara-Meji

Obara is the strength to see,
To lift the veil and let light be.
Perspective shapes the paths we take,
Transforming loss into what we make.

Obara Meji embodies the power of perspective, transformation, and the creative force of intention, teaching that reality is shaped not only by actions but also by words, thoughts, and focused purpose. Representing the ability to perceive life clearly and act with insight, this Odu guides the seeker to align energy with both material and spiritual goals, where light at the top symbolizes clarity and new awareness, and darkness below reflects the necessary release of old habits and limiting beliefs. True transformation under Obara Meji requires seeing life as it truly is and responding with purpose, discipline, and integrity, recognizing that repeated setbacks, conflicts, or failures are opportunities for learning and growth when approached with awareness and adaptability.

Speech is a powerful creative tool that influences circumstances, and by embracing change, mastering communication, and remaining adaptable, the practitioner turns scarcity into abundance, confusion into clarity, and inertia into purposeful action. Material wealth and spiritual growth are intertwined, with success measured not solely by possessions but by the alignment of action, intention, and ethical conduct. The path to prosperity is continuous, requiring vigilance, humility, and focused intent to transform limitations into opportunity.

When action aligns with integrity, Obara Meji bestows **Ire (blessings)** such as effective expression, proactive effort, goal achievement, recognition, and positive influence. However, when pride, misuse of words, procrastination, or unethical action take hold, **Osogbo (challenges)** arises, blocking progress, damaging relationships, and limiting success. Ultimately, Obara Meji teaches that transformation, turning poverty into wealth and cultivating both material and spiritual abundance, flows from one who moves with life's natural changes, using challenges as mirrors to refine character and strengthen resilience.

* * *

8. Okanran-Meji

Before you leap, think things through,
Don't let emotions cloud your view.
Balance is crucial, keep it in sight,
To navigate life, with all its might.

Okanran Meji is the Odu of the heart, guiding the seeker in navigating emotions that can either align them with destiny or lead them astray. Its central teaching is the integration of emotional intelligence, rational thought, and intuitive insight. Emotions are not obstacles to overcome, nor enemies to resist; they are powerful guides. When understood and managed consciously, they illuminate the path to fulfillment. Balance between heart and mind is essential: impulsive decisions made without reflection invite chaos, while emotional disconnection cuts off intuitive guidance.

When cultivated with awareness, Okanran bestows **Ire (blessings)** that turn adversity into strength. Self-mastery emerges as the ability to observe emotions without being consumed by them, responding thoughtfully instead of reacting impulsively. Strength in adversity becomes more than endurance; it becomes grace, maintaining integrity even through life's storms. Patience is active and deliberate, honoring sacred timing rather than forcing outcomes. Wise action under pressure develops through decisions that address both immediate needs and long-term growth. Enduring hardships ethically builds character of lasting value, teaching that how we handle challenges is as important as how we celebrate success.

However, when emotions are ignored or mismanaged, **Osogbo (challenges)** arise with destructive force. Impulsiveness leads to hasty decisions that may take years to correct. Aggression, whether directed inward or outward, generates compounding negative consequences. Words spoken in anger, destructive actions, or abandoned relationships create immediate setbacks and long-term instability. Lessons go unlearned when emotional storms pass without reflection, trapping the seeker in repeating patterns. Okanran also warns against emotional numbness or cold rationality, which dismisses the heart's wisdom and blocks access to destiny's guidance. Ultimately, Okanran teaches that mastery of the heart is not about suppressing feelings but understanding and directing them. True alignment comes from observing emotions, balancing them with reason, and letting intuition guide action, turning both trials and triumphs into sources of growth, wisdom, and fulfillment.

* * *

9. Ogunda-Meji

Ogun's the boss of iron and war,
Hunting, farming, and so much more.
We ask him for help when things get tough,
He gives us strength to be strong enough.

Ogunda Meji represents the forward-driving power that pushes us toward destiny by demanding we face responsibilities requiring immediate attention. Dominated by Ogun, the Orisha of iron, war, and transformation, this Odu teaches that confronting uncomfortable aspects of life is essential for progress. Ogun's machete clears external obstacles blocking our path, yet he also places challenges deliberately to foster growth, understanding that struggle builds character and capability. When emotions prove insufficient for navigating difficulties, Ogunda calls upon rational faculties to cut through confusion, overcome barriers, and forge new pathways forward. This Odu reminds us that avoidance only prolongs suffering, while confrontation, however uncomfortable, ultimately liberates.

Ire (blessings) manifest through achievement born of sustained effort, breakthroughs that follow persistent struggle, and the physical and mental strength developed through adversity. Success comes to those who harness willpower and determination, pushing through challenges with unwavering resolve. Every obstacle overcome under Ogunda's influence becomes a foundation stone for greater accomplishments, as the practitioner discovers capacities previously unknown.

Osogbo (challenges) arises when laziness takes hold, when avoidance of necessary confrontation becomes habitual, or when unpreparedness meets opportunity. These failures to engage invite wasted potential, stagnation that compounds over time, and deep frustration born of knowing what should have been done yet remained undone. Ogunda warns that the path does not wait opportunity missed through inaction may not return, and challenges avoided only grow larger in the shadows. True progress requires picking up Ogun's machete and cutting a path forward, no matter how dense the forest ahead.

* * *

<u>10. Osa-Meji</u>

When Osa Meji shows its face,
Sudden changes often take their place.
Oya, the Orisha, rules this sign,
Bringing shifts both fierce and fine.

Osa Meji governs the realm of sudden, unexpected change under the dominion of Oya, the Orisha of winds, transformation, and the cemetery gates. This Odu teaches that Oya arrives with abrupt shifts precisely when something in life requires transformation, whether relationships, circumstances, or stagnant patterns that have overstayed their purpose. These changes often feel distressing and chaotic in the moment, yet they consistently clear space for new beginnings, renewal, and growth that could not otherwise take root. Oya's nature is to warn before she strikes; she speaks through intuition, synchronicities, and restless feelings that signal preparation time. Trusting these inner nudges becomes essential, for those who heed Oya's whispers need not endure her screams. As fierce protector and guardian of the dead and ancestors, Oya ensures that transitions honor what came before while making way for what must come.

Ire (blessings) flow through heightened intuition that perceives change before it arrives, spiritual protection that shields during vulnerable transitions, and harmonious alignment with life's forces that transforms chaos into ordered renewal. Careful discernment during turbulent times allows the practitioner to ride Oya's winds rather than be crushed by them, emerging stronger and wiser on the other side.

Osogbo (challenges) manifests as deception that clouds perception, poor judgment that misreads warning signs, and ignorance of hidden dynamics operating beneath surface appearances. When change is resisted until the whirlwind forces it, losses multiply, and confusion deepens. Osa reminds us that transformation is not optional; it is life's constant rhythm. The only choice is whether we dance with Oya willingly or are swept away by forces we refused to acknowledge.

* * *

11. Ika-Meji

Pride bows to wisdom's gentle call,
Greed dissolves when compassion stands tall.
A life of virtue, steadfast and bright,
Becomes its own reward, its own light.

Ika Meji addresses the sacred responsibility of harnessing inner power and building personal Ashe to direct toward positive manifestation. This Odu teaches that ase, the divine life force and spiritual authority granted by Olodumare, is accumulated through disciplined living and must be intentionally directed to achieve desired goals. Loss of personal power is no small matter; when Ase diminishes or becomes blocked, it manifests as both physical illness and spiritual disconnection, signaling that something in one's character or conduct requires realignment. Ase is not freely given but earned; it is the reward from the divinities for consistent good character, ethical deeds, and the humility to make ebo (sacrifice) after divination reveals what requires adjustment. Ika emphasizes that power flows to those who respect its source and wield it with purpose.

Ire (Blessings) arises as the wisdom gained from challenges that might have overwhelmed a lesser spirit. Living ethically becomes its own reward, drawing opportunities and protection that dishonesty could never provide. Balanced decision-making combining heart, reason, and ancestral guidance yields results that benefit both the individual and their wider community. Healing occurs as blocked *Ase* begins to flow again, restoring vitality to body, mind, and spirit. Most importantly, accomplishment comes from focused, intentional action guided by cultivated inner *Ase*, showing that properly directed power can transform vision into reality.

Osogbo (Challenges) arises from rash decisions made without guidance or consideration of long-term consequences. Dishonesty undermines *Ase*, for power built on falsehood cannot endure. Destructive habits such as substance abuse, toxic relationships, or self-sabotaging patterns drain personal power, leaving little for constructive action. Ignoring repeated lessons invites recurring setbacks, each more costly than the last. One of the most dangerous misuses of power is turning *Ase* against oneself, using it destructively instead of purposefully. Equally perilous is giving energy or authority to those who exploit it, feeding on attention or influence without giving back. The Odu warns that power wasted is power lost, and lost power requires far greater effort to regain.

* * *

When whispers of illness linger near,
We act with swiftness, without fear.
For in addressing concerns before they grow,
We ensure that our wellness continues to glow.

Oturupon Meji governs the sacred domain of health, teaching that the physical body is the vessel through which destiny manifests and must be maintained with reverence and discipline. This Odu emphasizes proper nutrition, observing spiritual taboos, managing stress, and protecting the immune system as acts of spiritual devotion. When health concerns arise, Oturupon advises addressing both realms: spiritual practices, such as sacrifices or cleansing, support unseen influences, while medical care and checkups maintain the physical body. The body communicates through symptoms; ignoring these signals invites imbalance. Prevention through daily care requires less effort than recovery from a crisis, making attentive stewardship of the body a central spiritual responsibility.

Ire (Blessings): Ire under Oturupon manifests as recovery and restoration. Illnesses are overcome, relationships heal, and fortunes are renewed. Emotional and spiritual well-being flows naturally when the body is cared for, as vessel and occupant heal together. Rest and proper self-care create fresh beginnings, demonstrating that recovery is wisdom, not weakness. Gratitude becomes inherent, and those who honor their health often emerge as teachers, appreciating life as a precious gift. Renewal through disciplined care shows that tending the body is not indulgence but a sacred duty aligned with one's destiny.

Osogbo (Challenges): Osogbo arises when rest and self-care are repeatedly sacrificed for productivity. Burnout accumulates, energy is misused, and the mind's plans cannot be executed by an exhausted body. Neglecting preventive care forces longer recovery periods and magnifies health issues. Minor ailments can become major, and what could have healed naturally may become chronic. Oturupon warns that no spiritual or material achievement compensates for a neglected vessel. The body is the foundation upon which all else is built, and honoring it is essential for balance, resilience, and the fulfillment of destiny.

✳ ✳ ✳

13. Otura-Meji

For visions bright can blind the eye,
To faults within, we might deny.
Yet with humility as our guide,
Personal growth will surely abide.

Otura Meji governs the gift of perception, the ability to discern truth and receive guidance through dreams, spiritual sources, or deep insight beyond ordinary knowing. This Odu teaches that visions are not merely personal experiences but practical tools for growth, providing clarity that guides decision-making and illuminates paths toward goals. Seeing truth carries responsibility: acting on or teaching visions requires genuine understanding, not just confidence, because perception without preparation can mislead others, and vision without wisdom can be dangerous.

Ire (blessings) manifests as spiritual clarity that pierces illusion, revealing hidden patterns beneath surface appearances. Life's challenges become understandable, and disciplined application of insights transforms vision into practical action. When perceived truth aligns with purpose, living intentionally becomes natural, the seer becomes the doer, and destiny unfolds through focused effort.

Osogbo (challenges) arises when visions multiply without interpretation, creating confusion as insights contradict or overwhelm each other. Lack of focus scatters perception, sacrificing depth for breadth, while visions that replace action leave the seeker spiritually empty. Ignored guidance accumulates, and ungrounded visions can inflate the ego, fostering moral superiority and rigid judgment that blocks growth. Otura emphasizes that vision is a servant, not a master; insight must be tempered with discernment, humility, and ethical action. True mastery comes when the seeker interprets visions wisely, integrates guidance into daily life, and uses perception to illuminate both self and destiny, balancing the knowledge they hold with the truths yet to be discovered.

* * *

14. IRETE-MEJI

In Irete Meji's warning light,
We see the dangers, clear and bright.
Self-sabotage and premature fears,
May cloud our path, lead to tears.

Irete Meji delivers a profound warning against self-sabotage and the spiritual danger of prematurely seeking death, whether through literal self-destruction or the symbolic abandonment of one's destiny. This Odu promises wealth and good fortune to those who persevere, but blessings are conditional, requiring right action, ethical conduct, and spiritual alignment. Initiation and disciplined practice serve not as mere ritual but as pathways to personal transformation. Perseverance through difficulty, cultivation of good character, and consistent seeking of Ifá guidance are essential to claim Irete's rewards.

Ire (blessings) manifests as success earned through patient effort, with prosperity flowing responsibly to serve both self and community. Fulfillment accompanies material gain when purpose remains central, and wise stewardship of resources ensures that wealth multiplies rather than diminishes. Humility in maintaining blessings attracts further favor, for divinities honor those who acknowledge the source of their fortune.

Osogbo (challenges) arises when greed transforms abundance into obsession, when unethical behavior for gain incurs spiritual debt, or when wealth is misused through hoarding or ostentation. Arrogance leads to the withdrawal of blessings, teaching lessons that fortune alone cannot. Most critically, self-destructive choices turning from life toward death, from abundance toward emptiness, from destiny toward dissolution recreate the very patterns Irete warns against. This Odu teaches that wealth is both a test and a gift: prosperity demands a character equal to its acquisition, reminding the seeker that the true measure of success lies not in accumulation, but in integrity, purpose, and the responsible use of one's blessings.

* * *

15. Ose-Meji

When Oshe Meji rises high,
Patience is the reason why.
For in the calm, and steady wait,
Blessings come, not early, not late.

Ose Meji teaches the sacred discipline of patience and the wisdom of refraining from hasty decisions. This Odu emphasizes that carefully considering all options allows blessings to unfold naturally when timing aligns with divine will. Patience is not passivity but active trust, recognizing that prayers are acknowledged in the spiritual realm and manifest when conditions are right.

Ire (blessings) manifests as love that deepens through waiting, creativity that matures fully, and harmonious relationships built on understanding rather than impulse. Emotional balance steadies the seeker amid life's fluctuations, while abundance flows through compassion extended to self and others. Blessings arrive at exactly the right moment, not too early to be valued, not too late to fulfill their purpose.

Osogbo (challenges) arises when impatience disrupts life, straining relationships and situations. Vanity and the desire for immediate gratification mistake urgency for importance, while emotional instability fluctuates with every delay. Words spoken too quickly and decisions made in haste create discord, and forcing outcomes guarantees that blessings are missed. Oshe teaches that divine timing cannot be hurried; the practitioner's task is to trust the process, and the reward is that all blessings arrive precisely when needed, fully formed and enduring.

* * *

16. Ofun-Meji (Orangun)

In Ofun Meji's sacred space,
Miracles bloom, challenges face.
Pray with heart and seek the light,
Wisdom guides us through the night.

Ofun Meji is the sixteenth and final Odu of the foundational Ifá corpus, representing the culmination of a complete spiritual cycle. Known as the Odu of the "White Spirit," it embodies illumination, clarity, and transcendence, marking the end of a journey where the soul is purified and prepared for rebirth. Ofun Meji teaches that no new beginning can be sacred or stable until previous chapters are fully resolved: debts, promises, and unfinished actions must be completed with honesty and intention. Consistent prayer, reflection, and the sincere seeking of spiritual guidance are essential tools for this process. This Odu emphasizes transparency and purity of intent, guiding the practitioner to align fully with divine will so that prayers become powerful declarations rather than whispers into the void. Its wisdom reveals the interconnectedness of life's events and the deeper meaning behind struggles, offering clarity after periods of confusion or trial.

Ire (blessings) under Ofun Meji manifests as wholeness, spiritual mastery, fulfillment of purpose, readiness for new cycles, answered prayers, and the manifestation of miracles. It represents the achievement of balance and the preparation for the next stage of life or spiritual growth.

Osogbo (challenges) arises when lessons are ignored, tasks left incomplete, or insight is rejected, leaving one trapped in confusion, blocked from progress, or unwilling to embrace truth. Ofun Meji reminds the seeker that the ultimate tragedy is willful blindness: standing at the threshold of clarity yet clinging to familiar darkness. This Odu is both the final exam and the gateway to a new beginning, offering peace, wisdom, and the light needed to carry forward all that has been learned.

* * *

CHAPTER 15

THE MINOR ODU OF IFA
EXPLORING THE INTERPRETATION OF THE 240 COMBINED SIGNS

Beyond the sixteen major Ódù, the Ifá corpus also contains 240 minor Ódù, bringing the total number of Odù Ifá to 256. In this chapter, we examine the meanings and interpretations of these 240 minor Ódù. By studying them alongside the major Ódù, readers can gain a deeper, more comprehensive understanding of the entire Ifá divination system. These interpretations provide a foundational overview of each Ódù. While they are relatively basic, they serve as an essential starting point for new priests and dedicated practitioners, helping them recognize the specific energies of each Ódù and align with their spiritual significance. This foundational knowledge prepares the way for more detailed study and practical application.

THE CHILDREN OF EJI -OGBE
Common Themes found in the family of Ogbe include: Light, creation, clarity, destiny.

17. Ogbe-Oyeku: This Odu speaks of light fading into darkness and the cycles of endings and beginnings. **Message:** Growth comes from facing difficult truths and accepting that some things must end. Reconciliation and new opportunities are possible once wisdom is embraced. This Odu often signals that your current methods or efforts are failing or will fail in some aspect of your life. When Ogbe is followed by Oyekun, it may indicate minimal or no blessings (darkness) at this time in what you are pursuing, or that something must end before true blessings can arrive. **Iré (Positive Influences)**: Protection during change, deep resilience, spiritual insight, guidance through transitions, renewal. **Òsogbo (Challenges)**: Fear of change, stagnation, avoidance of necessary endings, confusion, emotional resistance to transformation.

18. Ogbe-Iwori: This Odu talks about illumination paired with inner insight and revelation. **Message:** Awareness of subtle truths and red flags prevents missteps; self-understanding is key. **Iré:** Clarity of mind, deep insight, wise discernment, revealing hidden truths, purposeful direction. **Òsogbo:** Misunderstanding, deception, lack of focus, ignoring inner wisdom.

19. Ogbe-Odi: This Odu talks about light applied to structure, stability, and protection. **Message:** Boundaries and personal integrity sustain growth; avoid over-attachment to others' approval. **Iré:** Security, dependable foundations, protection, stable progress. **Òsogbo:** Rigidity, feeling stuck, resistance to growth, clinging to the past.

20. Ogbe-Irosun: This Odu talks about illumination guided by ancestral lineage. **Message:** Spiritual purpose is strengthened by connection to heritage; ancestors shape destiny. **Iré:** Guidance from ancestors, lineage connection, spiritual continuity, fulfillment of potential. **Òsogbo:** Disconnection from heritage, repeating ancestral mistakes, emotional blocks from unresolved history.

21. Ogbe-Owonrin: This Odu talks about light in transformation and adaptability through change. **Message:** Life's shifts require trust, flexibility, and patience; breakthroughs may follow disruption. **Iré:** Effective adaptation, creative responsiveness, growth through change, new opportunities. **Òsogbo:** Restlessness, instability, inconsistency, chaos from resisting change.

22. Ogbe-Obara: This Odu talks about the power of communication and expression guided by clarity. **Message:** Patience in pursuing destiny or wealth; words can shape outcomes. **Iré:** Inspired communication, influence, collaboration, recognition, achievement. **Òsogbo:** Miscommunication, conflict through speech, pride, unwise words.

23. Ogbe-Okanran: This Odu talks about light through trial and courage forged in challenge. **Message:** Strength and resilience develop through tested character; caution is necessary. **Iré:** Courage, decisiveness, empowerment, overcoming obstacles. **Òsogbo:** Aggression without foresight, rash decisions, conflict, destructive impulses.

24. Ogbe-Ogunda: This Odu talks about illumination through effort and discipline. **Message:** Consistent, purposeful work produces progress and breakthroughs. **Iré:** Achievement through perseverance, productivity, success from dedication. **Òsogbo:** Burnout, wasted effort, frustration, stubborn conflict.

25. Ogbe-Osa: This Odu talks about light in spiritual awareness and unseen realms. **Message:** Respect divine timing and cultivate intuition; spiritual sensitivity guides life. **Iré:** Heightened intuition, spiritual protection, guidance from unseen realms, harmony. **Òsogbo:** Confusion, deception, poor discernment, fear of the unknown.

26. Ogbe-Ika: This Odu talks about clarity paired with ethical accountability. **Message:** Moral responsibility shapes destiny; integrity protects the path. **Iré:** Integrity, self-mastery, protection through right action, alignment with purpose. **Òsogbo:** Disorder from unethical behavior, destructive habits, conflict from poor choices.

27. Ogbe-Oturupon: This Odu talks about illumination through trial and karmic lessons. **Message:** True growth arises after challenge; healing follows hardship. **Iré:** Renewal, spiritual growth, resilience, breakthroughs after difficulty. **Òsogbo:** Suffering without learning, overwhelming obstacles, resistance to change.

28. Ogbe-Otura: This Odu talks about peace and clarity paired with divine guidance. **Message:** Spiritual growth and harmony require calm reflection; inner peace nurtures progress. **Iré:** Inner harmony, clear judgment, balanced direction, conflict resolution. **Òsogbo:** Illusion, indecision, superficial peace, avoidance of necessary confrontation.

29. Ogbe-Irete: This Odu talks about steady growth, patience, and long-term stability. **Message:** Persistence and thoughtful action produce enduring success. **Iré:** Consistent progress, lasting achievement, perseverance rewarded. **Òsogbo:** Delays, stagnation, impatience, giving up too early.

30. Ogbe-Ose: This Odu talks about harmony, joy, and creative expression. **Message:** Relationships and creativity flourish with emotional balance; joy enhances abundance. **Iré:** Love, creativity, emotional balance, harmonious relationships, abundance. **Òsogbo:** Emotional imbalance, indulgence without wisdom, vanity, relational discord.

31. Ogbe-Ofun: This Odu talks about divine authority and truth; completion and clarity. **Message:** Honest effort, integrity, and patience ensure success; pride and deception undermine destiny. **Iré:** Prosperity through honesty, wisdom, protection, hope after failure, good fortune. **Òsogbo:** Deceit, sexual misconduct, disrespect to elders, pride, spiritual stagnation, lies undermining progress.

* * *

THE CHILDREN OF OYEKU MÉJÌ

Common Themes found in the family of Oyeku include: Mystery of night, the unknown, ancestral wisdom, death and transitions.

32. Oyeku–Ogbe: This Odu talks about light emerging from mystery, ancestral wisdom guiding creation, and clarity born from darkness. **Message:** Destiny becomes clear when ancestral knowledge illuminates new beginnings and aligns one with their Ori. **Iré:** Clear direction, ancestral guidance, spiritual awakening, protection in new ventures, alignment with destiny. **Òsogbo:** Confusion, spiritual blindness, lack of direction, disconnection from ancestors, fear of the unknown.

33. Oyeku–Iwori: This Odu talks about hidden wisdom awakening consciousness and personal power through ancestral reflection. **Message:** Mastery of the self comes from understanding inner fire while honoring ancestral lessons. **Iré:** Self-awareness, awakened consciousness, disciplined power, wise decisions, spiritual insight. **Òsogbo:** Ego imbalance, impulsiveness, misuse of power, confusion from ignoring inner wisdom.

34. Oyeku–Odi: This Odu talks about ancestral protection, hidden gestation, and guarded growth within spiritual boundaries. **Message:** Stability and protection come from honoring ancestral foundations and maintaining strong boundaries. **Iré:** Protection, emotional security, stable growth, fertility of ideas or family, grounded progress. **Òsogbo:** Vulnerability, blocked growth, emotional insecurity, exposure to hidden dangers.

35. Oyeku–Irosun: This Odu talks about deep ancestral lineage, generational memory, and destiny shaped by inherited patterns. **Message:** True progress comes from understanding and healing ancestral influences. **Iré:** Strong ancestral connection, wisdom from lineage, destiny fulfillment, spiritual maturity. **Òsogbo:** Repeating generational cycles, unresolved ancestral issues, emotional burdens from the past.

36. Oyeku–Owonrin: This Odu talks about navigating change through the unknown with ancestral guidance at life's crossroads. **Message:** Adaptability and spiritual awareness ensure safe passage through transformation. **Iré:** Successful transitions, protection during change, wise decisions, adaptability. **Òsogbo:** Instability, poor choices, restlessness, confusion in uncertain situations.

37. Oyeku–Obara: This Odu talks about transforming hidden potential into abundance through spiritual wisdom and integrity. **Message:** Prosperity grows when transformation is guided by ancestral truth and balanced power. **Iré:** Financial growth, restored opportunities, abundance, empowerment, material and spiritual prosperity. **Òsogbo:** Financial instability, greed, misuse of influence, loss through poor judgment.

38. Oyeku–Okanran: This Odu talks about resilience forged in darkness and strength developed through emotional mastery. **Message:** Courage is strengthened when fear is confronted with ancestral support and discipline. **Iré:** Inner strength, patience, leadership ability, resilience through trials. **Òsogbo:** Anger, impulsiveness, emotional imbalance, destructive reactions.

39. Oyeku–Ogunda: This Odu talks about cutting through hidden obstacles and confronting darkness with decisive action. **Message:**

Victory requires courage, discipline, and the willingness to remove what blocks progress. **Iré:** Cleared paths, triumph over enemies, strength in adversity, successful breakthroughs. **Òsogbo:** Conflict, accidents, destructive anger, misuse of force, legal or physical struggles.

40. Oyeku–Osa: This Odu talks about spiritual storms, unseen forces, and the necessity of spiritual defense. **Message:**Protection comes through humility, discernment, and respect for hidden powers. **Iré:** Spiritual protection, heightened intuition, awareness of hidden matters, divine guidance. **Òsogbo:** Spiritual attacks, deception, fear, confusion, vulnerability to negative influences.

41. Oyeku–Ika: This Odu talks about moral accountability in hidden matters and the disciplined use of power. **Message:**Integrity and restraint prevent destructive consequences. **Iré:** Self-control, justice, protection through humility, stable progress. **Òsogbo:** Pride, misuse of authority, envy, conflict, karmic consequences of unethical behavior.

42. Oyeku–Oturupon: This Odu talks about endurance through hardship and restoration after loss. **Message:** Humility and perseverance allow recovery and long-term stability. **Iré:** Recovery from setbacks, resilience, divine intervention, restored opportunities. **Òsogbo:** Collapse from arrogance, prolonged suffering, bondage to poor decisions, resistance to correction.

43. Oyeku–Otura: This Odu talks about mystical reflection, deep truth, and spiritual alignment emerging from stillness. **Message:** Inner peace and honest self-examination restore balance and clarity. **Iré:** Spiritual vision, tranquility, clear understanding, restored harmony. **Òsogbo:** Illusion, denial, stubbornness, spiritual confusion.

44. Oyeku–Irete: This Odu talks about building character through ancestral discipline and steady moral effort. **Message:**Long-term blessings come through integrity, patience, and responsibility. **Iré:** Stable progress, rewarded patience, moral strength, lasting success. **Òsogbo:** Delays, instability, neglect of duties, loss through poor character.

45. Oyeku–Ose: This Odu talks about emotional renewal and the restoration of harmony after difficulty. **Message:**Cleansing and balance reopen the flow of abundance and relationships. **Iré:**

Emotional healing, restored peace, creative flow, prosperity returning. **Òsogbo:** Relationship conflict, emotional heaviness, indulgence, blocked blessings.

46. Oyeku–Ofun: This Odu talks about purification, completion of cycles, and emergence into clarity after darkness. **Message:** Endings serve as spiritual cleansing that leads to wisdom and renewal. **Iré:** Spiritual purification, completed cycles, clarity, divine protection, renewed destiny. **Òsogbo:** Resistance to endings, hidden enemies, destructive patterns, spiritual stagnation.

* * *

THE CHILDREN OF Ìwòrì Méjì

Common Themes found in the family of Iwori include: Fire, consciousness, ego, personal power, transformation, metamorphosis.

47. Iwori–Ogbe: This Odu shines light on the inner consciousness, teaching that self-reflection and honest evaluation of one's thoughts and actions reveal hidden potential. **Message:** By examining personal choices with clarity, one can identify strengths, weaknesses, and opportunities for growth. **Iré:** Insight, understanding of true purpose, clarity in relationships and work, improved decision-making. **Òsogbo:** Mental confusion, indecision, repeated mistakes, missing opportunities, misunderstanding one's own motives.

48. Iwori–Oyeku: This Odu represents insight emerging from silence, teaching that deep understanding comes through contemplation, meditation, and ancestral connection. **Message:** Listening to guidance from elders and spiritual sources unlocks hidden wisdom. **Iré:** Clarity on life paths, ancestral guidance, awakening to unseen truths. **Òsogbo:** Ignoring advice, fear of change, neglecting ancestral knowledge, repeating harmful patterns.

49. Iwori–Odi: This Odu emphasizes disciplined preparation, structure, and personal boundaries. **Message:** Patience and adherence to necessary processes support safe spiritual and personal growth. **Iré:** Protection from missteps, steady progress, renewed energy, visible transformation. **Òsogbo:** Stagnation, resistance to guidance, inability to release old habits, rushing processes.

50. Iwori–Irosun: This Odu brings focus to family, lineage, and inherited patterns. **Message:** Understanding ancestry reveals strengths and tendencies that shape current behavior. **Iré:** Guidance from ancestral wisdom, clarity about inherited talents, tools for resolving long-standing issues. **Òsogbo:** Neglecting heritage, failing to recognize recurring patterns, emotional wounds, repeating ancestors' mistakes.

51. Iwori–Owonrin (Iwori Ojuani): This Odu teaches mental adaptability and flexibility in thought. **Message:** Progress requires adjusting perspectives and responding effectively to new information. **Iré:** Adaptability, quick problem-solving, clarity in unexpected situations. **Òsogbo:** Rigidity, scattered thinking, inability to adjust, impulsive decisions.

52. Iwori–Obara: This Odu emphasizes expressing truth and ethical leadership. **Message:** Wisdom guides others best when combined with integrity and clear communication. **Iré:** Fair leadership, respect earned through honesty, inspiring collaboration. **Òsogbo:** Abusing authority, creating conflict, misleading others, pride compromising judgment.

53. Iwori–Okanran: This Odu teaches resolve, patience, and emotional stability under pressure. **Message:** Measured responses during challenges build character and inner strength. **Iré:** Courage, stress management, self-discipline, consistency under adversity. **Òsogbo:** Impulsive actions, fear-driven reactions, emotional instability, poor decision-making.

54. Iwori–Ogunda: This Odu teaches disciplined effort, self-knowledge, and constructive use of personal power. **Message:** Strength grows through focused, consistent effort and spiritual work. **Iré:** Inner power, ability to overcome challenges, persistence, long-term success. **Òsogbo:** Misdirected energy, burnout, wasted effort, inability to focus on priorities.

55. Iwori–Osa: This Odu teaches awareness of hidden spiritual and environmental forces. **Message:** Recognizing subtle energies prevents missteps and enables transformation. **Iré:** Spiritual intuition, understanding unseen influences, wise responses to hidden forces. **Òsogbo:** Ignorance, susceptibility to deception, spiritual imbalance, acting blindly.

56. Iwori–Ika: This Odu teaches discernment, ethical protection, and careful engagement with potentially harmful forces. **Message:** Awareness of intentions—personal and external—safeguards well-being. **Iré:** Protection from betrayal, clarity in complex situations, resilience in conflict. **Òsogbo:** Exposure to danger, involvement in conflict, manipulation, unethical choices.

57. Iwori–Oturupon: This Odu encourages balance, reflection, and renewal through contemplation of life cycles. **Message:** Understanding natural rhythms restores harmony and prepares for growth. **Iré:** Insight through meditation, personal restoration, harmonious decision-making, inner peace. **Òsogbo:** Stagnation, unresolved issues, imbalance, failure to learn from experience.

58. Iwori–Otura: This Odu emphasizes spiritual peace and alignment with universal truths. **Message:** Serenity comes through knowledge, reflection, and ethical living. **Iré:** Calmness, clarity in spiritual and practical matters, consistent ethical behavior. **Òsogbo:** Confusion, being misled, ignoring spiritual truths, moral misalignment.

59. Iwori–Irete: This Odu represents prosperity achieved through patient, consistent effort. **Message:** Ethical and reflective practice ensures lasting results. **Iré:** Stability, long-term progress, rewards from discipline, opportunities through patience. **Òsogbo:** Impatience, wasted effort, short-term thinking, setbacks from hasty decisions.

60. Iwori–Ose: This Odu embodies harmony, moderation, and alignment between action and spiritual principles. **Message:** Balanced behavior and ethical conduct bring fulfillment and joy. **Iré:** Peaceful relationships, spiritual satisfaction, ethical accomplishments, restored harmony. **Òsogbo:** Indulgence, imbalance, moral or spiritual decline, conflicts from selfishness.

61. Iwori–Ofun: This Odu represents completion, integration, and spiritual maturity. **Message:** Alignment with higher purpose comes from wisdom, ethical living, and self-understanding. **Iré:** Achievement of goals, clarity of purpose, spiritual fulfillment, life satisfaction. **Òsogbo:** Arrogance, misuse of knowledge, ethical failure, emotional or spiritual decline.

* * *

THE CHILDREN OF ÒDÍ MÉJÌ

Common Themes found in the family of Odi include: Seal of the womb, fertility, protection, maternal guidance

62. Odi–Ogbe: This Odu talks about protected growth, fertile beginnings, and creation within stable structure. **Message:**When intentions are clearly formed and properly protected, growth becomes stable and productive. **Iré:** Successful beginnings, stable foundations, protected opportunities, clarity of purpose, fruitful outcomes. **Òsogbo:** Poor planning, wasted effort, lack of direction, unstable foundations, blocked growth.

63. Odi–Oyeku: This Odu talks about sealing endings, protective closure, and preserving life's resources through transitions. **Message:** Proper closure protects future stability and maintains emotional and spiritual balance. **Iré:** Safe transitions, emotional protection, orderly endings, preserved resources, stability. **Òsogbo:** Disorder, unresolved cycles, loss through negligence, vulnerability during change.

64. Odi–Iwori: This Odu talks about containment of inner fire, emotional control, and disciplined self-mastery. **Message:**Mastering inner impulses protects one from harm and allows controlled transformation. **Iré:** Self-discipline, emotional balance, inner clarity, wise action, controlled growth. **Òsogbo:** Impulsiveness, emotional instability, rash behavior, loss of self-control.

65. Odi–Irosun: This Odu talks about maternal lineage, ancestral protection, and stability through heritage. **Message:**Security and protection come from honoring ancestry and inherited wisdom. **Iré:** Ancestral guidance, strong roots, inherited strength, stability through tradition. **Òsogbo:** Disconnection from ancestry, weak foundations, repeated generational problems.

66. Odi–Owonrin: This Odu talks about protected change, flexible stability, and transformation within safe boundaries. **Message:** Adaptation must occur without breaking essential structures that preserve life. **Iré:** Resilience, safe transformation, adaptability, steady progress. **Òsogbo:** Rigidity, resistance to change, confusion, instability.

67. Odi–Obara: This Odu talks about guarded authority, disciplined leadership, and maintaining clear boundaries. **Message:** True leadership protects others through integrity and responsible guidance. **Iré:** Respect, ethical authority, structured influence, harmonious relationships. **Òsogbo:** Abuse of power, broken trust, boundary violations, conflict.

68. Odi–Okanran: This Odu talks about endurance, emotional strength, and protection under pressure. **Message:**Stability is preserved through patience and emotional control during trials. **Iré:** Courage, perseverance, resilience, strong character. **Òsogbo:** Impulsive reactions, emotional weakness, instability during stress.

69. Odi–Ogunda: This Odu talks about disciplined labor, structured effort, and productive action. **Message:** Consistent work within proper structure produces lasting results. **Iré:** Endurance, practical success, effective work, steady achievement. **Òsogbo:** Disorganization, wasted energy, inefficiency, failure to complete tasks.

70. Odi–Osa: This Odu talks about protection from hidden forces and awareness of unseen influences. **Message:**Recognizing subtle spiritual and environmental forces preserves balance and prevents harm. **Iré:** Spiritual protection, foresight, awareness, guarded stability. **Òsogbo:** Ignorance of hidden dangers, deception, spiritual imbalance.

71. Odi–Ika: This Odu talks about responsibility, ethical conduct, and protective accountability. **Message:** Honoring obligations safeguards one's path and preserves harmony. **Iré:** Integrity, protection, trustworthy conduct, balanced relationships. **Òsogbo:** Negligence, misconduct, conflict, exposure to harm.

72. Odi–Oturupon: This Odu talks about renewal of boundaries, healing, and restoration of protection. **Message:**Reflection and healing restore strength and preserve integrity. **Iré:** Renewal, restored energy, strong boundaries, resilience. **Òsogbo:** Vulnerability, stagnation, weakened protection, unresolved issues.

73. Odi–Otura: This Odu talks about spiritual purity, divine order, and peaceful alignment. **Message:** Consistent spiritual discipline preserves harmony and protection. **Iré:** Serenity, spiritual clarity, moral order, inner peace. **Òsogbo:** Confusion, spiritual disorder, lack of direction.

74. Odi–Irete: This Odu talks about fertile prosperity, patient development, and stable growth. **Message:** Lasting abundance develops through disciplined and protected effort. **Iré:** Steady progress, abundance, stability, long-term success. **Òsogbo:** Impatience, failed plans, instability, inconsistency.

75. Odi–Ose: This Odu talks about harmony within boundaries, nurtured balance, and preserved well-being. **Message:**Moderation and order maintain peace and protect life's sweetness. **Iré:** Harmony, joy, balance, peaceful relationships. **Òsogbo:** Imbalance, disorder, conflict, excess.

76. Odi–Ofun: This Odu talks about sealed completion, perfected order, and fulfilled destiny. **Message:** Integrity and completion of responsibilities lead to wholeness and mastery. **Iré:** Fulfillment, completion, spiritual alignment, mastery, clarity. **Òsogbo:** Arrogance, unfinished work, misuse of knowledge, decline.

* * *

THE CHILDREN OF IROSUN MEJI
Common Themes found in the family of Irosun include: Ancestors,
generational consciousness, destiny shaped by lineage

77. Irosun–Ogbe: Ancestral wisdom, generational influence, inherited destiny, lineage consciousness, light, creation, clarity, alignment with one's higher self (Ori), new beginnings. **Message:** This Odu teaches that honoring ancestral guidance and carefully planning actions brings clarity, success, and safe progression toward one's destiny. Following proven guidance ensures that efforts are effective and aligned with purpose. **Iré:** Insight, protection, clear direction, alignment with destiny, and well-informed decisions. **Òsogbo:** Hidden dangers, betrayal, mistrust, spiritual confusion, and mistakes caused by ignoring advice or guidance.

78. Irosun–Oyeku: Letting go, release, endings, ancestral support, transformation, renewal, opening new paths, embracing change. **Message:** This Odu teaches that gracefully releasing the past and accepting endings allows ancestral guidance to open the way for renewal and new opportunities. Acceptance of change ensures smooth transitions. **Iré:** Peaceful transitions, support from ancestors, clarity, and access to new opportunities. **Òsogbo:** Fear of change, stagnation, feeling stuck, resistance, and missed opportunities.

79. Irosun–Iwori: Reflection, ancestral memory, personal and family history, wisdom, learning from experience, consciousness, personal power. **Message:** This Odu teaches that careful reflection on personal and family history strengthens decision-making and prevents repeated mistakes. Ancestral lessons provide insight for a clear path forward. **Iré:** Wisdom, clarity, careful planning, sound judgment, and strengthened decision-making. **Òsogbo:** Hasty decisions, ignoring tradition, repeating past errors, and lack of foresight.

80. Irosun–Odi: Discipline, structure, patience, protection, stability, guidance, ancestral alignment, purpose. **Message:** This Odu teaches that disciplined action guided by ancestral wisdom safeguards growth, ensures steady progress, and protects one's personal path. **Iré:** Grounded stability, alignment with purpose, protection in undertakings, and steady advancement. **Òsogbo:** Confusion, recklessness, ignoring guidance, impatience, and setbacks.

81. Irosun–Owonrin: Adaptability, flexibility, balance, being grounded, change, foresight, guidance. **Message:** This Odu teaches that adapting wisely to new circumstances while remaining anchored in ancestral guidance ensures stable and secure progress. **Iré:** Balanced adaptability, purposeful movement, secure transitions, and stable outcomes. **Òsogbo:** Instability, impulsive choices, lack of grounding, rushing, and errors caused by poor judgment.

82. Irosun–Obara: Honest communication, integrity, trust, relationships, harmony, ancestral guidance, listening, clear expression. **Message:** This Odu teaches that truthful speech and careful listening strengthen bonds, build trust, and prevent conflict in relationships. **Iré:** Harmonious relationships, clear expression, strong trust, and connectedness. **Òsogbo:** Gossip, conflict, broken trust, misunderstandings, and relationship challenges.

83. Irosun–Okanran: Emotional control, patience, resilience, inner strength, composure, self-mastery. **Message:** This Odu teaches that calm responses and emotional discipline create strength and stability, enabling one to navigate challenges successfully. **Iré:** Emotional balance, courage, patience under stress, self-mastery, and composure. **Òsogbo:** Anger, frustration, impulsive reactions, emotional outbursts, and instability.

84. Irosun–Ogunda: Hard work, persistence, effort guided by wisdom, growth, long-term achievement, ancestral counsel. **Message:** This Odu teaches that sustained effort combined with guidance from wisdom and ancestors produces lasting success and meaningful accomplishments. **Iré:** Persistence, growth, steady progress, achievements grounded in wisdom. **Òsogbo:** Wasted effort, misapplied energy, lack of direction, and failure to follow guidance.

85. Irosun–Osa: Sacred knowledge, spiritual awareness, discernment, protection, responsibility, clarity. **Message:** This Odu teaches that spiritual and sacred knowledge must be handled carefully and wisely to bring benefit, clarity, and protection rather than harm. **Iré:** Spiritual clarity, wise decisions, discernment, and protection from misguidance. **Òsogbo:** Confusion, oversharing secrets, vulnerability, misuse of knowledge, and harm.

86. Irosun–Ika: Accountability, integrity, responsibility, moral clarity, learning from mistakes, ancestral guidance. **Message:** This Odu teaches that accepting responsibility and correcting mistakes restores balance, strengthens character, and builds trust. **Iré:** Moral clarity, sound judgment, ethical behavior, and resilience. **Òsogbo:** Pride, stubbornness, poor choices, and negative consequences from ignoring lessons.

87. Irosun–Oturupon: Endurance, patience, perseverance, strength, preparation, overcoming obstacles, ancestral support. **Message:** This Odu teaches that challenges and delays are opportunities to strengthen resolve and prepare for future success. **Iré:** Resilience, endurance, preparation for growth, and ability to overcome difficulties. **Òsogbo:** Discouragement, giving up, stagnation, and missed opportunities.

88. Irosun–Otura: Reflection, heritage, ancestry, balanced judgment, wisdom, careful decision-making. **Message:** This Odu teaches that reflecting on ancestry, personal experience, and heritage fosters balanced and wise choices, preventing mistakes. **Iré:** Careful judgment, calm reasoning, wise decisions, and alignment with purpose. **Òsogbo:** Indecision, scattered thinking, poor alignment with goals, and confusion.

89. Irosun–Irete: Respect for tradition, family, ancestors, discipline, gratitude, consistency, lasting success. **Message:** This Odu teaches that honoring family, ancestors, and tradition creates a stable foundation for enduring achievements. **Iré:** Steady progress, recognition, support, and secure accomplishments. **Òsogbo:** Pride, ignoring guidance, mismanagement, and fragile outcomes.

90. Irosun–Ose: Harmony, cooperation, relationships, social balance, gratitude, community, ancestral guidance. **Message:** This Odu teaches that respect, cooperation, and gratitude create harmony in relationships and strengthen community well-being. **Iré:** Balanced relationships, happiness, clear communication, and social harmony. **Òsogbo:** Conflict, tension, imbalance, and difficulty connecting with others.

91. Irosun–Ofun: Renewal, completion, clarity, ancestral alignment, fulfillment, spiritual guidance, personal growth. **Message:** This Odu teaches that honoring one's roots and following ancestral guidance brings clarity, renewal, and successful completion of projects and life goals. **Iré:** Spiritual renewal, clarity, blessings, alignment with purpose, and fulfillment. **Òsogbo:** Avoidance of growth, stalled progress, loss of direction, and failure to honor responsibilities.

* * *

92. Òwónrín–Ogbe: Clarity of intention, purposeful action, ancestral guidance, careful progress, alignment with one's path. **Message:** This Odu teaches that success comes from acting with clear intention and guidance. Careful, deliberate steps lead to progress, while rushing creates obstacles and confusion. **Iré:** Clear direction, smooth progress, ancestral support, and well-planned actions. **Òsogbo:** Confusion, careless action, haste-induced mistakes, and obstacles caused by impulsiveness.

93. Òwónrín–Oyeku: Release, endings, acceptance, readiness for change, ancestral support, new opportunities. **Message:** This Odu teaches that letting go of what has ended allows new opportunities to enter. Proper closure and acceptance of change bring stability and growth. **Iré:** Peaceful transitions, insight, readiness for new beginnings, and ancestral support. **Òsogbo:** Fear of change, hesitation, resistance, and missed opportunities.

94. Òwónrín–Iwori: Reflection, foresight, planning, careful thinking, learning from experience. **Message:** This Odu teaches that thinking before acting prevents mistakes. Planning and reflection lead to wise, effective decisions. **Iré:** Thoughtful planning, clarity, protection during change, and wise choices. **Òsogbo:** Impulsive actions, poor decisions, wasted effort, and lack of foresight.

95. Òwónrín–Odi: Discipline, structure, patience, guidance, protection, steady progress. **Message:** This Odu teaches that disciplined action guided by wisdom safeguards growth and prevents setbacks. Careful planning ensures stability and success. **Iré:** Stability, protection, steady growth, and alignment with purpose. **Òsogbo:** Recklessness, ignoring guidance, frustration, and delays caused by poor preparation.

96. Òwónrín–Irosun: Ancestral reflection, learning from the past, personal history, family patterns, wisdom. **Message:** This Odu teaches that understanding the past and ancestral lessons prevents repeated mistakes and strengthens your path forward. **Iré:** Ancestral guidance, steady progress, and wisdom gained from experience. **Òsogbo:** Ignoring lessons, confusion, acting without foresight, and repeated errors.

97. Òwónrín–Obara: Honest communication, integrity, trust, listening, harmony in relationships. **Message:** This Odu teaches that clear speech and respectful listening strengthen relationships and foster trust. Speaking with integrity builds lasting bonds. **Iré:** Harmony, strong relationships, trust, and mutual understanding. **Òsogbo:** Gossip, dishonesty, misunderstandings, and broken trust.

98. Òwónrín–Okanran: Emotional control, patience, resilience, inner strength, composure. **Message:** This Odu teaches that managing emotions and responding calmly prevents conflict and supports steady progress. **Iré:** Emotional balance, inner strength, patience, and composure under stress. **Òsogbo:** Anger, impulsiveness, frustration, and emotional instability.

99. Òwónrín–Ogunda: Hard work, persistence, effort guided by wisdom, growth, lasting achievement. **Message:** This Odu teaches that consistent effort, guided by ancestral or wise counsel, leads to meaningful and lasting success. **Iré:** Steady growth, meaningful accomplishments, protection through effort, and progress. **Òsogbo:** Wasted energy, lack of direction, impatience, and setbacks.

100. Òwónrín–Osa: Spiritual awareness, careful handling of knowledge, discernment, insight, responsibility. **Message:** This Odu teaches that knowledge, especially sacred or spiritual knowledge, must be used with care and wisdom to prevent harm. **Iré:** Insight, clarity, wise decision-making, and protection from misguidance. **Òsogbo:** Confusion, carelessness, oversharing, and misuse of knowledge.

101. Òwónrín–Ika: Responsibility, honesty, integrity, moral clarity, ethical behavior. **Message:** This Odu teaches that acting with integrity and accountability protects your path and maintains balance. **Iré:** Accountability, good judgment, ethical behavior, and spiritual protection. **Òsogbo:** Stubbornness, unethical actions, poor choices, and conflict.

102. Òwónrín–Oturupon: Endurance, patience, resilience, strength through experience, preparation for growth. **Message:** This Odu teaches that challenges and hardships strengthen resolve and prepare you for future success when met with patience. **Iré:** Resilience, personal growth, strength through experience, and perseverance. **Òsogbo:** Discouragement, giving up, stagnation, and missed opportunities.

103. Òwónrín–Otura: Reflection, balance, thoughtful judgment, ancestral insight, careful action. **Message:** This Odu teaches that reflection and careful consideration lead to wise choices and steady progress. **Iré:** Calm judgment, clarity, wise decisions, and steady advancement. **Òsogbo:** Indecision, scattered thinking, mistakes from rushing, and poor alignment with goals.

104. Òwónrín–Irete: Responsibility, humility, respect for ancestors, discipline, gratitude, steady success. **Message:** This Odu teaches that honoring duties, ancestors, and traditions ensures lasting achievements and stability. **Iré:** Steady progress, recognition, support, and secure accomplishments. **Òsogbo:** Pride, neglect of responsibilities, mismanagement, and fragile outcomes.

105. Òwónrín–Ose: Harmony, cooperation, ethical conduct, relationships, community balance, gratitude. **Message:** This Odu teaches that balanced actions, respect, and cooperation bring joy, peace, and harmony in relationships and community life. **Iré:** Happiness, harmonious relationships, social balance, and mutual respect. **Òsogbo:** Conflict, imbalance, tension, and challenges in connecting with others.

106. Òwónrín–Ofun: Completion, renewal, spiritual alignment, fulfillment, honoring roots, clarity. **Message:** This Odu teaches that honoring ancestral guidance and completing what you begin brings clarity, blessings, and spiritual fulfillment. **Iré:** Renewal, spiritual alignment, successful completion, clarity, and fulfillment. **Òsogbo:** Avoidance of responsibility, unfinished tasks, loss of direction, and stalled progress.

* * *

THE CHILDREN OF OBARA MÉJÌ

Common Themes found in the family of Obara include: Transformation, turning poverty into wealth, material and spiritual abundance.

107. Obara-Ogbe: New beginnings in transformation, emerging clarity after struggle, turning adversity into opportunity, material and spiritual potential. **Message:** True transformation occurs when you embrace challenges openly and use wisdom to navigate adversity. Material and spiritual growth come from clarity and proactive action. **Ire:** Success in leadership and personal endeavors, recognition, prosperity, clear decision-making, growth in spiritual and material life. **Osogbo:** Arrogance, misuse of authority, pride, conflicts, broken relationships, failure to learn from struggles.

108. Obara-Oyeku: This Odu teaches that facing hidden fears and emotional struggles leads to growth and inner strength. **Message:** Maintaining discipline and caution in relationships protects you and ensures spiritual stability. **Ire:** emotional resilience, spiritual protection, victory over hidden obstacles, inner strength. **Osogbo:** depression, conflict in relationships, being manipulated, hidden dangers.

109. Obara-Iwori: This Odu teaches that intelligence, careful planning, and strategic thinking solve complex problems. **Message:** Patience and reflection prevent mistakes and unnecessary conflict. **Ire:** wisdom, insight, successful planning, clear judgment. **Osogbo:** confusion, poor decisions, deceit, misuse of knowledge.

110. Obara-Odi: This Odu teaches that challenges are overcome through patience, steady effort, and emotional control. **Message:** Stability comes from disciplined action and careful handling of obstacles. **Ire:** endurance, stability, strong foundations, resilience. **Osogbo:** stagnation, emotional burden, blocked progress, impatience.

111. Obara-Irosun: This Odu teaches that listening to ancestors and learning from family traditions provides guidance, protection, and spiritual insight. **Message:** Honoring heritage strengthens your path. **Ire:** ancestral guidance, protection, wisdom, support from lineage. **Osogbo:** neglect of tradition, repeated mistakes, spiritual confusion.

112. Obara-Owonrin: This Odu teaches that sudden changes and movement require flexibility, awareness, and emotional balance. **Message:** Adapting quickly while staying grounded ensures progress and avoids unnecessary loss. **Ire:** adaptability, quick success, opportunity through change, balanced decisions. **Osogbo:** instability, chaos, scattered energy, rash actions.

113. Obara-Okanran: This Odu teaches that controlling strong emotions and acting with discipline leads to success. **Message:** Courage, tempered by wisdom, allows you to navigate challenges without creating conflict. **Ire:** patience, courage, emotional control, decisive action. **Osogbo:** anger, impulsiveness, aggression, conflict.

114. Obara-Ogunda: Cutting through obstacles, decisive action in transformation, clearing paths for progress, forging ahead with strength and clarity. **Message:** Steady effort and decisive action remove obstacles. Strength and clarity produce progress and lasting achievement. **Ire:** Achievement, progress through effort, resilience, strength, breakthrough success. **Osogbo:** Overexertion, wasted energy, burnout, frustration, forcing outcomes.

115. Obara-Osa: Spiritual defense in transformation, facing hidden consequences, navigating storms in life, protection against misuse of spiritual power. **Message:** Surrender to guidance and trust in spiritual support to navigate life's storms. Spiritual vigilance ensures successful transformation. **Ire:** Spiritual awakening, renewal, protection, successful transformation, resilience in challenges. **Osogbo:** Fear, confusion, instability, spiritual crisis, vulnerability to unseen dangers.

116. Obara-Ika: Transforming restraint into wisdom, self-control as a tool for success, understanding limits of power, careful navigation of challenges. **Message:** Ethical behavior and self-discipline protect you and maintain balance. Responsible action ensures safety and personal mastery. **Ire:** Protection, ethical decisions, self-mastery, victory in disputes, controlled power. **Osogbo:** Betrayal, hostility, unethical behavior, conflict, misuse of authority.

117. Obara-Oturupón: Sustained transformation, enduring hardships to achieve stability, perseverance leading to long-term abundance, steadfastness in trials. **Message:** Enduring challenges with discipline ensures long-term stability and prosperity. Responsibility and integrity bring spiritual and material success. **Ire:** Spiritual renewal, transformation, stability, resilience, long-term abundance. **Osogbo:** Sudden loss, destructive actions, misfortune, delayed results, burnout.

118. Obara-Otura: Transformational insight, mystical understanding, reflecting on divine guidance, inner alignment as a path to clarity and peace. **Message:** Reflection, calm judgment, and alignment with spiritual guidance bring clarity, harmony, and wise decisions. **Ire:** Spiritual insight, clarity, peace, harmony, effective decision-making. **Osogbo:** Confusion, poor judgment, emotional imbalance, setbacks, misinterpretation of guidance.

119. Obara-Irete: Ethical transformation, developing integrity, cultivating blessings through virtue, building personal character as a foundation for prosperity. **Message:** Steady, disciplined effort and ethical conduct ensure long-term growth and lasting achievement. **Ire:** Progress, stability, endurance, reliable results, personal integrity. **Osogbo:** Impatience, setbacks, unstable growth, neglect of responsibility.

120. Obara-Ose: Flowing transformation, harnessing creativity for abundance, prosperity through aligned action, opening channels of wealth and joy. **Message:** Align creativity with ethical action and harmonious energy to manifest prosperity, joy, and social success. **Ire:** Happiness, balanced enjoyment, prosperity, ethical relationships, creative success. **Osogbo:**Overindulgence, temptation, conflict, missed opportunities, excess.

121. Obara-Ofun: Completion and integration of transformation, full cycles realized, emergence into clarity, ultimate understanding of spiritual and material lessons. **Message:** Fulfillment comes from ethical leadership, maturity, and honoring responsibilities. Complete cycles with integrity bring clarity and success. **Ire:** Spiritual wisdom, fulfillment, achievement of goals, clarity, mastery. **Osogbo:** Pride, dishonesty, misuse of knowledge, loss of direction, incomplete lessons.

✳ ✳ ✳

Common Themes found in the family of Okanran include: Strength of heart, resilience, trials that shape leadership, Emotions, Could indicate a restless heart.

122. Okanran–Ogbe: This Odu speaks of a restless and emotionally driven heart seeking clarity, light, and alignment with destiny. Strong feelings must be guided by wisdom to lead to successful new beginnings. **Message:** When emotions align with clarity and purpose, they create inspired action and forward movement. When feelings override wisdom, confusion and self-sabotage follow. **Ire:** Clear direction, inspired action, emotional alignment, successful beginnings. **Osogbo:** Impulsiveness, emotional confusion, blocked destiny, poor decisions.

123. Okanran–Oyekun: Emotional strength built through confronting hidden fears; facing inner struggles; mystery of night, the unknown, ancestral wisdom. **Message:** This Odu teaches that confronting hidden fears and inner darkness allows transformation, protection, and emotional resilience. Facing the unknown with discipline and reflection strengthens the heart and supports spiritual growth. **Ire:** Spiritual awakening, inner strength, overcoming fear, protection. **Osogbo:** Emotional turmoil, hidden enemies, depression, spiritual imbalance.

124. Okanran–Iwori: This Odu centers on the relationship between strong emotions and personal power, showing how ego shapes emotional expression and leadership. **Message:** Balanced self-awareness transforms emotional intensity into wise leadership. When ego controls the heart, pride and poor judgment lead to downfall. **Ire:** Emotional intelligence, confident leadership, balanced authority. **Osogbo:** Arrogance, misuse of power, reactive behavior, damaged reputation.

125. Okanran–Odi: This Odu represents emotional restlessness seeking stability, protection, and nurturing foundations that allow growth and security. **Message:** The heart must be protected and grounded to create lasting results. Emotional instability blocks growth, while patience and emotional security allow steady development. **Ire:** Protection, stability, fertility, emotional security. **Osogbo:** Blocked progress, emotional immaturity, delays, vulnerability.

126. Okanran–Irosun: This Odu addresses emotional patterns connected to ancestry and generational influences that shape destiny. **Message:** Recognizing inherited emotional behaviors allows transformation and spiritual maturity. Ignoring them leads to repeated cycles and karmic repetition. **Ire:** Ancestral healing, wisdom, emotional awareness, destiny correction. **Osogbo:** Repeated mistakes, family conflict, karmic burdens, stagnation.

127. Okanran–Owonrin: Flexibility and composure forged through sudden changes; adaptability and flexibility; crossroads, unpredictability, change. **Message:** This Odu teaches that leaders who remain flexible, prepared, and observant can navigate sudden changes with clarity and composure. Emotional balance ensures survival and opportunity through transitions. **Ire:** Adaptability, quick solutions, creative change, survival through flexibility. **Osogbo:** Instability, confusion, unexpected problems, scattered energy.

128. Okanran–Obara: This Odu explores how emotional passion can either block or create transformation, turning hardship into abundance when properly directed. **Message:** Disciplined passion transforms struggle into prosperity. Emotional excess or pride can lead to financial and spiritual loss. **Ire:** Wealth creation, transformation, material and spiritual abundance. **Osogbo:** Loss through emotional decisions, pride, instability.

129. Okanran–Ogunda: This Odu reflects emotional drive combined with hard work and persistent effort. **Message:** When strong feelings are channeled into disciplined labor, progress is inevitable. When emotions fuel anger or conflict, effort is wasted. **Ire:** Productivity, perseverance, strength through effort, leadership. **Osogbo:** Burnout, frustration, conflict, wasted energy.

130. Okanran–Osa: This Odu represents emotional storms that can create sudden upheaval and disruption. **Message:** Uncontrolled emotions can bring rapid destruction. A steady and disciplined heart transforms upheaval into renewal instead of chaos. **Ire:** Protection during crisis, emotional maturity, renewal. **Osogbo:** Sudden loss, chaos, emotional instability.

131. Okanran–Ika: This Odu focuses on emotional intensity that must be restrained to prevent harm and conflict. **Message:** Self-control protects destiny. Mastering emotional reactions prevents destruction and preserves peace. **Ire:** Protection, victory through restraint, disciplined strength. **Osogbo:** Conflict, aggression, betrayal, reckless behavior.

132. Okanran–Oturupon: This Odu speaks of emotional intensity tested through hardship, requiring endurance and correction. **Message:** Challenges refine the heart and build resilience. Refusing correction leads to prolonged suffering. **Ire:** Endurance, renewal, emotional strength, transformation. **Osogbo:** Stubbornness, repeated hardship, destructive patterns.

133. Okanran–Otura: This Odu centers on calming the restless heart through reflection and spiritual clarity. **Message:** Insight and contemplation bring emotional balance and wise decision-making. Acting without reflection leads to confusion. **Ire:** Insight, peace, clarity, wise choices. **Osogbo:** Illusion, misunderstanding, poor judgment.

134. Okanran–Irete: This Odu emphasizes building good character by grounding emotional strength in integrity and discipline. **Message:** Strong emotions must be stabilized by ethical behavior and responsibility. Character ensures lasting success. **Ire:** Stability, earned respect, disciplined growth. **Osogbo:** Irresponsibility, loss of trust, stagnation.

135. Okanran–Ose: This Odu teaches that emotional balance creates flow, harmony, and prosperity. **Message:** When the heart is balanced, life flows with ease and abundance. Emotional excess disrupts peace and blocks blessings. **Ire:** Harmony, prosperity, emotional flow, joyful balance. **Osogbo:** Imbalance, tension, relational or financial instability.

136. Okanran–Ofun: Mastery and completion achieved through overcoming trials and integrating lessons; completion, integration, spiritual and material fulfillment; completion of cycles, clarity, emergence into light. **Message:** This Odu teaches that ethical conduct, gratitude, and spiritual alignment ensure fulfillment, wisdom, and lasting blessings.

Disciplined action brings completion and mastery over lessons learned. **Ire:** Fulfillment, spiritual maturity, completion, alignment with divine principles. **Osogbo:** Pride, spiritual arrogance, lost blessings, unfinished outcomes.

* * *

THE CHILDREN OF OGUNDA MÉJÌ
Common Themes found in the family of Ogunda include: Iron and war, hard work to cut obstacles and clear paths in life to move forward.

137. Ogunda–Ogbe: Iron and war, clearing obstacles, persistence, light, clarity, alignment with Ori. **Message:** This Odu teaches that enduring effort and disciplined action cut through obstacles like iron in battle. By staying persistent and strategic, even in difficult conditions, one moves toward clarity, success, and alignment with destiny. **Ire:** Victory through effort, courage, protection, prosperity, strategic achievement. **Osogbo:** Conflict, impatience, repeated struggles, wasted effort, poor planning.

138. Ogunda–Oyekun: Mystery of night, the unknown, ancestral guidance, endurance in hardship. **Message:** This Odu represents being in the most challenging part of a battle, when it's hard to see the path or success. Hardships here teach resilience and trust in inner strength. Spiritual and emotional trials, though unclear, guide transformation. **Ire:** Resilience, renewal, spiritual strength, protection, personal growth. **Osogbo:** Loss, fear, depression, destructive behavior, emotional collapse.

139. Ogunda–Iwori: This Odu teaches that restless or scattered energy must be guided by careful thought and planning. Success comes from mental discipline, reflection, and making decisions based on insight rather than impulse. **Message:** Ignoring wisdom leads to mistakes and unnecessary conflict. **Ire:** clarity, intelligent action, wise planning, insight, informed decisions. **Osogbo:** confusion, impulsiveness, poor judgment, wasted effort, hasty decisions.

140. Ogunda–Odi: This Odu emphasizes the power of hard work, the importance of cutting through obstacles with persistence, and the need for patience, stability, and protective guidance, like the nurturing strength of a mother. **Message:** Ogunda–Odi teaches that challenges are part of the journey, and true progress comes from steady, disciplined effort. By combining hard work with patience and self-control, one can overcome obstacles and create a stable, protected foundation. Persistence and careful action ensure security, growth, and long-term success. **Ire:** Stability, endurance, overcoming obstacles, persistent effort, grounded progress. **Osogbo:** Stagnation, blockages, frustration, resistance to guidance, slow or failed progress.

141. Ogunda–Irosun: teaches that persistent effort and hard work are essential for overcoming life's challenges. When this dedication is combined with the wisdom of elders and guidance from ancestors, one can navigate hidden obstacles, avoid mistakes, and strengthen both personal and generational growth. **Message:** Success comes not just from action, but from listening, learning, and aligning one's efforts with spiritual insight. **Ire:** Achievement through effort, protection and guidance from ancestors, spiritual clarity, personal and family growth. **Osogbo:** Ignoring advice, wasted effort, emotional turmoil, setbacks from poor decisions, spiritual confusion.

142. Ogunda–Owonrin: This Odu teaches that sudden changes and unpredictable events require adaptability and alertness. **Message:** Success comes from flexible thinking, responsiveness, and careful decision-making during unstable circumstances. **Ire:** adaptability, opportunity through change, quick solutions, alertness. **Osogbo:** chaos, accidents, instability, rash decisions, disorganization.

143. Ogunda–Obara: This Odu teaches that strong ambition, hard work and responsible leadership brings recognition, material wealth and influence. **Message:** Using authority wisely and communicating honestly strengthens relationships and fosters trust. **Ire:** leadership, influence, recognition, success, responsible authority. **Osogbo:** ego, domination, conflict with others, misuse of power, pride.

144. Ogunda–Okanran: Hard work, strength, resilience, courage, discipline, leadership through hardship. **Message:** This Odu teaches that facing challenges with discipline and effort builds strength and resilience, qualities that forge effective leaders. Courage guided by wisdom transforms obstacles into breakthroughs while avoiding harm to oneself or others. Ogunda emphasizes that consistent hard work is the foundation for personal growth and leadership. **Ire:** Strength, breakthrough, courage, rapid progress, disciplined action. **Osogbo:** Aggression, violence, reckless actions, destructive impulses.

145. Ogunda–Osa: Ogunda–Osa emphasizes spiritual defense, storms, hidden consequences, humility, and trust in guidance. It teaches that one must remain prepared for sudden challenges, whether literal storms or unexpected disruptions, to protect what has been built through hard work. **Message:** By preparing before something happens and looking forward one gains protection, insight, and insures success in hard work and plans. **Ire:** Preparedness, spiritual protection, safeguarding achievements, guided insight, transformation. **Osogbo:** Sudden loss, disruption, spiritual confusion, instability, misguidance.

146. Ogunda–Ika: Ogunda–Ika emphasizes restraint, self-control, vigilance, ethical action, and the dangers of misusing power. **Message:** It teaches that conflict and danger must be approached with careful strategy, moral integrity, and ethical conduct. Long-term safety, protection, and justice come from disciplined restraint and ethical vigilance. **Ìrè:** Protection, justice, overcoming enemies, ethical vigilance. **Osogbo:** Danger, hostility, betrayal, harm from negligence.

147. Ogunda–Oturupon: Endurance, stability, resilience, adaptability, transformation, personal growth. **Message:** This Odu teaches that crises and hardships are opportunities for transformation and personal correction. By facing challenges with humility, openness to change, and effort, one strengthens character, restores balance, and grows spiritually and personally. Ogunda here emphasizes hard work and perseverance as essential tools for overcoming difficulties. **Ire:** Renewal, correction, transformation, personal growth. **Osogbo:** Disaster, loss, resistance to change, stagnation.

148. Ogunda–Otura: Reflection, careful planning, wisdom, patience, discernment, spiritual alignment. **Message:** This Odu teaches that thoughtful, disciplined action prevents mistakes and ensures success.

Reflecting on circumstances, exercising patience, and seeking understanding before acting cultivates clarity, good judgment, and alignment with divine guidance. It highlights that careful effort and attention are key to achieving the desired outcome. **Ire:** Wisdom, clarity, successful decisions, careful planning. **Osogbo:** Confusion, poor judgment, misguided action, hasty mistakes.

149. Ogunda–Irete: Ethical behavior, responsibility, discipline, consistency, integrity, work ethic. **Message:** This Odu teaches that ethical behavior and consistent effort in one's work build long-term stability and success. By honoring commitments and acting responsibly, one ensures progress, rewards, and growth. Irete emphasizes that moral integrity in effort is as important as hard work itself. **Ire:** Progress, stability, reward through effort, disciplined growth. **Osogbo:** Failure from laziness, setbacks, negligence, inconsistency.

150. Ogunda–Ose: Flow, balance, moderation, gratitude, harmonious prosperity, creativity. **Message:** This Odu teaches that life's blessings and prosperity flow best when approached with balance, gratitude, and moderation. Acting ethically and harmoniously ensures that abundance is enjoyed without excess or disruption. Ose emphasizes the natural flow of effort and reward, showing that when work and energy move smoothly, fulfillment follows. **Ire:** Harmony, flow, balance, peace, joyful moderation. **Osogbo:** Indulgence, imbalance, loss through excess, moral lapses.

151. Ogunda–Ofun: Completion, fulfillment, spiritual maturity, wisdom, responsibility, clarity. **Message:** This Odu teaches that cycles come to completion when effort, discipline, and alignment with higher principles are applied. Ofun emphasizes that finishing tasks responsibly and thoughtfully brings clarity, spiritual growth, blessings, and lasting success. Completion is the reward of consistent effort and ethical action. **Ire:** Fulfillment, spiritual wisdom, clarity, blessings, responsible leadership. **Osogbo:** Arrogance, spiritual decline, moral failure, misuse of knowledge.

* * *

Common Themes found in the family of Osa include: Storms, spiritual defense, hidden consequences, witchcraft.

152. Osa–Ogbe: Osa brings storms, sudden upheaval, hidden forces, and the exposure of what was concealed. Ogbe brings light, clarity, truth, and new beginnings. Together, this Odu shows a storm that clears away deception so truth can emerge. **Message:** A disruption will reveal what has been hidden. Though the exposure may be sudden or uncomfortable, it removes illusion and opens the way for a fresh start. The storm is not destruction, it is purification leading to clarity. **Ire:** Truth revealed, sudden clarity, deep insight, new beginnings after chaos. **Osogbo:** Shocking revelations, emotional upheaval, exposed deception, loss of control.

153. Osa–Oyekun: Osa brings turbulence and spiritual disturbance. Oyekun represents darkness, depth, and hidden emotional or ancestral matters. This Odu speaks of an inner storm uncovering buried issues. **Message:** Hidden fears, grief, or spiritual heaviness may surface. Withdrawal and reflection are necessary. If you surrender and cleanse emotionally, renewal follows. If you resist, emotional stagnation deepens. **Ìrè:** Inner purification, emotional release, spiritual awareness, renewal after darkness. **Osogbo:** Fear of surrender, depression, resistance to change, lingering emotional weight.

154. Osa–Iwori: Osa creates disruption and reveals hidden consequences. Iwori governs thought, ego, and personal perception. This Odu shows a storm affecting the mind and judgment. **Message:** Do not let ego react to chaos. Careful thinking is required. The upheaval is exposing flawed reasoning or hidden motives. Insight and self-awareness will stabilize the situation. **Ìrè:** Clear judgment during crisis, self-awareness, wise decisions. **Osogbo:** Rash reactions, confusion, prideful missteps, acting without reflection.

155. Osa–Odi: Osa brings external storms and instability. Odi represents protection, structure, fertility, and guarded foundations. This Odu speaks of protecting what is vulnerable during upheaval. **Message:** Secure your foundations. Emotional discipline and practical planning protect your home, projects, or family during instability. If you panic or act impatiently, hidden weaknesses may be exposed. **Ìrè:** Stability during disruption, protection, disciplined structure. **Osogbo:** Blocked growth, hidden vulnerabilities exposed, impatience causing loss.

156. Osa–Irosun: Osa reveals hidden spiritual forces. Irosun governs ancestry and inherited patterns. This Odu speaks of ancestral matters surfacing through turbulence. **Message:** If life feels like a sudden storm, look at your roots, the cause might be older than you are. This Odu reveals that current upheavals are often echoes of unresolved family patterns or ancestral "debts." Your ancestors are essentially texting you through your intuition and dreams. Don't just fight the wind; listen to what it's saying. By acknowledging your spiritual heritage and the patterns you've inherited, you turn a chaotic crisis into a moment of deep, multi-generational healing. **Ìrè:** Ancestral protection, intuitive clarity, spiritual alignment. **Osogbo:** Repeated generational problems, ignoring spiritual warnings, inner unrest.

157. Osa–Owonrin: Osa brings sudden upheaval. Owonrin represents unpredictability and rapid shifts. This Odu intensifies instability and unexpected change. **Message:** When the ground shifts and the winds change at the same time, your only option is to be like water. This Odu is a masterclass in flexibility. The more you fight a "new normal" you didn't ask for, the more chaos you invite. Stay calm, keep your eyes open, and pivot. What looks like a disaster is often a shortcut to a breakthrough, but only if you're quick enough to move with it. **Ìrè:** Adaptability, breakthrough through change, resilience. **Osogbo:** Chaos, scattered focus, instability from rigidity.

158. Osa–Obara: Osa exposes hidden motives. Obara governs expression, expansion, and material growth. This Odu shows storms affecting communication and prosperity. **Message:** Be truthful in speech and action. Hidden intentions may surface suddenly. Honest communication protects relationships and finances during unstable periods. **Ìrè:** Honest communication, restored harmony, growth after exposure. **Osogbo:** Conflict from deception, financial disruption, broken trust.

159. Osa–Okanran: Emotional intensity, internal storms, and the power of self-control. **Message:** When external pressures hit the heart, the reaction can be explosive; this Odu warns that your greatest risk during a crisis isn't the problem itself, but your own temper. If you let raw anger or impulsive reactions drive your choices, you will only magnify the destruction, but by maintaining emotional discipline and staying in the "eye of the storm," you can transform that intense energy into unshakable resilience. **Ìrè:** Emotional maturity, calm strength, and the power to remain steady under pressure. **Osogbo:** Blind rage, emotional sabotage, and causing permanent damage through a temporary feeling.

160. Osa–Ogunda: Disciplined effort, repairing foundations, and persistence through upheaval. **Message:** This Odu teaches that when the storms of life cause disruption, stability will not return on its own; it must be actively rebuilt through grit and consistent work. Passivity only invites further chaos, but by applying strategic, grounded action, you can protect what is threatened and restore order to your environment. Your willingness to put in the "sweat equity" right now is exactly what transforms a period of instability into a foundation for lasting success. **Ìrè:** Rebuilding success, perseverance, and the triumph of constructive action. **Osogbo:** Instability fueled by laziness, neglect of duty, and effort wasted through lack of discipline.

161. Osa–Ika: Hidden conflict, moral accountability, and strategic caution. **Message:** This Odu acts as a spotlight that exposes underlying betrayals or wrongdoings that were previously concealed; it warns that while the truth may be jarring, your reaction must be governed by restraint rather than retaliation. By taking immediate moral accountability and correcting mistakes before they spiral, you prevent a temporary conflict from becoming a permanent disaster. True protection in this moment comes from holding yourself to a higher ethical standard and choosing discipline over impulsive anger. **Ìrè:** Moral clarity, restored balance, and safety through self-control. **Osogbo:** Reckless retaliation, the pain of betrayal, and conflict that lingers due to a lack of correction.

162. Osa–Oturupon: Osa brings collapse or upheaval. Oturupon represents hardship and endurance. This Odu speaks of difficult endings. **Message:** This Odu marks a difficult "closing of the door," reminding you that fighting a cycle that has already ended only turns pain into a long-term struggle. By accepting the end with humility and finding the strength to let go, you clear the space for a much-needed renewal. **Ìrè:** Closure, resilience, renewal after struggle. **Osogbo:** Stagnation, repeated hardship, refusal to release the past.

163. Osa–Otura: Osa creates turbulence. Otura brings reflection and spiritual insight. This Odu shows clarity emerging after chaos. **Message:** When the dust settles from a recent upheaval, your first instinct might be to rush forward—but this Odu advises the opposite. Use this pause to reflect on the "why" behind the chaos. The spiritual insight you gain right now is what prevents the same storm from returning later. Silence the noise and look for the lesson; it is your map to a smoother path. **Ìrè:** Wisdom, peaceful resolution, clear direction. **Osogbo:** Confusion, misjudgment, repeating mistakes.

164. Osa–Irete: Osa exposes hidden consequences. Irete governs character, discipline, and ethical responsibility. This Odu emphasizes moral correction during upheaval. **Message:** When the winds of change blow, it is your character that keeps you anchored. This Odu reminds you that integrity isn't just a moral choice, it's your best survival strategy. Your conduct during a crisis determines whether the storm breaks you or builds you. If you stay disciplined and own your responsibilities, you will find that the upheaval actually clears a path for steady, long-term growth. **Ìrè:** Ethical strength, steady growth, disciplined prosperity. **Osogbo:** Pride, moral failure, instability through poor character.

165. Osa–Ose: Compassion, hidden blessings, and social cooperation. **Message:**This Odu teaches that true prosperity is found in the way we treat others during times of transition; even when things are changing rapidly, nurturing your relationships with kindness and generosity creates a protective shield of joy. Harmony isn't just a feeling, but a strategic choice to act with compassion, ensuring that your social foundations remain strong while the world shifts around you. **Ìrè:** Lasting joy, supportive connections, and prosperity born from a generous spirit. **Osogbo:** Bitter envy, social discord, and fractured relationships that drain your peace.

166. Osa–Ofun: Higher wisdom, completion, and the power of truth. **Message:**This Odu marks the arrival of spiritual maturity, teaching that true fulfillment is only possible through absolute honesty and a disciplined life. By purifying your intentions and aligning your daily actions with divine truth, you allow your destiny to unfold with effortless grace and clarity. When you move with reverence and integrity, the confusion of the world falls away, revealing a path of profound peace and sacred purpose. **Ìrè:** Spiritual completion, divine alignment, and the clarity of higher wisdom. **Osogbo:** Arrogance, moral decline, and the confusion that comes from misusing sacred knowledge.

* * *

THE CHILDREN OF IKA-MEJI

Common Themes found in the family of Ika include: Restraint, self-control, dangers of misusing power, Self-control, restraint, the importance of self mastery as the way to true power.

167. Ika–Ogbe: Disciplined authority, visibility, and accountable progress. **Message:**Leadership and success require strict restraint and integrity; while opportunities for advancement will appear in the open, only disciplined action and humility can secure them long-term. Acting from pride or impulse may bring quick recognition, but without the self-control demanded by Ika, your results will remain unstable. **Ìrè:** Disciplined leadership, honorable progress, and victory through patience. **Osogbo:** Misuse of authority, impulsive decisions, and public conflict.

168. Ika–Oyekun: Moral testing, shadow work, and emotional accountability. **Message:** True growth comes from facing your inner battles and hidden guilts honestly rather than suppressing them; this Odu demands that you acknowledge your "shadows" to transform darkness into wisdom. Self-discipline and the courage to confront internal fears are the only ways to prevent hidden conflicts from surfacing painfully later. **Ìrè:** Emotional clarity, inner strength, and renewal through deep reflection. **Osogbo:** Denial of truth, emotional stagnation, and the weight of hidden guilt.

169. Ika–Iwori: Discernment, foresight, and thoughtful planning. **Message:** You must think deeply before you act, as careful planning is the only shield against avoidable mistakes. When your discipline is guided by wisdom and reflection, success is steady and sustainable, but rash decisions born of a lack of foresight will bring unnecessary setbacks. **Ìrè:** Strategic success, perceptive judgment, and wise decision-making. **Osogbo:** Poor judgment, impulsive errors, and confusion.

170. Ika–Odi: Moral accountability, boundaries, and structural integrity. **Message:**Stability is built through unwavering responsibility and the courage to do the right thing even when it is difficult; guard your commitments and maintain a clear structure in your life to ensure your success lasts. Neglecting your duties or cutting corners weakens your spiritual foundation and invites instability into your home and work. **Ìrè:** Strong foundations, structured growth, and reliable stability. **Osogbo:** Instability, neglected responsibilities, and fractured progress.

171. Ika–Irosun: Ancestral memory, traditional guidance, and accountability. **Message:** Learn from the past and respect the traditions of those who came before you; this Odu warns that ignoring inherited wisdom leads to the repetition of painful mistakes. By heeding the guidance of elders and the lessons of your ancestors, you find a path of moral clarity and protection that bypasses modern confusion. **Ìrè:** Ancestral protection, moral clarity, and guided decisions. **Osogbo:** Repeating past errors, ignoring heritage, and emotional imbalance.

172. Ika–Owonrin: Disciplined flexibility and navigating unpredictability. **Message:**While change is inevitable and often sudden, disciplined flexibility allows you to turn disruption into a distinct advantage. Resisting change out of fear only creates more confusion, but if you adapt responsibly and keep your head clear, you can find a creative way through any instability. **Ìrè:** Creative adaptability, resilient growth, and strategic flexibility. **Osogbo:**Instability, confusion, and resistance to necessary change.

173. Ika–Obara: Communication, social influence, and the power of words. **Message:**Your words shape your reality and your relationships, so you must speak with both integrity and careful intention. Honest and ethical communication builds a foundation of trust that can weather any storm, whereas careless speech or gossip will inevitably fracture your bonds and damage your reputation. **Ìrè:** Trustworthy influence, diplomatic success, and harmonious bonds. **Osogbo:** Gossip, disputes, and a damaged reputation.

174. Ika–Okanran: Emotional discipline, and self-control. **Message:** You must master your emotions before they master you; this Odu warns that anger and frustration must be tightly disciplined to avoid destructive consequences. When you channel your passionate energy through a filter of restraint, you gain a powerful, calm strength that commands respect. **Ìrè:** Emotional maturity, calm strength, and controlled passion. **Osogbo:** Impulsive anger, heated conflict, and emotional instability.

175. Ika–Ogunda: Ethical labor, focused achievement, and channeled strength. **Message:** Strength is only a virtue when it is purposeful and guided by a clear moral compass; hard work that follows ethical principles leads to undeniable achievement. Using force or aggression without discipline will only cause setbacks and wasted energy, so focus your power into constructive, honorable labor. **Ìrè:** Constructive effort, focused achievement, and productive strength. **Osogbo:** Conflict from aggression, wasted energy, and destructive force.

176. Ika–Osa: Hidden dynamics, spiritual defense, and sudden upheaval. **Message:** Be aware that not everything is visible on the surface, and unseen forces may be moving against you; disciplined awareness is your best protection against sudden disruptions. By staying alert and spiritually grounded, you can navigate hidden conflicts and destabilizing revelations without losing your footing. **Ìrè:** Spiritual protection, insight into hidden matters, and wise caution. **Osogbo:** Confusion, exposure to hidden conflict, and sudden instability.

177. Ika–Oturupon: Humility, transformation, and letting go. **Message:** Transformation requires the accountability to recognize what no longer serves you and the humility to let it go. Releasing outdated patterns is a responsibility, not a choice; clinging to the past out of fear or pride only prolongs your struggle and prevents your spiritual renewal. **Ìrè:** Empowered renewal, spiritual transformation, and humble growth. **Osogbo:** Stagnation, fear of change, and prolonged hardship.

178. Ika–Otura: Balanced judgment, clarity, and thoughtful action. **Message:**Reflection must come before decision-making, as calm discernment is the only way to achieve harmonious and lasting results. Hastiness and impulsive jumping to conclusions will only disrupt your alignment with your higher purpose, so seek a higher understanding before you commit to a path. **Ìrè:** Balanced judgment, peaceful direction, and thoughtful success. **Osogbo:** Indecision, scattered priorities, and a lack of clarity.

179. Ika–Irete: Ethical consistency, patience, and sustainable growth. **Message:**Long-term success is the result of patience and a steady commitment to ethical behavior; there are no shortcuts to a destiny that lasts. The discipline you exercise today in your character and work ensures the rewards of tomorrow, building a legacy that cannot be easily shaken. **Ìrè:** Steady progress, responsible achievement, and sustainable rewards. **Osogbo:**Impatience, negligence, and inconsistent effort.

180. Ika–Ose: Relational prosperity, harmony, and generosity. **Message:** Prosperity grows most abundantly where integrity and generosity meet; your ethical conduct is what strengthens your relationships and ensures communal success. By acting with kindness and maintaining high moral standards, you expand the joy and cooperation in your life, turning success into a shared blessing. **Ìrè:** Harmonious relationships, joyful cooperation, and balanced prosperity. **Osogbo:** Envy, selfishness, and relational conflict.

181. Ika–Ofun: Spiritual completion, higher wisdom, and ultimate accountability. **Message:** True fulfillment is the crown of spiritual maturity and unwavering integrity; you must align every action with your highest principles to secure your blessings. Arrogance or the misuse of your knowledge will lead to a rapid decline, but a humble heart and a clear purpose will lead to the ultimate completion of your destiny. **Ìrè:** Spiritual maturity, clarity of purpose, and fulfillment through integrity. **Osogbo:** Ethical downfall, arrogance, and spiritual confusion.

* * *

182. Oturupon–Ogbe: This Odu speaks of Oturupon's restraint, endurance, and lessons through hardship, strengthened by Ogbe's clarity, expansion, and new beginnings. Because Oturupon stands first, renewal comes only after discipline and careful correction. **Message:** A new beginning is available, but only through responsible action and self-control. Recovery and growth require patience and ethical choices. Acting impulsively may delay restoration. **Ire:** Renewal, restored health, fresh clarity, disciplined new beginnings. **Osogbo:** Stagnation, neglect of well-being, hasty decisions blocking progress.

183. Oturupon–Oyekun: This Odu reflects Oturupon's endurance and accountability combined with Oyekun's endings and deep transitions. Oturupon demands responsible release, while Oyekun closes old cycles. **Message:** Let go with discipline and humility. Endings are necessary for renewal, but clinging to the past prolongs hardship. Accept closure with maturity. **Ire:** Peaceful closure, release of burdens, renewal after transition. **Osogbo:** Fear of change, stagnation, delayed healing.

184. Oturupon–Iwori: This Odu blends Oturupon's restraint with Iwori's insight and reflection. Oturupon calls for controlled behavior; Iwori adds thoughtful discernment. **Message:** Reflect carefully on habits and decisions. Disciplined self-examination restores balance. Impulsiveness disrupts wellness and progress. **Ire:** Self-awareness, balanced judgment, holistic improvement. **Osogbo:** Confusion, poor choices, imbalance through neglect.

185. Oturupon–Odi: This Odu joins Oturupon's controlled endurance with Odi's structure and protection. Oturupon requires responsibility; Odi builds firm foundations. **Message:** Structure and routine stabilize recovery. Maintain discipline in daily responsibilities. Disorder and shortcuts weaken your foundation. **Ire:** Stability, resilience, structured progress. **Osogbo:** Chaotic behavior, neglect, preventable setbacks.

186. Oturupon–Irosun: This Odu combines Oturupon's accountability with Irosun's ancestral memory and lineage wisdom. Endurance is strengthened through tradition and inherited guidance. **Message:** Follow ancestral counsel with humility. Respect family patterns and lessons to avoid repeating hardship. **Ire:** Ancestral protection, emotional resilience, guided growth. **Osogbo:** Repeated family mistakes, ignoring heritage, unresolved patterns.

187. Oturupon–Owonrin: This Odu reflects Oturupon's disciplined restraint alongside Owonrin's unpredictable change. Controlled flexibility is required. **Message:** Adapt carefully. Sudden changes can be navigated through patience and ethical awareness. Resistance or recklessness creates instability. **Ire:** Successful adaptation, resilience, creative solutions. **Osogbo:** Rigidity, confusion, instability from poor reactions.

188. Oturupon–Obara: This Odu blends Oturupon's self-control with Obara's influence and communication. Words and authority must be handled responsibly. **Message:** Speak with restraint and integrity. Leadership requires ethical communication. Careless influence damages trust. **Ire:** Trustworthy leadership, harmonious connections, responsible influence. **Osogbo:** Gossip, dishonesty, fractured relationships.

189. Oturupon–Okanran: This Odu combines Oturupon's endurance with Okanran's emotional intensity and testing. Trials require emotional restraint. **Message:** Face pressure with calm strength. Emotional control transforms hardship into long-term resilience. **Ire:** Perseverance, emotional maturity, steady endurance. **Osogbo:** Anger, frustration, reactive decisions under stress.

190. Oturupon–Ogunda: This Odu unites Oturupon's disciplined restraint with Ogunda's labor and forceful action. Effort must be controlled and purposeful. **Message:** Consistent, focused work overcomes obstacles. Reckless use of energy wastes opportunities. **Ire:** Breakthrough through effort, constructive progress, improved vitality. **Osogbo:** Wasted energy, aggression, blocked advancement.

191. Oturupon–Osa: This Odu reflects Oturupon's caution combined with Osa's storms, hidden forces, and spiritual mysteries.Discipline protects during unseen upheaval. **Message:** Be vigilant of hidden influences. Spiritual awareness and restraint prevent avoidable disruption. **Ire:** Spiritual protection, insight, safe navigation of uncertainty. **Osogbo:** Confusion, overlooked warning signs, destabilizing revelations.

192. Oturupon–Ika: This Odu joins Oturupon's self-mastery with Ika's moral consequences and accountability. Ethical discipline is doubly emphasized. **Message:** Take responsibility for your choices. Recovery and growth depend on correcting behavior with humility. **Ire:** Responsible action, ethical progress, restored stability. **Osogbo:** Avoidance of duty, harmful conduct, repeated setbacks.

193. Oturupon–Otura: This Odu blends Oturupon's restraint with Otura's clarity and peace. Calm reflection stabilizes hardship. **Message:** Thoughtful discipline leads to inner peace. Impulsiveness disrupts clarity and direction. **Ire:** Harmony, balanced judgment, peaceful outcomes. **Osogbo:** Indecision, scattered focus, imbalance.

194. Oturupon–Irete: This Odu combines Oturupon's steady endurance with Irete's growth and aligned prosperity. Long-term effort yields stable rewards. **Message:** Consistency and responsibility build lasting success. Impatience undermines steady progress. **Ire:** Sustainable growth, persistence rewarded, stable well-being. **Osogbo:** Neglect, inconsistency, preventable delays.

195. Oturupon–Ose: This Odu reflects Oturupon's ethical restraint with Ose's harmony and joyful connection. Joy must be grounded in discipline. **Message:** True fulfillment comes from moral living and balanced relationships. Selfishness disrupts harmony. **Ire:** Joy, harmonious relationships, balanced prosperity. **Osogbo:** Envy, selfishness, relational conflict.

196. Oturupon–Ofun: This Odu unites Oturupon's disciplined integration of lessons with Ofun's spiritual completion and higher wisdom.-Completion comes after endurance and ethical refinement. **Message:** Spiritual maturity arises from self-control and alignment with higher principles. Arrogance or misuse of knowledge prevents full restoration. **Ire:** Completion, spiritual maturity, holistic restoration. **Osogbo:** Ethical decline, arrogance, incomplete healing.

$$* * *$$

THE CHILDREN OF OTURA-MEJI

Common Themes found in the family of Otura include: Mystical visions, reflection, alignment with the divine, tranquility, dreams.

197. Otura-Ogbe: This Odu focuses on the manifestation of mystical visions and the attainment of divine alignment through the light of destiny. **Message:** This Odu represents a powerful synergy where spiritual peace meets the clarity of a new beginning; it teaches that when you quiet the mind through reflection, you can finally see your true purpose manifesting. By aligning your daily actions with higher principles, you move from mere existence into a state of disciplined spiritual growth and illumination. **Iré:** Spiritual clarity, alignment with purpose, and steady progress. **Òsogbo:** Confusion, misdirection, and wasted potential due to neglecting guidance.

198. Otura-Oyekun: This Odu explores the achievement of inner calm while navigating the mysterious transitions and endings of life. **Message:** Otura brings a steadying inner peace to the inevitable endings and transitions governed by Oyekun; this Odu teaches that true harmony is found when we gracefully release past struggles. By letting go of old conflicts with a calm heart, you resolve deep-seated tensions and transition into a space of profound spiritual tranquility. **Iré:** Inner peace, harmonious transitions, and the resolution of conflict. **Òsogbo:** Clinging to the past, spiritual stagnation, and delayed peace.

199. Otura-Iwori: This Odu emphasizes the cultivation of tranquility and heightened consciousness through the fire of sharp discernment. **Message:** This Odu teaches that spiritual awareness is not accidental but comes through the intentional study and contemplation of sacred truths. By combining a tranquil mind with sharp discernment, you gain the ability to see through surface-level ego and understand the deeper divine patterns of the universe. **Iré:** Divine insight, enlightened understanding, and disciplined study. **Òsogbo:** Shallow understanding, lack of focus, and misinterpretation of truth.

200. Otura-Odi: This Odu highlights the importance of spiritual grounding and structural stability as a means of protecting one's growth. **Message:** Otura-Odi teaches that your spiritual growth must be housed within a strong structure of consistent ritual and ethical behavior to remain safe; it is the "seal" that protects your inner peace. Disciplined devotion acts as a shield, ensuring that your orientation remains steady even when external distractions attempt to scatter your focus. **Iré:** Structured practice, spiritual protection, and steady progress. **Òsogbo:** Neglect of discipline, vulnerability to distraction, and scattered energy.

201. Otura-Irosun: This Odu centers on the use of calm reflection to connect with generational consciousness and inherited wisdom. **Message:** This Odu emphasizes that your spiritual foundation is strengthened when you honor the wisdom and mandates inherited from your lineage. By reflecting on ancestral lessons, you find the moral clarity needed to make ethical decisions in the present, fulfilling a spiritual contract that spans generations. **Iré:** Ancestral guidance, inherited wisdom, and a strengthened moral foundation. **Òsogbo:** Ignoring your heritage, repeating ancestral mistakes, and ethical confusion.

202. Otura-Owonrin: This Odu examines the necessity of calm awareness when standing at the crossroads of unpredictable change. **Message:** Otura-Owonrin teaches that spiritual resilience is found in the ability to adapt to divine cues with a calm and open heart. Faith is not rigid; it is a responsive movement that embraces unpredictable shifts as opportunities for growth, showing that flexibility is the key to staying aligned with guidance during times of change. **Iré:** Spiritual adaptability, faith-driven change, and resilience. **Òsogbo:** Rigidity, resistance to divine direction, and missed opportunities.

203. Otura-Obara: This Odu addresses the role of spiritual reflection in manifesting ethical leadership and the flow of abundance. **Message:** True spiritual authority is expressed through humble leadership and the consistent application of moral integrity; this Odu teaches that your influence over others is a reflection of your own inner peace. By maintaining a devotional heart, you inspire those around you and ensure that your leadership remains aligned with higher truths rather than personal ego. **Iré:** Ethical leadership, influence through integrity, and spiritual authority. **Òsogbo:** Arrogance, misuse of influence, and loss of respect.

204. Otura-Okanran: This Odu demonstrates how inner peace provides the strength to endure the most difficult trials. **Message:** This Odu teaches that the strength to endure testing times comes from a deep well of spiritual grounding and inner awareness. When you are tested by life's hardships, maintaining your emotional balance and inner peace ensures that you do not waver in your purpose, allowing you to move through trials with steady grace. **Iré:** Inner resilience, emotional balance, and steady growth. **Òsogbo:** Instability, wavering focus, and weakened resolve.

205. Otura-Ogunda: Otura represents spiritual stability, while Ogunda embodies effort, discipline, and action. **Message:** Combined, Otura-Ogunda teaches labor for the spirit, clearing obstacles, and overcoming challenges through disciplined effort, showing that constructive action and diligence bring spiritual breakthroughs. **Ire:** Focused spiritual effort, clearing obstacles, disciplined action, progress through work. **Osogbo:** Neglect, scattered effort, stagnation, failure to overcome challenges.

206. Otura-Osa: Otura signifies calm reflection and spiritual insight, while Osa embodies mystery, subtlety, and hidden forces. **Message:** Otura-Osa teaches discovering hidden spiritual revelations and divine mysteries, emphasizing that awareness of unseen forces encourages trust in the divine and deepens wisdom. **Ire:** Spiritual insight, revelation, trust in divine guidance, inner peace. **Osogbo:** Misunderstanding hidden truths, fear, disconnection from divine wisdom.

207. Otura-Ika: Otura represents spiritual peace, while Ika embodies moral responsibility, ethical correction, and accountability. **Message:** Otura-Ika teaches correcting one's orientation through wisdom and responsible action, ensuring alignment with spiritual principles. **Ire:** Wisdom, moral correction, responsible action, realignment. **Osogbo:** Ethical lapses, misjudgment, ignoring guidance, confusion.

208. Otura-Oturupon: Otura signifies calm, reflective insight, while Oturupon embodies restoration, protection, and holistic balance. **Message:** Combined, Otura-Oturupon teaches restoration through the balance of physical and spiritual study, showing that integrating learning, reflection, and practical action brings holistic healing and renewal. **Ire:** Restoration, balance, spiritual and physical integration, holistic recovery. **Osogbo:** Neglect of balance, partial effort, stagnation, incomplete restoration.

209. Otura-Irete: Otura represents spiritual calm and awareness, while Irete embodies clarity, expansion, and alignment. **Message:** Otura-Irete teaches success through total spiritual alignment, showing that harmonizing thought, emotion, and action ensures long-term prosperity, fulfillment, and spiritual well-being. **Ire:** Alignment, prosperity, spiritual success, harmonious living. **Osogbo:** Imbalance, disconnection, stagnation, incomplete fulfillment.

210. Otura-Ose: Otura signifies peace and reflection, while Ose embodies joy, harmony, and relational sweetness. **Message:** Combined, Otura-Ose teaches harmony and joy in connection with the divine, showing that ethical conduct, gratitude, and cooperation cultivate spiritual happiness and harmonious relationships. **Ire:** Joy, harmony, ethical living, spiritual satisfaction. **Osogbo:** Envy, conflict, broken relationships, disrupted peace.

211. Otura-Ofun: Otura represents spiritual tranquility and reflection, while Ofun embodies divine completion, fulfillment, and alignment with higher principles. **Message:** Otura-Ofun teaches the divine completion of the spiritual journey and awareness, emphasizing that spiritual maturity, reflection, and disciplined practice culminate in fulfillment, clarity, and alignment with higher purpose. **Ire:** Completion, spiritual maturity, fulfillment, alignment with divine purpose. **Osogbo:** Arrogance, misuse of spiritual knowledge, incomplete understanding, stagnation.

* * *

212. Irete-Ogbe: Irete represents growth and moral clarity, while Ogbe embodies initiative and forward movement. **Message:** Together, this Odu teaches that prosperity comes from clear vision, disciplined effort, and ethical action. Success follows when one acts with integrity, patience, and responsibility. **Ire:** Prosperity, clarity in growth, new opportunities, ethical decision-making, expansion of resources. **Osogbo:** Stagnation, ignoring opportunities, impulsive choices, poor planning, missed growth.

213. Irete-Oyeku: Irete signifies clarity and ethical living, while Oyeku represents endings and transitions. **Message:** This Odu teaches that releasing limiting habits, fears, or negative patterns allows abundance and renewal. Success arises through reflection, courage, and moral integrity. **Ire:** Financial renewal, stability, new beginnings, ethical transitions, end of scarcity. **Osogbo:** Fear of change, clinging to old patterns, repeated mistakes, stagnation.

214. Irete-Iwori: Irete embodies insight and growth, while Iwori represents reflection and discernment. **Message:** Together, this Odu emphasizes understanding patterns and making thoughtful, ethical decisions to ensure sustainable prosperity and personal development. **Ire:** Clarity of purpose, strategic planning, sustainable growth, ethical insight, understanding consequences. **Osogbo:** Confusion, shortsightedness, impulsive spending, neglect of reflection, missed opportunities.

215. Irete-Odi: Irete signifies clarity and expansion, while Odi embodies structure and discipline. **Message:** This Odu teaches that long-term success requires responsible management, ethical action, and a strong foundation in all endeavors. **Ire:** Structured wealth, disciplined management, secure resources, long-term stability, responsible oversight. **Osogbo:** Neglect, poor management, instability, shortcuts, inconsistency.

216. Irete-Irosun: Irete embodies clarity and growth, while Irosun represents ancestral guidance and family wisdom. **Message:** This Odu teaches that prosperity flows when one honors lineage, learns from elders, and acts ethically. **Ire:** Ancestral support, inherited abundance, responsible stewardship, family prosperity, fulfillment through lineage. **Osogbo:** Ignoring heritage, ethical lapses, blocked opportunities, repeating past mistakes.

217. Irete-Owonrin: Irete signifies opportunity and clarity, while Owonrin embodies adaptability and change. **Message:** This Odu emphasizes that ethical flexibility, responsiveness, and moral awareness allow one to navigate transitions and achieve success. **Ire:** Adaptability, resilience, ethical decision-making, opportunity through change, flexible success. **Osogbo:** Rigidity, failure to adapt, missed opportunities, stubbornness, loss.

218. Irete-Obara: Irete embodies clarity and positive energy, while Obara represents leadership and ethical influence. **Message:** This Odu teaches that honest, responsible, and ethical action attracts trust, recognition, and supportive relationships. **Ire:** Confident leadership, social influence, ethical guidance, strong relationships, recognized success. **Osogbo:** Arrogance, misuse of authority, relational conflict, unethical behavior, loss of respect.

219. Irete-Okanran: Irete represents clarity and growth, while Okanran embodies challenges and endurance. **Message:** This Odu teaches that moral discipline, patience, and ethical perseverance ensure steady progress during trials. **Ire:** Resilience, disciplined growth, endurance through trials, emotional maturity, steady progress. **Osogbo:** Reckless decisions, giving in to pressure, instability, financial stress, loss of direction.

220. Irete-Ogunda: Irete embodies clarity, while Ogunda represents effort and disciplined action. **Message:** This Odu teaches that material and personal success comes through consistent, ethical labor, guided by responsibility and focus. **Ire:** Achievement through effort, responsible action, material success, constructive energy, persistent work. **Osogbo:** Laziness, misdirected effort, fragmented progress, burnout, unethical shortcuts.

221. Irete-Osa: Irete signifies clarity and insight, while Osa embodies hidden influences and subtlety. **Message:** This Odu teaches that ethical discernment and awareness of unseen forces protect resources and ensure successful outcomes. **Ire:** Spiritual wealth, informed decisions, protection of resources, ethical insight, understanding hidden dynamics. **Osogbo:** Ignorance, mismanagement, superficial judgment, unexpected setbacks, lost opportunities.

222. Irete-Ika: Irete embodies growth and clarity, while Ika represents accountability and moral responsibility. **Message:** This Odu teaches that ethical stewardship, transparency, and integrity preserve wealth and success. **Ire:** Accountability, wise resource management, ethical oversight, responsibility in wealth, financial integrity. **Osogbo:** Irresponsibility, unethical actions, mismanagement, exploitation, loss of prosperity.

223. Irete-Oturupon: Irete signifies clarity and growth, while Oturupon represents restoration and protection. **Message:** This Odu teaches that disciplined correction of past errors, ethical action, and renewal restore balance and abundance. **Ire:** Restoration, financial recovery, holistic renewal, recovered stability, ethical renewal. **Osogbo:** Neglect, unresolved problems, stagnation, lost opportunities, failure to correct mistakes.

224. Irete-Otura: Irete embodies clarity and balance, while Otura signifies spiritual peace and contentment. **Message:** This Odu teaches that ethical and mindful decisions create harmony between material and spiritual life. **Ire:** Material-spiritual harmony, peace of mind, balanced living, secure prosperity, ethical clarity. **Osogbo:** Overemphasis on materialism, stress, imbalance, insecurity, scattered efforts.

225. Irete-Ose: Irete represents clarity and attraction of positive energies, while Ose embodies joy, harmony, and generosity. **Message:** This Odu teaches that ethical sharing and moral engagement with others bring joy, relational harmony, and blessings. **Ire:** Joy, harmony, ethical enjoyment, relational prosperity, community support, balance. **Osogbo:** Envy, selfishness, conflict, mismanagement of resources, disruption of peace.

226. Irete-Ofun: Irete embodies clarity and ethical growth, while Ofun represents divine completion and fulfillment. **Message:** This Odu teaches that alignment of intention, effort, and morality leads to ultimate blessings and realization of life's potential. **Ire:** Divine favor, ultimate prosperity, fulfillment, completion of cycles, alignment with higher purpose. **Osogbo:** Arrogance, misuse of blessings, stagnation, misalignment with principles, ethical decline.

* * *

THE CHILDREN OF OSE MEJI
Common Themes found in the family of Ose include: Abundance, creativity, wealth, the flow of prosperity.

227. Ose-Ogbe: This Odu focuses on the manifestation of potential through the attraction of positive energies and the initiation of clear, harmonious new beginnings. **Message:** This Odu signals a vibrant phase of growth where your sincere actions and relational sweetness align perfectly with the light of a new path. It teaches that by moving forward with a clear heart and positive intent, you naturally attract the blessings required to manifest your highest destiny. **Iré:** Smooth beginnings, supportive relationships, and success in new ventures. **Òsogbo:** Stagnation caused by a lack of initiative or failing to nurture the connections that open doors.

228. Ose-Oyeku: This Odu centers on the transition from difficult or bitter cycles into a space of emotional healing and renewed joy. **Message:** Ose softens the finality of Oyeku, turning a potentially painful ending into a graceful transition characterized by forgiveness and relief. It teaches that when a challenging cycle concludes, the arrival of positive energy facilitates a deep emotional release, allowing light to return where there was once only darkness. **Iré:** Healing, reconciliation, and protection from the weight of past burdens. **Òsogbo:** Clinging to old grudges or refusing to accept the necessary end of a cycle.

229. Ose-Iwori: This Odu emphasizes the use of deep reflection to understand the spiritual patterns and motives governing one's attractions and relationships. **Message:** By combining relational sweetness with inward consciousness, Ose-Iwori encourages a thoughtful evaluation of how you love and who you attract. It teaches that true harmony is sustained when you gain the insight to recognize your own emotional patterns, allowing for more honest and strengthened bonds with others. **Iré:** Emotional clarity, harmonious romantic ties, and strengthened family bonds. **Òsogbo:** Ignorance of one's own motives or repeating unhealthy emotional patterns without reflection.

230. Ose-Odi: This Odu highlights the importance of establishing strong structures and protective boundaries to secure long-term harmony and creative growth. **Message:** Ose-Odi teaches that joy and attraction must be "sealed" within a stable structure—such as marriage, a committed partnership, or a solid career—to truly thrive. By placing your creative and emotional energies into a disciplined framework, you protect your blessings and ensure that your growth is both fertile and permanent. **Iré:** Strong family ties, long-term stability, and successful creative manifestation. **Òsogbo:** Preventable setbacks caused by chaotic behavior or a lack of commitment.

231. Ose-Irosun: This Odu explores the continuity of family harmony and the ancestral support that sustains a lineage filled with joy. **Message:** The sweetness of Ose is tied here to your ancestral roots, reminding you that the harmony you cultivate today becomes a legacy for future generations. It teaches that by honoring your family and mentoring the young, you maintain a flow of generational blessings that keeps your home peaceful and your lineage spiritually vibrant. **Iré:** A peaceful home, happy children, and the active support of the ancestors. **Òsogbo:**Ethical confusion or family discord caused by ignoring your heritage and responsibilities.

232. Ose-Owonrin: This Odu examines how adaptability and flexibility allow one to maintain inner joy during periods of rapid transformation. **Message:** Ose-Owonrin teaches that movement and change do not have to disrupt your peace; instead, they can be the very catalysts for new opportunities. By embracing the unpredictable shifts of life with grace, you find that your ability to stay fluid and positive leads to a more resilient and spiritually insightful path. **Iré:** Personal growth, resilience, and smooth transitions during times of change. **Òsogbo:**

Rigidity or resistance to change that creates unnecessary confusion and loss.

233. Ose-Obara: This Odu addresses the expression of authority and social influence through empathy, kindness, and effective communication. **Message:** True leadership in this Odu is defined not by dominance, but by the ability to attract others through generosity and relational skill. It teaches that when you lead with an open heart and communicate with compassion, your influence grows naturally, earning you the respect and support of your peers and community. **Iré:** Social influence, successful leadership, and receiving respect from peers. **Òsogbo:** Pride or the misuse of influence that fractures social bonds and trust.

234. Ose-Okanran: This Odu demonstrates how patience and loyalty allow one to maintain harmony even when tested by struggle or strife. **Message:** Ose-Okanran teaches that the strength of a connection is proven through its ability to endure hardship without losing its sweetness. It emphasizes that while you may face trials or testing periods, staying loyal and persistent in your values will eventually transform that struggle into a deeply rooted and unshakable success. **Iré:** Enduring love, spiritual growth through adversity, and strengthened connections. **Òsogbo:** Impulsive reactions to stress or losing heart during a period of testing.

235. Ose-Ogunda: This Odu focuses on the disciplined action and consistent labor required to maintain a prosperous and harmonious life. **Message:** This Odu serves as a reminder that a "sweet life" is not a passive gift, but something earned through effort and moral discipline. It teaches that prosperity and harmony are sustainable only when they are backed by hard work, showing that the most lasting rewards come to those who commit to their duties with joy. **Iré:** Sustainable prosperity, material abundance, and earned recognition. **Òsogbo:** Wasted energy or the loss of blessings due to laziness and a lack of discipline.

236. Ose-Osa: This Odu explores the spiritual power of beauty, elegance, and the awareness of subtle energies in social influence. **Message:** Ose-Osa reveals that there is a mystical quality to attraction; by cultivating inner and outer grace, you enhance your personal magnetism and spiritual influence. It teaches that moving through the world with elegance and awareness of the "subtle" allows you to navigate social dynamics with a unique and favorable power. **Iré:** Favorable connections, personal magnetism, and spiritual influence. **Òsogbo:** Disconnection from subtle truths or neglecting the grace required to maintain influence.

237. Ose-Ika: This Odu centers on the relationship between ethical conduct, social responsibility, and the preservation of trust. **Message:** Harmony in your community and your relationships is maintained through the practice of accountability and justice. This Odu teaches that taking responsibility for your actions and acting with fairness ensures that your bonds remain sweet and your reputation remains untarnished, preventing the discord that follows moral lapses. **Iré:** Restored harmony, justice, and the gain of trust and respect. **Òsogbo:** Social instability and fractured relationships caused by a lack of integrity.

238. Ose-Oturupon: This Odu highlights how compassion and forgiveness can lead to the holistic healing of broken emotional bonds. **Message:** Ose-Oturupon emphasizes that even the most damaged relationships can be renewed through the active application of kindness and restoration. It teaches that by choosing to forgive and seeking to mend what is broken, you invite a powerful healing energy that restores peace to your heart and joy to your connections. **Iré:** Emotional restoration, joyful reconnection, and peace in relationships. **Òsogbo:** Refusing to forgive or neglecting to mend a bond that requires attention.

239. Ose-Otura: This Odu examines how spiritual balance and the appreciation of beauty lead to profound serenity and contentment. **Message:** Ose-Otura teaches that love and spiritual practice should be beautiful and refined; by engaging with art, nature, and divine beauty, you enhance your inner peace. It emphasizes that a refined perception and a balanced spirit allow you to find "heaven on earth," where your relationships and your soul are in a state of constant, joyful harmony. **Iré:** Spiritual inspiration, contentment, and refined perception. **Òsogbo:** Disrupted peace caused by a lack of balance or aesthetic neglect.

240. Ose-Irete: This Odu highlights how collective success and social prosperity are achieved through the power of cooperation. **Message:** Ose-Irete teaches that while personal effort is good, collaboration is the true key to amplified rewards. It emphasizes that by working harmoniously with others and valuing partnerships, you create a "sweetness" in your ventures that leads to recognition and long-term success that could not be achieved alone. **Iré:** Strong partnerships, successful collaborations, and social recognition. **Òsogbo:** Isolation or failing to work collaboratively, leading to incomplete success.

241. Ose-Ofun: This Odu represents the peak of spiritual fulfillment where all life cycles culminate in divine harmony and illumination. **Message:** Ose-Ofun marks the ultimate fulfillment of your efforts, where every lesson has been learned and every blessing manifests in its most perfect form. It teaches that by maintaining your alignment with higher principles, you reach a state of total contentment and divine protection, though it warns that arrogance at this final stage is the only thing that can cloud your illumination. **Iré:** Total harmony, divine protection, and the fulfillment of all blessings. **Òsogbo:**Arrogance or moral decline that interrupts the completion of a cycle.

* * *

THE CHILDREN OF OFUN MEJI

Common Themes found in the family of Ofun include: Completion of cycles, clarity, emergence into light, understanding.

242. Ofun-Ogbe: This Odu focuses on the arrival of divine illumination and the manifestation of potential through clear, forward-moving beginnings. **Message:** Ofun-Ogbe reflects a powerful culmination phase where the "Source" reveals the path ahead, bringing expanded understanding after a period of uncertainty. It teaches that when divine light meets clear intention, your accomplishments become visible to all, signaling that you are now ready to lead with integrity and wisdom. **Iré:** Clear insight, revealed opportunities, and accomplishments that are finally visible after long effort. **Òsogbo:** Neglecting to acknowledge your progress or failing to align your next steps with the wisdom you have gained.

243. Ofun-Oyeku: This Odu centers on the divine illumination that accompanies the closing of major karmic cycles and the release of the past. **Message:** By bringing light into the darkness of Oyeku, this Odu signals the total resolution of old burdens and the end of long-standing struggles. It teaches that grace is found in the transition, allowing for a deep spiritual renewal where forgiveness and reconciliation pave the way for entirely new opportunities to emerge. **Iré:** The release of heavy burdens, spiritual renewal, and the resolution of past challenges. **Òsogbo:** Refusing to let go of a cycle that has ended or failing to forgive those involved in past conflicts.

244. Ofun-Iwori: This Odu emphasizes the internal transformation and heightened consciousness that arise when divine insight is applied to self-reflection. **Message:** This Odu represents the moment of ultimate "Aha!" at the end of a spiritual journey, where your inner clarity finally aligns perfectly with your destiny. It teaches that true enlightenment is the result of reflecting on every lesson learned, allowing that knowledge to transform your very being into a vessel of divine truth. **Iré:** Spiritual enlightenment, inner clarity, and the perfect alignment of thought and purpose. **Òsogbo:** Shallow interpretation of life lessons or failing to apply discovered insights to your future actions.

245. Ofun-Odi: This Odu highlights the structural completion and protective boundaries that result from divine alignment and manifestation. **Message:** Ofun-Odi signifies the final "protective seal" placed upon your life's work, representing a structure that has reached its perfect, divine form. It teaches that once a foundation is spiritually coherent and structurally sound, it becomes a fortress of stability that preserves your results and safeguards your future growth. **Iré:** Secure foundations, spiritual protection, and the integration of successful results. **Òsogbo:** Failing to guard your achievements or neglecting the stability of the foundation you have built.

246. Ofun-Irosun: This Odu explores the manifestation of inherited potential and the fulfillment of ancestral promises through divine revelation. **Message:** This Odu reveals that you are the living manifestation of your ancestors' prayers, emphasizing that your success is a continuation of their legacy. It teaches that by respecting tradition and fulfilling your spiritual obligations, you activate a powerful flow of lineage blessings that ensures family harmony and spiritual continuity. **Iré:**Ancestral support, a realized legacy, and harmonious family continuity. **Òsogbo:** Repeating ancestral mistakes or ignoring the spiritual traditions that provide your foundation.

247. Ofun-Owonrin: This Odu examines how sudden transformation and unpredictable movement can lead to the final completion of a cycle. **Message:** Ofun-Owonrin teaches that completion often arrives through unexpected shifts that clear away stagnant energy; these sudden changes are actually divine interventions. By remaining adaptable and open, you allow these "stormy" movements to become the very breakthroughs that resolve long-standing issues and bring you to a state of spiritual clarity. **Iré:** Rapid breakthroughs, spiritual insight, and the successful resolution of stagnation. **Òsogbo:** Rigidity or fear of change that prevents a necessary transformation from reaching completion.

248. Ofun-Obara: This Odu addresses the power of words and the alignment of will with divine revelation to manifest one's intentions. **Message:** This Odu highlights the ultimate authority found in truthful speech, where your words act as the final "stamp" that brings intentions into reality. It teaches that when your expression is aligned with divine light, your eloquence becomes a tool for leadership and influence, allowing you to finalize projects and command respect through integrity. **Iré:**Influential communication, eloquence, and the alignment of will with expression. **Òsogbo:** Careless speech or using one's influence to spread untruths rather than wisdom.

249. Ofun-Okanran: This Odu demonstrates how endurance and steady balance allow one to overcome the final test in any personal or spiritual trial. **Message:** Ofun-Okanran represents the strength found at the very end of a struggle, teaching that resilience during the "last mile" is what secures ultimate success. It emphasizes that by facing final obstacles with a steady heart and divine clarity, you transform past adversity into a crown of spiritual maturity and undeniable victory. **Iré:** Victory after long struggle, emotional endurance, and growth through adversity. **Òsogbo:** Losing resolve at the final moment or allowing frustration to unbalance your success.

250. Ofun-Ogunda: This Odu focuses on the disciplined effort and creative labor that culminate in the full realization of one's potential.

Message: This Odu signals a breakthrough into true mastery, where your skills, discipline, and effort align with divine light to create sustainable prosperity. It teaches that your dedication to your craft has prepared you for a position of respected authority, showing that you have forged a path that others can now follow. **Iré:** Skill mastery, sustainable prosperity, and the attainment of respected authority. **Òsogbo:** Failing to refine your gifts or neglecting the discipline required to maintain your status.

251. Ofun-Osa: This Odu explores the discovery of hidden spiritual forces and the revelation of divine secrets through spiritual depth. **Message:** Ofun-Osa represents the unveiling of the "final mystery," where your spiritual depth grants you access to blessings and insights that were previously hidden. It teaches that through meditation, prayer, and awareness of the unseen, you can perceive the subtle forces of the universe, leading to a profound trust in divine guidance. **Iré:** Intuitive revelation, spiritual insight, and awareness of hidden blessings. **Òsogbo:** Disconnection from spiritual wisdom or failing to heed intuitive warnings.

252. Ofun-Ika: This Odu centers on the relationship between ethical accountability and the restoration of harmony at the end of a cycle. **Message:** This Odu emphasizes that divine justice is the final word as a cycle closes, ensuring that integrity and fairness are rewarded. It teaches that by upholding ethical standards and remaining accountable for your actions, you find yourself in a state of restored harmony where your character is your greatest shield and your best recommendation. **Iré:** Realized justice, restored harmony, and the recognition of ethical conduct. **Òsogbo:** Ethical lapses or failing to take responsibility, which leads to a difficult closing of the cycle.

253. Ofun-Oturupon: This Odu highlights the total restoration of health and physical balance through divine purification. **Message:**Ofun-Oturupon marks the end of illness or imbalance, signaling a time of total physical and emotional renewal; it is the manifestation of wholeness. It teaches that by maintaining routines that honor the body and mind, you sustain a state of purity and vitality that allows your spirit to shine at its brightest. **Iré:** Renewed health, restored vitality, and perfect physical-emotional balance. **Òsogbo:** Neglecting self-care or failing to maintain the rituals that sustain your well-being.

254. Ofun-Otura: This Odu represents the attainment of spiritual peace and stability as the ultimate result of a life in coherence. **Message:**Ofun-Otura signifies the deep serenity that comes when your life's orientation is perfectly aligned with divine principles. It teaches that spiritual contentment is the highest form of success, manifesting as harmonious relationships and a clarity of purpose that remains unshakable regardless of external circumstances. **Iré:** Spiritual contentment, clarity of purpose, and unshakable serenity. **Òsogbo:** Scattered priorities or allowing external noise to disrupt your inner peace.

255. Ofun-Irete: This Odu explores how determination and spiritual alignment manifest as total fulfillment and ultimate good fortune. **Message:** This Odu indicates a time of "ultimate luck," where your determination and discipline finally bear the fruit of total abundance. It teaches that your success is a divine gift that must be preserved through gratitude and generosity, ensuring that your prosperity continues to multiply and benefit those around you. **Iré:** Total prosperity, favorable circumstances, and positive recognition. **Òsogbo:** Ingratitude or inconsistency that interrupts the flow of good fortune.

256. Ofun-Ose: This Odu represents the peak of divine manifestation where joy and universal harmony become the final law of existence. **Message:** Ofun-Ose reflects the ultimate state of "joyful co-creation," where your thoughts and words move in perfect sync with the harmony of the universe. It teaches that when you act with sincerity and joy, you fulfill your spiritual destiny, manifesting a life of contentment that serves as a beacon of light for others. **Iré:** Universal harmony, spiritual contentment, and fulfillment in all things. **Òsogbo:** Acting with insincerity or allowing discord to interrupt your state of joy.

* * *

A simple and direct way to determine which Orishas are connected to an Odu is to always ask during divination which Orishas are speaking or willing to accept the *ebo* to help the client. This step is essential. However, if you need a general idea of which Orishas are associated with a particular Odu, you can use the following method as a guide:

1. If the Odu is a **principal Odu** (for example, *Ogbe Meji / Eji-Ogbe*), examine the Orishas clearly associated with that Odu family.
2. If the Odu is a **composite Odu** (for example, *Ogbe–Osa*), examine the Orishas associated with both Odu families and determine which are primarily speaking in that combination.

EXAMPLE:

- **Ogbe Meji** → look at Orishas of the Ogbe family.
- **Ogbe–Osa** → consider both Ogbe and Osa families and determine which energies are most active.

Below is a general guide to the Orishas and their deeper themes within each Odu family.

<u>ORISHAS BY ODU FAMILY</u>

<u>1. OGBE FAMILY</u>

- **Primary Orishas:** Obatala, Ori, Orunmila, Oduduwa
- **Themes:** Light, creation, spiritual clarity, divine consciousness, alignment with one's Ori.

2. OYEKUN FAMILY

- **Primary Orishas:** Egun, Eshu
- **Themes:** Mystery, darkness, the unknown, ancestral forces, death and transitions.

3. IWORI FAMILY

- **Primary Orishas:** Shango, Aganju, Ibeji, Ori
- **Themes:** Fire, consciousness, ego, power of awareness, transformation and metamorphosis.

4. ODI FAMILY

- **Primary Orishas:** Yemoja, Olokun
- **Themes:** The womb, containment, protection, deep emotional and spiritual waters.

5. IROSUN FAMILY

- **Primary Orishas:** Egun, Ori, Shango
- **Themes:** Ancestral influence, generational consciousness, destiny shaped by lineage.

6. OWONRIN FAMILY

- **Primary Orishas:** Eshu, Orunmila
- **Themes:** Crossroads, change, unpredictability, adaptability.

7. OBARA FAMILY

- **Primary Orishas:** Shango, Oshun, Aje, Olokun
- **Themes:** Transformation, turning poverty into wealth, prosperity.

8. Okanran Family

- **Primary Orishas:** Ochosi, Shango, Orunmila
- **Themes:** Strength of heart, resilience, trials that shape leadership, Emotions, could indicate a restless heart.

9. Ogunda Family

- **Primary Orishas:** Ogun, Ochosi
- **Themes:** Iron and war, hard work to cut obstacles and clear paths in life to move forward.

10. Osa Family

- **Primary Orishas:** Oya, Iyami, Egbe, Egun, Yewa
- **Themes:** Storms, wind, spiritual warfare, protection, hidden actions, consequences, witchcraft.

11. Ika Family

- **Primary Orishas:** Ori, Oro, Shango
- **Themes:** Self-control, restraint, responsible use of power, self mastery as the way to true power.

12. Oturupon Family

- **Primary Orishas:** Orunmila, Ogun, Ori, Eshu, Aganju
- **Themes:** Endurance, stability, surviving hardship.

13. Otura Family

- **Primary Orishas:** Obatala, Orunmila, Ori, Egbe, Olodumare, Oya
- **Themes:** Mystical vision, divine alignment, reflection, tranquility, dreams

<u>**14. IRETE FAMILY**</u>

- **Primary Orishas:** Ori, Onile, Ochosi, Orunmila, Eshu
- **Themes:** Good character brings blessings.

<u>**15. OSE FAMILY**</u>

- **Primary Orishas:** Oshun, Aje, Olokun
- **Themes:** Abundance, creativity, wealth.

<u>**16. OFUN FAMILY**</u>

- **Primary Orishas:** Obatala, Orunmila, Ori, Olofin, Oduduwa, Yemaya
- **Themes:** Completion of cycles, clarity, enlightenment, spiritual illumination.

* * *

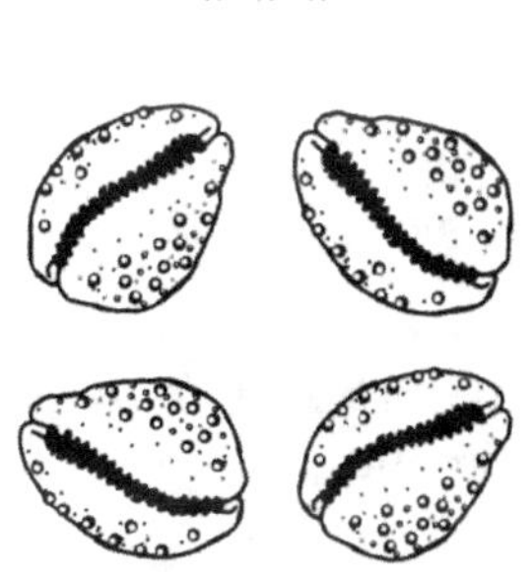

CHAPTER 16

SPIRITUAL SIGNATURES OF PLANTS

In the sacred worldview of Ifá, plants are not merely physical organisms, they are living vessels of spiritual intelligence. Each plant carries a pattern of consciousness that aligns with one or more energy matrices associated with a particular Odu family or multiple Odu families. Through these energetic patterns, plants embody specific forces of creation, transformation, protection, destiny, and ancestral memory.

Single and Multiple Odu Associations

Plants with concentrated energy: Some plants embody the energy of a single Odu family in a clear and focused way. These plants are considered energetically pure because they reflect the core vibration of that Odu without significant blending.

Plants with layered energy: Other plants carry composite or layered energies. They resonate with multiple Odu families at once, which is why a single plant may traditionally be associated with more than one Odu. Their spiritual expression is multidimensional rather than singular.

Factors That Influence a Plant's Spiritual Expression

A plant's spiritual quality is not fixed. Its expression can vary depending on several conditions:

- **Region:** The geographical location where a plant grows influences its energetic character. Climate, soil composition, and local spiritual traditions all shape how its energy manifests.
- **Environment:** Plants exist in relationship with surrounding vegetation. The energetic field created by neighboring plants can influence and modify a plant's spiritual expression.
- **Plant Part:** Different parts of the same plant carry different energetic signatures. For example, the roots of all plants are associated with the Odu family of Irete, which represents virtue, stability, and strong foundations. Just as roots anchor and nourish the plant, Irete governs grounding and moral structure.

It is also important to understand that Odu family groupings do not limit a plant's potential. A plant aligned primarily with one Odu may still participate in the work of another when guided by divination, ritual context, or ancestral instruction. The Odu family indicates its core vibration, but spiritual application depends on wisdom and proper alignment. With this framework in mind, we now begin examining the plants according to their dominant Odu families, starting with the family of Ogbe, the current of light, creation, and revealed destiny.

* * *

A Personal Note on Safety

Before handling, consuming, or burning any plant mentioned in this book, please consult a qualified healthcare professional. The information provided here is strictly for educational purposes and should never replace professional medical advice, diagnosis, or treatment. Please approach every plant with extreme caution and keep the following risks in mind:

1. **Severe Toxicity:** Some plants listed are highly toxic and can cause serious illness, poisoning, coma, or even death if touched, ingested, or inhaled.

2. **Allergies and Interactions:** Even plants that are not explicitly labeled as "toxic" can trigger severe, life-threatening allergic reactions. Furthermore, they can interact dangerously with prescription medications or worsen existing health conditions.

3. **Inhalation Risks:** Burning a plant can release its natural toxins directly into the air you breathe.

4. **Incomplete Labels:** While I have flagged certain plants as toxic, this is not an exhaustive list of every potential side effect or danger. A lack of a **"toxic"** label does not guarantee a plant is completely safe or non toxic.

Because exact safe dosages are often unknown, you should never use this information for medical experimentation. Enjoy learning about these plants, but prioritize your physical health and safety first.

* * *

1. OGBE FAMILY

Plants associated with the family of Ogbe carry energies primarily connected to the Orishas Obatala, Ori, Orunmila, and Oduduwa. They carry the energies of light in creation, destiny, and clarity through the truth being revealed in the light of day.

- **Bermuda Grass (Couch Grass)** – *Cynodon dactylon* – Eji Ogbe
- **Celery** – *Apium graveolens* – Eji Ogbe
- **Coconut** – *Cocos nucifera* – Eji Ogbe
- **Copal (Resin)** – *Bursera bipinnata* – Eji Ogbe
- **Cotton (Sea Island)** – *Gossypium barbadense* – Ogbe Odi – toxic if touched or ingested
- **Cucumber** – *Cucumis sativus* – Eji Ogbe
- **Green Tea** – *Camellia sinensis* – Eji Ogbe
- **Indian Shot** – *Canna indica* – Eji Ogbe
- **Kola Nut (Obi)** – *Cola nitida* – Eji Ogbe
- **Lemongrass** – *Cymbopogon citratus* – Eji Ogbe
- **Mint** – *Mentha spp.* – Eji Ogbe

- **Parsley** – *Petroselinum crispum* – Eji Ogbe
- **Red Palm Oil** – *Elaeis guineensis* – Eji Ogbe
- **Rosemary** – *Salvia rosmarinus* – Eji Ogbe
- **Thyme** – *Thyme vulgaris* – Ogbe Bara
- **Wandering Jew** – *Zebrina pendula* – Ogbe Roso – toxic if touched or ingested
- **White Commelina** – *Commelina elegans* – Eji Ogbe
- **Spreading Hogweed** – *Boerhavia diffusa* – Eji Ogbe
- **Four O'clock** – *Mirabilis jalapa* – Eji Ogbe – toxic if touched or ingested
- **Plantain Broadleaf** – *Plantago major* – Eji Ogbe
- **Purslane** – *Portulaca oleracea* – Eji Ogbe
- **Soursop** – *Annona muricata* – Eji Ogbe – toxic if ingested
- **White Mallow** – *Waltheria indica* – Eji Ogbe
- **Wild Spinach** – *Amaranthus viridis* – Eji Ogbe – toxic if ingested
- **Bitter Melon** – *Momordica charantia* – Ogbe Sa
- **Castor Bean** – *Ricinus communis* – Ogbe Yonu – toxic if touched or ingested, can cause death
- **Guava** – *Psidium guajava* – Ogbe Irosun
- **Jack-in-the-Bush** – *Newbouldia laevis* – Ogbe Ogunda
- **Elephant Ear** – *Xanthosoma sagittifolium* – Ogbe Wale (Ogbe Iwori) – toxic if touched or ingested
- **White Pepper** – *Piper nigrum* – Eji Ogbe
- **Coriander Seed** – *Coriandrum sativum* – Eji Ogbe

2. OYEKU FAMILY

Plants associated with the family of Oyekun carry energies primarily connected to the Orishas Eshu, Yewa and Egun, they carry the energies that surround the mysteries of night, darkness, death, transition, endings, rest, and ancestral wisdom. They support reflection and communion with ancestors.

- **Ackee** – *Blighia sapida* – Oyeku Meji – toxic if ingested (unripe fruit), can cause death
- **Beetroot** – *Beta vulgaris* – Oyeku Meji
- **Billygoat Weed** – *Ageratum conyzoides* – Oyeku Meji – toxic if ingested

- **Coffee** – *Coffea arabica* – Oyeku Meji
- **Garlic** – *Allium sativum* – Oyeku Meji
- **Onion** – *Allium cepa* – Oyeku Meji
- **Dragon Tree** – *Dracaena fragrans* – Oyeku Ose – toxic if ingested, can cause poisoning
- **Sassafras** – *Sassafras albidum* – Oyeku Irete – toxic if ingested in large amounts
- **Star Apple (Agbalumo)** – *Chrysophyllum cainito* – Oyeku Obara
- **Umbrella Sedge** – *Cyperus alternifolius* – Oyeku Ka
- **Nigella Seed (Black Cumin)** – *Nigella sativa* – Oyeku Meji – toxic if ingested in large amounts
- **Fenugreek** – *Trigonella foenum-graecum* – Oyeku Meji
- **Cloves (Whole)** – *Syzygium aromaticum* – Oyeku Ose
- **Hibiscus** — *Hibiscus rosa-sinensis* — Oyeku -Osa

3. Iwori Family

Plants associated with the family of Iwori carry energies primarily connected to the Orishas Shango, Aganju, Ibeji, and Ori. They carry the energies that surround consciousness, personal power, ego, transformation, metamorphosis, and awakening.

- **Grape Ivy** – *Cissus debilis* – Iwori Meji
- **Odundun** – *Kalanchoe crenata* – Iwori Meji – toxic if ingested
- **Rosary Pea (Crab's Eye)** – *Abrus precatorius* – Iwori Meji – highly toxic if touched or ingested, can cause death
- **Shiny Bush (Pepper Elder)** – *Peperomia pellucida* – Iwori Meji
- **Sweet Basil** – *Ocimum basilicum* – Iwori Meji
- **Whipstick Tree** – *Glyphaea brevis* – Iwori Meji
- **Paprika** – *Capsicum annuum* – Iwori Ogunda
- **Fennel** — *Foeniculum vulgare* - Iwori- Ogbe
- Mandrake (European Mandrake) — *Mandragora officinarum*- Iwori- Otura - highly toxic if touched or ingested, can cause death.
- **Hawthorn** (English Hawthorn) — *Crataegus laevigata* - Iwori- Okana

- **Ground Ivy** (Creeping Charlie) — *Glechoma hederacea* - Iwori-yeku
- **Clover** (White Clover) — *Trifolium repens*- Iwori -Ofun
- **Scotch Broom** — *Cytisus scoparius*— Iwori- Ose
- **St. John's Wort** — *Hypericum perforatum* — Iwori- Obara
- **May apple** —(American Mandrake) —*Podophyllum peltatum* - Iwori-Otura—highly toxic if touched or ingested, can cause coma or death.

4. Odi Family

Plants associated with the family of Odi carry energies primarily connected to the Orishas Yemoja and Olokun. They carry the energies that surround the seal of the womb, fertility, protection, maternal guidance, nurturing force in creation.

- **Cluster Fig** – *Ficus sur* – Odi Meji
- **Peony** – *Paeonia officinalis* – Odi Bara – toxic if ingested
- **Striped Inch Plant (Boat Lily)** – *Tradescantia spathacea* – Odi Ogunda – toxic if touched
- **White Water Lily** – *Nymphaea lotus* – Odi Meji – toxic if ingested
- **Chicory** – *Cichorium intybus* – Odi Meji
- **Sea Kelp / Seaweed** — *Various species (e.g., Fucus vesiculosus, Ascophyllum nodosum)* — Odi -Obara
- **Water Lily / Lotus** — *Nymphaea spp. / Nelumbo nucifera* -Odi -Ogbe
- **Magnolia** — *Magnolia grandiflora* -Odi- Ofun
- **Lilac** -*Syringa vulgaris* — Odi -Osa

5. Irosun Family

Plants associated with the family of Irosun carry energies primarily connected to the Orishas Egun, Ori, and Shango. They carry the energies that surround ancestors, generational consciousness, lineage, family destiny, inherited wisdom and what is passed on through spiritual and ancestral lineages.

- **African Rosewood (Camwood)** – *Pterocarpus erinaceus* – Irosun Meji
- **Allspice** – *Pimenta dioica* – Irosun Meji
- **Bay Leaf** – *Laurus nobilis* – Irosun- bara
- **Cashew** – *Anacardium occidentale* – Irosun Meji – toxic if ingested raw or contact with skin
- **Nutmeg** – *Myristica fragrans* – Irosun Meji – toxic if ingested in large amounts
- **Sweet Potato** – Ipomoea batatas – Irosun Meji
- **Thatch Grass** – *Hyparrhenia spp.* – Irosun Meji
- **Road Opener (Abrecamino)** – *Eupatorium villosum* – Irosun Meji – toxic if ingested
- **Red Sandalwood** – *Pterocarpus santalinus* – Irosun Meji
- **Bloodroot** – *Sanguinaria canadensis* – Irosun Meji – toxic if ingested or touched
- **Tree of Heaven** – *Ailanthus altissima* – Irosun Meji – toxic if ingested
- **Golden Rod** – *Solidago virgaurea* – Irosun Meji
- **Annatto (Achiote)** – *Bixa orellana* – Irosun Meji
- **Sumac** – *Rhus coriaria* – Irosun Meji – toxic if ingested in large amounts
- **Saw Palmetto** —— *Serenoa repens* ——Irosun Meji

6. Owonrin Family

Plants associated with the family of Owonrin carry energies primarily connected to the Orishas Eshu and Orunmila. They carry the energies that surround crossroads, unpredictability, open/ closed doors and infinite possible potential as well as destiny.

- **Banana / Plantain** – *Musa spp.* – Owonrin Meji
- **Bitter Leaf** – *Vernonia amygdalina* – Owonrin Meji
- **Black-Eyed Peas** – *Vigna unguiculata* – Owonrin Meji
- **Cabbage** – *Brassica oleracea* – Owonrin- Irete
- **Papaya (Pawpaw)** – *Carica papaya* – Owonrin Meji
- **Snakeweed (Brazilian Tea)** – *Stachytarpheta spp.* – Owonrin Meji

- **Broomweed** – *Sida acuta* – Owonrin Meji
- **Tamarind** – *Tamarindus indica* – Owonrin Meji
- **Indian Jujube** – *Ziziphus mauritiana* – Owonrin Meji
- **Nettle** – *Urtica dioica* – Owonrin Meji
- **Yarrow** – *Achillea millefolium* – Owonrin Meji
- **Horseradish** – *Armoracia rusticana* – Owonrin Meji
- **Dry Mustard** – *Sinapis alba* – Owonrin Meji
- **Epazote** – *Dysphania ambrosioides* – Owonrin Sidogbe

7. OBARA FAMILY

Plants associated with the family of Obara carry energies primarily connected to the Orishas Shango, Oshun, Aje, and Olokun. They carry the energies that surround transformation, turning poverty into wealth, material and spiritual abundance, prosperity, and growth.

- **Lemon** – *Citrus limon* – Obara Meji
- **Lime** – *Citrus aurantiifolia* – Obara Meji
- **Dandelion** — *Taraxacum officinale* Obara- Rosu
- **Okra** — *Abelmoschus esculentus* -- Obara-Rosu
- **Peanuts** – *Arachis hypogaea* – Obara Meji
- **Pomegranate** – *Punica granatum* – Obara Meji
- **Pumpkin / Squash** – *Cucurbita maxima* – Obara Meji
- **Watermelon** – *Citrullus lanatus* – Obara Meji
- **Maize** (Corn) – *Zea mays* – Obara Meji
- **Sunflower** – *Helianthus annuus* – Obara Meji
- **Sesame** – *Sesamum indicum* – Obara Meji
- **African Fan Palm** – *Borassus aethiopum* – Obara Meji
- **Cantaloupe** – *Cucumis melo* – Obara Meji
- **Saffron** – *Crocus sativus* – Obara Meji
- **Yellow Mustard Seed** – *Brassica alba* – Obara Meji

8. Okanran Family

Plants associated with the family of Okanran carry energies primarily connected to the Orishas Ochosi, Shango, and Orunmila. They carry the energies that surround the strength and resilience of the heart, trials that forge leaders, courage, endurance, and empowerment. They support developing leadership, perseverance, and inner fortitude.

- **Cumin** – *Cuminum cyminum* – Okanran Meji
- **Wild Leadwort** – *Plumbago zeylanica* – Okanran Meji
- **Black Locust** – *Robinia pseudoacacia* – Okanran Meji
- **Prickly Poppy** – *Argemone mexicana* – Okanran Meji
- **African Myrrh** – *Commiphora africana* – Okanran Meji
- **Thistle** – *Cirsium spp.* – Okanran Meji
- **Pears (Peras)** — *Pyrus communis*- Okana Meji
- **Green Apples** (*Manzanas verdes*) — *Okana- Ogbe*

9. Ogunda Family

Plants associated with the family of Ogunda carry energies primarily connected to the Orisha Ogun. They carry the energies that surround iron, war, cutting obstacles, clearing paths, determination, and action. They support decisiveness, removing barriers, and opening the way for progress.

- **Cayenne** — *Capsicum annuum* —Ogunda Meji
- **Avocado** – *Persea americana* – Ogunda Meji
- **Black Pepper** – *Piper nigrum* – Ogunda Meji
- **Ginger** – *Zingiber officinale* – Ogunda Meji
- **Pineapple** – *Ananas comosus* – Ogunda Meji
- **Snake Plant** – *Dracaena trifasciata* – Ogunda Meji (Toxic if ingested)
- **Yam** – *Dioscorea spp.* – Ogunda Meji
- **Tobacco** – *Nicotiana tabacum* – Ogunda Meji (Toxic if ingested)
- **Hog Plum** – *Spondias mombin* – Ogunda Meji
- **Ironwood** – *Lophira alata* – Ogunda Meji
- **Bamboo** – *Bambusa vulgaris* – Ogunda Meji

- **Arrowroot** – *Maranta arundinacea* – Ogunda Meji
- **Alligator Pepper** – *Aframomum melegueta* – Ogunda-Tura

10. Osa Family

Plants associated with the family of Osa carry energies primarily connected to the Orishas Oya, Iyami, Egbe, Egun, and Yewa. They carry the energies that surround storms, spiritual defense, hidden consequences, witchcraft, and transformation. They support protection, discernment, and navigating powerful unseen forces.

- **African Mistletoe** – *Loranthus spp.* – Osa Meji
- **Tomato** – *Solanum lycopersicum* – Osa Meji
- **Wild Adenia (Lace-leaf)** – *Adenia lobata* – Osa Meji
- **Dragon Fruit** – *Hylocereus undatus* – Osa Meji
- **Eucalyptus Leaf** – *Eucalyptus globulus* – Osa Meji
- **Eggplant** -*Solanum melongena*— Osa Meji
- **Plum**- *Prunus domestica* - Osa Meji
- **Purple Heart** — *Tradescantia pallida* —Osa Meji
- **Oxalis Triangularis** — *Oxalis triangularis* —Osa Meji
- **Persian Shield** — *Strobilanthes dyerianus* —Osa Meji
- **Smoke Bush** — *Cotinus coggygria.* —Osa Meji
- **Blackberries** — *Rubus fruticosus* —Osa Meji
- **Blueberries** — *Vaccinium sect. Cyanococcus*— Osa Meji
- **Concord Grapes** — *Vitis vinifera / Vitis labrusca.* — Osa Meji
- **Acai Berries** — *Euterpe oleracea* — Osa Meji
- **Elderberries** — *Sambucus nigra*— Osa Meji
- **Blackcurrants** — *Ribes nigrum* — Osa Meji
- **Mangosteen** — *Garcinia mangostana* ——Osa Meji
- **Purple Passion Fruit** — *Passiflora edulis* —Osa Meji

11. Ika Family

Plants associated with the family of Ika carry energies primarily connected to the Orishas Ori, Oro, and Shango. They carry the energies that surround restraint, self-control, discipline, and the dangers of misusing power, mastery over the self.

- **Lavender Croton** – *Croton zambesicus* – Ika Meji
- **Sea Bean (Monkey Ladder)** – *Entada gigas* – Ika Meji
- **Black Nightshade** – *Solanum nigrum* – Ika Meji (Highly Toxic)
- **Yaya / Yaya Tree**— *Oxandra lanceolata*— Ika Mji
- **Juniper** —*Juniperus communis* —Ika Mjei
- **Rue** — *Ruta graveolens*—Ika-Yeku
- **Vervain** — *Verbena officinalis* — Ika Meji
- **Wormwood** — *Artemisia absinthium*— Ika Meji

12. OTURUPON FAMILY

Plants associated with the family of Oturupon carry energies primarily connected to the Orishas Orunmila, Ogun, Ori, Eshu, and Aganju. They carry the energies that surround endurance, stability, perseverance, and navigating hardships. They support resilience, balance, and strength in challenging circumstances.

- **Fagara** – *Zanthoxylum spp.* – Oturupon Meji
- **Watercress** – *Nasturtium officinale* – Oturupon Meji
- **Sacred Fig (Bo Tree)** – *Ficus religiosa* – Otrupon Bara
- **Garden Cress** – *Lepidium sativum* – Otrupon Sa
- **Wild Date Palm** – *Phoenix reclinata* – Oturupon Meji
- **Mustard Plant** – *Brassica nigra* – Oturupon Meji

13. OTURA FAMILY

Plants associated with the family of Otura carry energies primarily connected to the Orishas Obatala, Orunmila, Ori, Egbe, and Olodumare, Oya. They carry the energies that surround mystical visions, dreams, self reflection, alignment with the divine, tranquility, intuition and psychic abilities.

- **Mugwort (Artemisa)** – *Artemisia vulgaris* – Otura-Osa – toxic if ingested
- **Chamomile** – *Matricaria chamomilla* – Otura Ose
- **Valerian** – *Valeriana officinalis* – Otura Meji
- **Calea zacatechichi (Dream Herb)** – Otura Meji
- **Passionflower** – *Passiflora incarnata* – Otura Melji

- **Hops** – *Humulus lupulus* – Otura Meji
- **Blue Lotus** – *Nymphaea caerulea* – Otura Meji
- **Salvia** - *Salvia divinorum* - Otura Meji
- **Star Anise** – *Illicium verum* – Otura Meji
- **Tropical Almond** – *Terminalia catappa* – Otura Meji
- **Royal Palm** – *Roystonea regia* – Otura Meji
- **False Yam** – *Icacina trichantha* – Otura Meji
- **Frankincense** – *Boswellia sacra* – Otura Meji
- **Marjoram** – *Origanum majorana* – Otura Meji

14. IRETE FAMILY

Plants associated with the family of Irete carry energies primarily connected to the Orishas Ori, Onile, Ochosi, Orunmila, and Eshu. They carry the energies that surround building good character, personal integrity, virtue, and blessings through ethical living. They support moral clarity, personal growth, and alignment with spiritual principles.

- **Buttercup** – *Ranunculus spp.* – Irete Meji
- **River Fern** – *Bolbitis heudelotii* – Irete Meji
- **Spiny Amaranth** – *Amaranthus spinosus* – Irete Kutan
- **Collard Greens** – *Brassica oleracea* – Irete Ogunda
- **Licorice Root**— *Glycyrrhiza glabra* — Irete Meji
- **Carrot** — *Daucus carota* — Irete Meji
- ***The root of any plant carries the energy of Irete, as it nourishes the plant and holds it firmly upright.***

15. OSE FAMILY

Plants associated with the family of Ose carry energies primarily connected to the Orishas Oshun, Aje, and Olokun. They carry the energies that surround abundance, creativity, wealth, prosperity, and the flow of resources. They support artistic expression, manifestation of gifts, and harmonious expansion.

- **Cinnamon** – *Cinnamomum verum* – Oshe Meji
- **Orange** – *Citrus sinensis* – Oshe Meji
- **Sugar Cane** – *Saccharum officinarum* – Oshe Meji

- **Turmeric** – *Curcuma longa* – Oshe Meji
- **Vanilla** – *Vanilla planifolia* – Oshe Meji
- **Lemon Balm** – *Melissa officinalis* – Oshe Meji
- **Honeysuckle** – *Lonicera spp.* – Oshe Meji
- **Sweet Pea** – *Lathyrus odoratus* – Oshe Meji
- **Orchid** – *Orchidaceae spp.* – Oshe Meji
- **Cardamom (Green)** – *Elettaria cardamomum* – Oshe Meji
- **Lavender Flowers (Culinary)** – *Lavandula angustifolia* – Oshe Meji

16. Ofun Family

Plants associated with the family of Ofun carry energies primarily connected to the Orishas Obatala, Orunmila, Ori, Olofin, Oduduwa, Yemaya, They carry the energies that surround completion of cycles, clarity, emergence into light, understanding, and fulfillment after a cycle took place and looking back. They support resolution, spiritual illumination, and the harmonious culmination of processes. This is a different type of light, it is the light of looking backwards and the illumination that comes from living through a cycle and completing it.

- **Aloe Vera** – *Aloe vera* – Ofun Meji
- **Silver Grass** – *Miscanthus floridulus* – Ofun Meji
- **White Chalk** – *Calcium carbonate* – Ofun Meji
- **Mango** – *Mangifera indica* – Ofun Yemilo
- **Indian Head Ginger** – *Costus spicatus* – Ofun Meji
- **White Rose** – *Rosa alba* – Ofun Meji
- **Gardenia** – *Gardenia jasminoides* – Ofun Meji
- **Salvia** – *Pluchea adorata* – Ofun Meji

* * *

In Ifá, plants are living beings that carry spiritual intelligence and a sacred power called *ase*. This power can be used in many ways, but its strength and effect depend on several factors: the Odu the plant is linked to, the Orishas it serves, the region where it grows, its natural purpose or role in the ecosystem, its surroundings, and the specific part

212

of the plant being used. Each of these influences determines how well the plant's *ase* works for a particular ritual or healing. Orisha teachings remind us that the natural world is alive with energy, offering guidance, protection, and healing when we approach it with respect and understanding.

CHAPTER 17

SACRED HERBS OF THE ORISHAS

RITUAL AND SPIRITUAL USES OF PLANTS IN ORISHA DEVOTION

Plants known as (*ewe*)hold a central role in the spiritual traditions of the Orishas, serving as vessels of *ase* (spiritual power) and bridges between the physical and spiritual worlds. Through their leaves, roots, fruits, and essences, plants are used in offerings, cleansings, initiations, and ritual work to invoke, honor, and communicate with the divine. The relationship between plants and the Orishas is not fixed, but varies across lineage, region, and spiritual house. Traditions such as Lukumí, Candomblé, and Umbanda each preserve their own interpretations, ritual uses, and symbolic meanings for herbs and plants. These differences reflect the living nature of the tradition, shaped by geography, culture, and ancestral transmission.

The correspondences presented in this chapter are intended as general, cross-traditional references rather than strict rules. They offer a foundation for understanding common associations between specific plants and the energies of the Orishas, but they should not replace direct instruction. Practitioners are strongly encouraged to follow the guidance of their elders and the teachings of their specific lineage when applying these associations in spiritual practice. Below are examples of several Orishas and their commonly associated herbs, leaves, and plants, along with their general spiritual uses and symbolic meanings.

* * *

A PERSONAL NOTE ON SAFETY

This guide is intended for educational purposes only and should not be considered medical advice. Consult a healthcare professional before handling, consuming, or burning any plant mentioned in this book. Approach all flora with extreme caution:

Toxicity: Some listed plants are highly toxic and can cause severe illness or death if touched, ingested, or inhaled.

Allergies & Interactions: Even "non-toxic" plants can trigger life-threatening allergic reactions or dangerously interfere with medications and existing health conditions.

Inhalation Risks: Burning plants can release harmful toxins directly into the air.

Incomplete Labels: The absence of a "toxic" warning does not guarantee a plant is safe. Safe botanical dosages are often unknown.

Enjoy learning about these traditions, but never use this information for medical experimentation. Prioritize your physical health and safety above all else.

* * *

THE ORISHA OBATALA

Obatala's plants are typically found in high-altitude environments such as mountains, hills, and elevated, unspoiled landscapes where the air is cool and the light is clear and pure. His flora is characterized by white-flowering and silver-toned plants, often with soft or velvety leaves, growing in calm, shaded areas or on high peaks. These plants thrive in "cooling" environments, near clean springs, in misty forests, and away from the heat and noise of lower regions, and are often associated with sacred groves containing ancient, stable trees that symbolize longevity, purity, and peace.

Rosemary (*Rosmarinus officinalis* – Mental clarity, purification, and bridging celestial energy with grounded spiritual protection.

Angelica (*Angelica archangelica*) - Protection from malign influences, neutralizing negative waves, and raising environmental vibrations for peace.

True Vanilla (*Vanilla planifolia*) - Protecting ritual spaces, enhancing the "sweetness" of energy, and supporting fertility and emotional balance.

Carnauba Palm (*Copernicia prunifera*) - Illuminating the spiritual path, strengthening the aura, and providing structural focus during rituals.

Clove Vine (*Tynanthus panurensis*) - Calming the spirit for meditation or divination and clearing energy for inner wisdom.

Gardenia (*Gardenia jasminoides*) - Believed to bring peace, emotional balance, and heightened intuition. Its gentle fragrance calms the spirit, while its waxy petals symbolize renewal and healing.

White Rose (*Rosa x alba*) - Believed to bring purity, tranquility, and heart-centered healing, opening the heart to love, compassion, and self-acceptance.

White Yarrow (*Achillea millefolium*) - Believed to bring protection, courage, and energetic clarity. It is believed to help protect against negativity and emotional exhaustion.

Peace Lily – (*Spathiphyllum spp.*) - Promotes peace, harmony, and emotional balance. Used for cleansing negative energy and creating calm in the home or meditation spaces. Associated with the heart chakra and sometimes used in offerings to Obatala for purity and wisdom.

White Poppy (*Papaver somniferum*) - This plant is spiritually and magically significant, associated with tranquility, restful sleep, and the journey into the afterlife.

Lemon Balm (*Melissa officinalis*) - It calms restless energies, dispels negative influences, and restless spirits, has been used to elevate weary hearts. It is often linked to the moon and the feminine and emotional healing.

Holy Basil (*Ocimum tenuiflorum*) – Promotes protection, purification, and spiritual clarity; often used in rituals to ward off negative energy and invite healing.

Moonflower (*Ipomoea alba*) – Enhances intuition, dreams, and psychic awareness; used in meditation to connect with lunar energies and inner guidance.

White Lotus (*Nymphaea lotus*) – Symbolizes spiritual awakening, purity, and enlightenment; used in meditation and offerings to deepen spiritual insight and transcendence.

Coconut (*Cocos nucifera*) – Represents abundance, protection, and fertility; used in offerings, blessings, and ritual baths for prosperity and spiritual cleansing.

Cotton (*Gossypium spp.*) – Symbolizes purity, protection, and comfort; used in spiritual baths, offerings, and talismans to absorb negativity and promote peace.

White Rice (*Oryza sativa*) – Represents purity, abundance, and prosperity; used in offerings, rituals, and spiritual baths to attract wealth, blessings, and positive energy.

Mint (*Mentha spp.*) - is a cooling botanical sacred to Obatala, used to "cool the head" and restore mental clarity

Spearmint (*Mentha spicata*) – Used for purification, mental clarity, and protection. Often added to ritual baths, offerings, or used in hear cleanses to cool down the head and promote calmness.

* * *

Oshun's plants are found in "sweet" environments along the lush, fertile banks of rivers, waterfalls, and freshwater streams. Her flora thrives at the water's edge or floats upon it, including aquatic plants like watercress, water lilies, and lotus, and is often marked by yellow and golden hues that reflect warmth, beauty, and abundance. These plants are typically aromatic and inviting, such as cinnamon, basil, mint, and chamomile, used to attract love and prosperity, while fertile trees and vines produce sweet fruits like oranges, pumpkins, and melons in well-watered, sunlit lowlands, embodying the richness and sweetness of life.

SOME COMMON PLANTS ASSOCIATED WITH OSHUN

Aloe Vera (*Aloe barbadensis*) – In some traditions, it is associated with love, emotional healing, and harmony, helping to attract affection, strengthen relationships, and nurture the heart's energy.

Cinnamon (*Cinnamomum verum, zeylanicum*) – Used for prosperity, protection, and love. Spiritually, it attracts abundance, enhances passion, strengthens relationships, and is added to rituals, baths, or charms for success, energy, and spiritual empowerment.

Calendula (*Calendula officinalis*) – Used for protection, healing, and love. Spiritually, it attracts positive energy, promotes emotional healing, aids in purification, and is often used in blessings, charms, and ritual baths to draw love and harmony.

Sunflower (*Helianthus annuus*) – Prosperity, positivity, and devotion; used to attract happiness, success, and spiritual growth.

Pumpkin (*Cucurbita spp.*) – Abundance, protection, and fertility; used in rituals for prosperity, harvest blessings, and safeguarding the home.

Sweet Melon (*Cucumis melo*) – Love, attraction, and healing; used to draw affection, sweeten relationships, and enhance emotional well-being.

Honey – Love, sweetness, and attraction; used to "sweeten" situations, enhance love and harmony, and attract blessings.

Oranges (*Citrus sinensis*) – Abundance, purification, and happiness; used in rituals and baths to invite prosperity, joy, and positive energy.

Mango (*Mangifera indica*) – Attracts love, sweetness, and abundance; used in love charms, prosperity rituals, and offerings to Orishas.

Papaya (*Carica papaya*) – Promotes healing, protection, and fertility; used in cleansing baths, spiritual offerings, and rituals to remove negative energy.

Peaches (*Prunus persica*) – Draws love, happiness, and longevity; used in love spells, emotional healing rituals, and charms to improve relationships.

Figs (*Ficus carica*) – Encourages abundance, wisdom, and fertility; used in prosperity rituals, divination, and fertility spells.

Yellow Squash (*Cucurbita pepo*) – Invites abundance, protection, and prosperity; used in harvest rituals, offerings, and protective charms.

Lemon (*Citrus limon*) – Provides purification, protection, and clarity; used in cleansing baths, space clearing, and rituals to remove negativity.

Chamomile (*Matricaria chamomilla, nobile*) – Promotes calm, love, and protection; used in baths, teas, and charms for emotional healing and attracting love.

Goldenrod (*Solidago spp.*) – Used for prosperity, protection, strength, and positive energy; attracts abundance, safeguards spaces, boosts confidence and endurance, and encourages optimism and guidance in spiritual work.

Turmeric (*Curcuma longa*) – Offers purification, protection, and healing; used in cleansing rituals, protective charms, and spiritual baths.

Apricot (*Prunus armeniaca*) – Brings love, fertility, and sweetness; used in love charms, emotional healing baths, and fertility rituals.

Golden Apple (*Malus domestica, golden variety*) – Attracts love, wisdom, and prosperity; used in baths, offerings, and spells for affection, clarity, and abundance.

Dandelion (*Taraxacum officinale*) – Used for wish fulfillment, abundance, divination, and protection; its seeds carry intentions and prayers, while the plant attracts prosperity, clears negativity, and enhances spiritual insight.

Yellow/Golden Flowers (*various*) – Attract prosperity, joy, and energy; used in rituals, baths, and offerings to uplift spiritual energy.

* * *

The Orishas Shango & Aganju

Chango's plants are typically found in sunny, elevated environments and within the high canopy of the forest, reflecting his connection to lightning, fire, and celestial power. His flora is most strongly associated with towering royal palms that stand in open, sun-filled landscapes, vibrant red-flowering trees that thrive in intense heat and light, and sturdy fruit-bearing trees that grow in fertile, well-watered lowlands, symbolizing strength, vitality, and royal abundance. Aganju's plants on the other-hand thrive in harsh, dramatic landscapes such as volcanoes, deserts, and untamed wilderness, reflecting his association with the earth's molten core and raw elemental power. His flora includes botanicals that grow in mineral-rich, heated soils near craters and lava fields, as well as resilient desert plants like cacti, succulents, and hardy scrub that endure extreme sun and aridity. Most species of cacti are sacred to Aganju and thrive in the harsh, dramatic landscapes he governs, including deserts, volcanic slopes, and untamed wilderness. These resilient plants, along with succulents and hardy scrub, reflect his connection to the earth's raw power and elemental strength, surviving in extreme heat, sun, and mineral-rich soils.

Some Common Plants Associated with Shango

Flamboyant Tree (*Delonix regia*) - This is Shango's primary "throne." Its fiery red-orange flowers mirror his lightning. The large seed pods are used as rattles to "call" Shango to the ceremony. The leaves are used in baths to give a person the "radiance" and authority of a leader.

Cedar (*Cedrela odorata*) - Cedar is the most sacred wood for Shango. Most of his ritual tools (like the *Oshe* or double-headed axe) are carved from it. The leaves and bark are used in baths for protection and victory. Burning cedar as a smudge is believed to drive away "dark spirits" that cannot withstand Shango's heat.

Eritrina / Mulungu (*Erythrina mulungu*) - Used specifically to provide clarity and strength before a major conflict or legal proceeding. Sometimes carried before a legal proceeding. It is also commonly utilized to ease anxiety, treat emotional trauma, and promote tranquil sleep or dream work, acting as a spiritual "stillness after the storm". (toxic).

Quebra-pedra (Stonebreaker) – (*Phyllanthus niruri*) - Used to "break" through obstacles and stubborn problems. In Shango's domain, it is used to "crush" the power of enemies or legal opposition.

Aperta-ruao (*Piper aduncum*) - A "warrior" herb used to "tighten" or secure a victory. It is often included in baths taken by those who need to stand their ground or command respect.

Marjoram – (*Origanum majorana*) - Used in "sweet" baths for Shango to attract wealth and success. It balances his fiery nature with the "coolness" required for strategic thinking.

Okra (*Abelmoschus esculentus*) - Shango's most famous food offering (*Amalá*). The "slime" of the okra is spiritually used to "slick" one's path so that negativity slides right off. It is offered to Shango to ask for his protection and to "cool" his anger when justice has been served.

Pomegranate (*Punica granatum*) - Filled with "crown-like" seeds and blood-red juice. Used in offerings to represent the many followers or "subjects" of the King. The peel is used in baths for **personal magnetism and power.**

Pineapple (*Ananas comosus*) – Invites abundance, hospitality, and protection; used in prosperity rituals, offerings, and blessing baths.

Banana (*Musa spp.*) - Used for nourishment and vitality. Spiritually, bananas attract abundance, prosperity, and happiness. Can be offered in rituals for fertility and family harmony.

Plantain (*Musa paradisiaca*) – Provides strength and grounding; used in protection and prosperity rituals.

Ceiba (*Ceiba pentandra*) – Often associated with connection to the ancestors, spiritual protection, and wisdom. Its wood, seeds, and leaves are used in rituals, offerings, and sacred spaces to invite guidance, strength, and divine blessings.

Charcoal – Used in baths, soaps, or ritual work to draw out stagnant or harmful energy, stabilize the aura, and restore balance after spiritual stress; associated with fire and earth elements.

Red Carnations (*Dianthus caryophyllus*) – Offered to Shango or used to decorate his altar; considered one of his most sacred flowers in offerings and ritual devotion.

Pineapple Sage (*Salvia elegans*) – Burned for spiritual purification, emotional calm, and harmony, clearing spaces of negative energy.

Pineapple (*Ananas comosus*) / Leaves – Used to banish negativity, attract abundance, and invite positive energy; commonly placed on altars or included in ritual baths and offerings.

Red Bell Pepper (*Capsicum annuum*) – Enhances vitality, strength, and protection; used to ward off negative energy and promote courage.

Palm Oil (*Elaeis guineensis*) – Palm oil is Shango's "blood." It is the primary ingredient in his favorite offering, **Amala** (made with okra). It is used to "cool" his anger while simultaneously providing him the "heat" (energy) to execute justice. Without palm oil, Shango's energy is considered "dry" and ineffective.

Figs (*Ficus carica*) – Promotes fertility, wisdom, and spiritual clarity; used in abundance and health rituals.

Royal Palm Leaves (*Roystonea spp.*) – Used in rituals for protection, blessings, and spiritual elevation; often placed on altars or incorporated in offerings to invite divine favor and positive energy.

St. John's Wort (*Hypericum perforatum*) – Used to remove negative energies, promote emotional balance.

Arrowleaf Elephant Ear (*Xanthosoma sagittifolium*) – Traditionally used for cleansing and protection in spiritual or folk practices. Its leaves are sometimes burned or placed in spaces to remove negative energy and promote harmony.

* * *

THE ORISHA YEMAYA

Yemaya's plants are found in maritime and coastal environments, including oceans, salt marshes, and sandy shorelines, reflecting her role as mother of the salt waters and mistress of the moon. Her flora includes oceanic plants like seaweeds, kelp, and algae that symbolize the hidden mysteries of the deep, as well as coastal species such as sea grapes, sea oats, and hardy vines that thrive in sandy, saline soil. Many of her plants display blue, indigo, or silvery tones, echoing the moon's reflection on water, and succulent, water-rich textures, like water hyacinths and aloe, embody her nurturing, cooling, and life-giving energy.

SOME COMMON PLANTS ASSOCIATED WITH YEMAYA

Parsley (*Petroselinum crispum*) - Parsley is used in spiritual baths and cleansings to draw in positive energy and harmony. It helps to restore balance, encourage growth, and calm the mind and spirit.

Lettuce (*Lactuca sativa*) - Lettuce represents Yemayá's nurturing and life-giving qualities and is used in offerings or ritual arrangements. It supports emotional healing, inner peace, and calm energies.

Seaweed (*various marine algae*) - Used for deep cleansing, protection, and emotional healing; it absorbs and removes stagnant or negative energy while restoring spiritual flow. It represents the ever-moving ocean, symbolizing adaptability, renewal, and connection to deeper emotional currents.

Salt (*Sea Salt*) - Salt represents the ocean and Yemayá's purifying power and is sprinkled in sacred spaces or water. It cleanses negativity, protects, and brings clarity and emotional balance.

Vervain (*Verbena spp.*) -Vervain is used for protection, purification, and healing rituals. Its energy uplifts and soothes, resonating with Yemayá's calming and restorative influence.

Florida Water / Lavender – (*Lavandula spp.*) - While lavender is a Mediterranean herb, its cooling scent and purple-blue flowers make it a standard in Yemaya rituals. Used to "calm the waves" of a person's life and promote deep, restful sleep.

Kelp (*Laminaria spp., Macrocystis spp.*) - Used for grounding and purification; it helps release heavy energy and stabilize the spirit after emotional or spiritual stress. Its long, flowing form symbolizes resilience, strength, and the ability to remain rooted while navigating change.

Bladderwrack (*Fucus vesiculosus*)- Used for protection, strength, and energetic cleansing; it is believed to draw out harmful influences and reinforce spiritual boundaries. It symbolizes endurance and survival, thriving in harsh coastal conditions while maintaining balance.

Irish Moss (*Chondrus crispus*) - Used for soothing, healing, and restoration; it gently cleanses while promoting emotional balance and inner peace. It represents nourishment, comfort, and the quiet healing power of the ocean.

Sargassum (*Sargassum spp.*) - Used to attract abundance and encourage movement in stagnant situations; it helps shift blocked energy and promote forward motion. It symbolizes flow, prosperity, and the natural cycles of gathering and release.

Sea Lettuce (*Ulva lactuca*) - Used for light purification and renewal; it refreshes the spirit and clears minor energetic disturbances. It represents freshness, clarity, and new beginnings.

Rockweed (Ascophyllum nodosum) - Used for grounding, protection, and stability; it anchors energy and strengthens emotional resilience. It symbolizes endurance, structure, and steady growth through changing tides.

Wakame (*Undaria pinnatifida*) - Used for transformation and emotional release; it supports letting go of past burdens and embracing renewal. It represents fluid transformation, adaptability, and rebirth.

Nori (*Porphyra spp.*) - Used for balance and harmony; it encourages flexibility and emotional equilibrium. It symbolizes adaptability and the ability to move with changing conditions while maintaining inner stability.

Celery (*Apium graveolens*) - Celery is used in ritual baths, offerings, and cleanings to attract clarity, protection, and emotional balance. It is believed to help remove stagnant energy and support spiritual focus and harmony.

* * *

THE ORISHA OGUN

Ogun's plants are typically found in dense, wild forests near large, sturdy trees, as well as along railroad tracks, near blacksmith shops, or in areas rich in iron ore. They often grow in rugged, sun-baked soil that has been "disturbed" and contains high levels of iron or other heavy metals. These plants usually display a mix of dark brown, black, and green hues. Many have high mineral content or sharp, serrated edges, like Saw Palmetto or Spear Thistle, echoing the shape of Ogun's machete. While hardwoods and towering trees are associated with Ogun, the very tallest trees in the forest are more often linked to Shango. Ogun is said to reside in the strongest trees of the forest, such as Guay-acán and Oak, where his energy is most potent.

SOME COMMON PLANTS ASSOCIATED WITH OGUN

Snake Plant (*Sansevieria trifasciata*) – Note: This is the version without the yellow border (the all-green variety). Planted at the front of a home to act as a spiritual "sentry." It is used for protection, purification, and energy stabilization; often placed in homes or near altars to ward off negative energy, cleanse the space, and support spiritual focus.

Alamo plant (*Randia formosa*): Also known as thorny poison-wood, it is associated with the warrior's energy, used in spiritual baths for protection.

Guava (*Psidium guajava*) - Used for protection, strength, and spiritual cleansing; it reinforces resilience and removes negative influences. Associated with Ogun, it supports endurance, grounding, and the strengthening of one's spiritual defenses.

Guinea Pepper /Alligator Pepper (*Aframomum melegueta*) - Used for protection, courage, and spiritual empowerment; it is often employed to strengthen personal will before fighting a spiritual battle, it helps to also enhance focus, and repel negative energy.

Mariwó (*Palm Fronds*) – *Elaeis guineensis* - This is Ogun's most iconic sacred material; the shredded young fronds represent his "clothing." Hung over the entrance of a house or a shrine to protect against evil and signify that the space is under Ogun's guard. It "cuts" negative energy before it can enter.

Peregun – (*Dracaena fragrans*) - Known as the "King of Herbs," it is essential for the consecration of almost all Orishas but is specifically used by Ogun to "anchor" energy. Used to mark the perimeter of a sacred space. It is believed to represent resilience and the ability to "stay standing" through any conflict.

Akoko – (*Newbouldia laevis*) - Known as the "Tree of Life" or "Fertility Tree. The leaves are used to crown kings and leaders. In Ogun's context, they represent the authority to lead and the power of ancestral lineage.

Guiné (Guinea Hen Weed) – (*Petiveria alliacea*) - A very powerful herb with a strong, garlic-like scent. Used to make a person invisible to their enemies. It is highly effective at breaking "iron-clad" hexes or negative patterns that won't go away.

Clove (*Syzygium aromaticum*) – Supports protection, love, and prosperity; used in incense and spiritual cleansing. Due to the tree's rugged nature and its has an association with the "wild" edges of the forest.

The wood of the fig tree is sometimes used to craft handles for tools or as a base for protection charms. It is believed to provide the "spine" or structural integrity needed to finish a difficult job.

Purple Bellyache Bush – (*Jatropha gossypiifolia)* **-** Identified by its deep purple leaves and caustic sap. Used for heavy protection and "charging" Ogun's shrine. The sap is considered a potent spiritual "acid" that dissolves negative spells.

Eucalyptus – (*Eucalyptus globulus)* **-** Used in steam baths or floor washes to clear stagnant energy. Its sharp, cooling scent is believed to sharpen the mind for strategic planning and "battle."

Brazilian Peppertree – (*Schinus terebinthifolia***)** **-** A dominant "hot" herb used in Candomblé and Umbanda for Ogun. Used in aggressive cleansing baths to "burn away" spiritual parasites. It is also used to wash Ogun's iron tools.

Ginger (*Zingiber officinale***)** – Boosts energy, courage, and protection; used in love, healing, and purification rituals.

* * *

SACRED WOODS OF OGUN

Although Ogun is widely recognized as the Orisha of iron, technology, and warfare, his primordial essence is grounded in the forest where his journey first began. Long before the discovery of metallurgy, wood was the primary tool of humanity, and for this reason, Ogun holds all timber as sacred, viewing it not as a predecessor to iron but as its vital partner. In his hands, wood stabilizes iron, providing the necessary handle and heart that give direction, support, and endurance to the blade's raw power. As the first Orisha to descend into the physical world, Ogun acted as the ultimate pioneer, using his strength to clear the dense, impenetrable wilderness so that civilization and life could finally take root. While iron represents the piercing force of action, wood serves as the guiding spirit that sustains it, reflecting Ogun's unique ability to move through untamed land and transform it through purposeful labor. Within ritual practice, this sacred connection is further refined, as the wood of each specific tree carries a unique spiritual vibration. Below is a list of woods, their trees, and the spiritual powers they carry:

Foundational Trees

- **Ceiba (Ceiba pentandra)** - *Connects practitioners with ancestors and spiritual entities while grounding rituals and energies.*
- **Palo Yaya (Oxandra lanceolata)** - *Command, enforcement, discipline, control.*
- **Palo Ramón (Trophis racemosa)** - *Endurance, longevity, sustaining spiritual force.*
- **Palo Mulato (Phoebe elongata)** - *Grounding, stabilization, mental clarity*

Protection and Defense Woods

- **Guayacán (Guaiacum officinale)** - *Protection, resilience, spiritual hardening.*
- **Quiebra Hacha (Copaifera hymenaeifolia)** - *Resistance, deflection, blocking harm.*
- **Palo Caja (Allophylus psidium)** - *Containment, binding, trapping negativity.*

Force, Aggression, and Control

- **Palo Diablo (Capparis cynophallophora)** - *Forceful action, rapid clearing, aggressive energy.*
- **Palo Verraco (Picrodendron baccatum)** - *Dominance, willpower, assertive control.*

Movement, Attraction, and Change

- **Palo Yamao (Guarea guidonia)** - *Attraction, magnetism, drawing conditions.*
- **Abre Camino (Eupatorium villosum)** - *Road opening, obstacle removal.*

- ***Cambia Camino (Casearia sylvestris)*** *- Redirection, change, breaking stagnation.*

Justice, Cleansing, and Balance

- ***Palo Justicia (Stifftia chrysantha)*** *- Justice, truth, fair outcomes.*
- ***Palo Santo (Bursera graveolens)*** *- Purification, blessing, clarity.*
- ***Palo Cenizo (Behaimia cubensis)*** *- Cooling, neutralizing, restoring balance.*

* * *

NORTHERN HEMISPHERE TREES & WOODS

Power, Strength & Authority

- ***Oak (Quercus spp.)*** *- Strength, protection, authority, endurance.*
- ***Ash (Fraxinus excelsior)*** *- Connection between realms, spiritual pathways, protection.*
- ***Yew (Taxus baccata)*** *- Death, rebirth, ancestral connection, longevity.*

Protection & Warding

- ***Rowan (Sorbus aucuparia)*** *- Protection, warding evil, psychic defense*
- ***Hawthorn (Crataegus monogyna)*** *- Protection, boundaries, spirit thresholds*
- ***Holly (Ilex aquifolium)*** *- Protection, vitality, defense against negativity*

Cleansing & Renewal

- ***Birch (Betula spp.)*** *- Purification, new beginnings, renewal.*
- ***Pine (Pinus spp.)*** *- Cleansing, protection, clearing stagnation.*
- ***Juniper (Juniperus spp.)*** *- Purification, protection, banishing negativity.*

Healing & Emotional Work

- ***Willow (Salix spp.)*** *- Emotional healing, intuition, lunar energy.*
- ***Elder (Sambucus nigra)*** *- Healing, protection, communication with spirit.*
- ***Apple (Malus domestica)*** *- Love, healing, connection to the Otherworld.*

Wisdom & Knowledge

- ***Hazel (Corylus avellana)*** *- Wisdom, inspiration, divination.*
- ***Beech (Fagus sylvatica)*** *- Knowledge, learning, memory.*
- ***Maple (Acer spp.)*** *- Balance, insight, mental clarity.*

Grounding, Stability & Balance

- ***Elm (Ulmus spp.)*** *- Stability, inner strength, support.*
- ***Alder (Alnus glutinosa)*** *- Courage, protection, balance between elements.*
- ***Poplar (Populus spp.)*** *- Transformation, communication, adaptability.*

Attraction & Prosperity

- ***Cherry (Prunus spp.)*** *- Attraction, love, fertility.*
- ***Linden / Basswood (Tilia spp.)*** *- Love, harmony, calming energy.*
- ***Walnut (Juglans regia)*** *- Intellect, strategy, protection, manifestation.*

* * *

THE ORISHA OYA

Many of Oya's plants are multi-colored or shades of purple, burgundy, or dark red, and are connected to the dead and ancestors, making them strongly associated with this Orisha. Her herbs are often found near cemeteries, along riverbanks, or in wetlands where the wind blows strongly.

SOME COMMON PLANTS ASSOCIATED WITH OYA

Garden Croton – (*Codiaeum variegatum* **)** -In Jamaican and broader Caribbean folk traditions, the Garden Croton is regarded as a sacred and spiritually protective plant. It is commonly used in healing rituals and funeral ceremonies to ward off negative energy. Its vibrant, multicolored foliage symbolizes transformation, personal growth and vitality.

Mulberry – (Morus alba / nigra) – Mulberry leaves and small twigs are used in ancestral ceremonies for cleansing, protection, and absorbing negative energies. This plant helps calm restless ancestors, maintain harmony between the living and the spirit world, and strengthen the connection to ancestral guidance. It is also used to facilitate mediumship, and in some lineages, the wood is crafted into a *palo de muerto* (ancestor staff) for its strength and deep spiritual significance.

Hibiscus – (*Hibiscus sabdariffa***)** - In some lineages, the flowers of this plant are used to adorn shrines of the ancestors. They are also valued for healing emotional grief, aiding recovery after the loss of a loved one, and clearing negative energy. The tea is sometimes used in "baths " to cleanse the aura after visiting a cemetery or hospital. In some lineages Hibiscus wood is used to craft the *palo de muerto* (ancestor staff) instead of the *Morus alba/ nigra.*

Eggplant – (*Solanum melongena***)** – This is Oya's most sacred food in some traditions. It is common to offer nine eggplants to her. Used to "clean" the head or home of negative influences *(osogbo)*. It is believed to act as a spiritual sponge, absorbing the "shade" of death or illness before it takes hold.

Purple Grapes (*Vitis vinifera***)** - Represent the abundance of the marketplace, which Oya owns. Placed on ancestor altars to sweeten the relationship with the deceased. They are often used in *ebó* (offerings) to ensure that the "winds of change" bring financial or emotional prosperity rather than destruction.

Red Wine (Fermented Grape) - Oya is one of the few Orishas who is frequently offered red wine rather than clear spirits. Its deep red juice is often used also as a blood substitute in non-animal offerings.

Plums (*Prunus domestica*) - Often included in Oya's *adimu* (offerings) due to their dark skin and sweet interior. Symbolize the "sweetness of the soul" that survives death. They are offered to ask Oya for a smooth transition through a difficult life change.

Purple & Red Cabbage (*Brassica oleracea*) - The layered structure represents the "nine skirts" of Oya. The leaves are sometimes used as "plates" for other offerings to Oya. Ritually, the layers symbolize the unveiling of secrets or the protection of one's inner core from external spiritual attacks.

Blackberries & Raspberries (*Rubus spp.*) - Berries represent the "fruits of the wild" and Oya's connection to the forest edge. Used in charms to "catch" or snag negative energy. Because of their brambles/thorns, they are used to build spiritual "fences" around a person's property. Sometimes the thorns are worn as protection agains the evil eye.

Elderberries (*Sambucus nigra*) - Known as the "Elder" or the "Queen of Herbs" in many traditions. Strongly associated with the wisdom of grandmother ancestors. Used in washes to protect the home from "wandering spirits" (abiku or ghosts) that Oya governs.

Cypress (*Cupressus sempervirens*) - Known globally as the "tree of the cemetery," it is perhaps the most sacred tree for the ancestors. Its branches are used to sweep a space to remove "heavy" or "dark" spirits. The wood can be used to carve staffs (palo) for ancestor communication.

Camphor – (*Cinnamomum camphora*) – Camphor is burned or placed in water at ancestor shrines to purify the air and enhance the connection between the physical and spiritual realms. It is believed to dissolve barriers, allowing easier communication and harmony between these two worlds.

Geranium (*Pelargonium spp.*) - Specifically the red and purple varieties. Used to attract success in the marketplace (business and career) and to harmonize her fierce energy with one's personal aura.

Wandering Jew / Inch Plant (*Tradescantia zebrina*) - A trailing plant with purple-striped leaves. Used in *sacudimentos* (cleansing rituals) to "carry away" bad luck. Its ability to grow quickly mirrors Oya's association with rapid change.

Marigold (*Tagetes spp.*) - While famous for the Day of the Dead, in many Orisha lineages, it is used for its bright, sun-like energy. Used to "brighten" the spirit of a deceased loved one and help them find their way to the light.

Nutmeg (*Myristica fragrans*) – Scattered in homes or businesses to attract wealth, prosperity, and improved financial conditions.

* * *

The Orisha Eshu / Elegua

Plants that are red and black are most often associated with this Orisha and are typically found at crossroads or along forest edges. Common, low-growing grasses, often stepped on but never die, symbolize Elegua's humility and omnipresence and are frequently used in floor washes to help ground the energy of a household.

Some Common Plants Associated with Eshu / Elegua

Sugar Cane (*Saccharum officinarum*) – Brings sweetness, prosperity, and love; used to "sweeten" situations, attract blessings, and enhance romantic energy.

Corn / Maize – (*Zea mays*) - Symbol of abundance, sustenance, and fertility. Used in rituals to bless crops, promote prosperity, and ensure food security. Often offered in ceremonies for protection, prosperity, and spiritual nourishment. This plant is also associated with the *Orishas, Oshun, Oko* and *Babalu-aye.*

Rosary Pea – (*Abrus precatorius*) Striking red and black seeds used as talismans for protection and good luck. **Caution**: Seeds contain abrin, a highly toxic substance; ingestion or handling broken seeds can be fatal.

Tobacco – (*Nicotiana tabacum*) - Blown as smoke over both Eshu and Ogun's elements to "feed" them with heat and breath. It is a catalyst that activates the power of other herbs. (Toxic)

Rue (*Ruta graveolens*) – Rue is Eshu's "broom." It is used to sweep away obstacles and "bad luck" before a major ritual begins. It is often included in the first bath of a series to "strip" the person of all external negativity so that the subsequent "sweet" baths can actually penetrate the aura.

Anise – (*Pimpinella anisum*) - Anise seeds are often added to Eshu's lamps or burned as incense to ask Eshu to help with communication.

Licorice (*Glycyrrhiza glabra*) - Placing a piece of Licorice root at the base of Elegua's shrine is a traditional way to ask for constant sweetness in the home. It is used to ensure that no "bitterness" or arguments enter through the front door.

black pepper- (*Piper nigrum*) - Black pepper is frequently used in *polvos* (spiritual powders) dedicated to Eshu to drive away negative spirits, "pepper" an enemy's path to make them move away,

* * *

THE ORISHA OCHOSI

Many of Ochosi's plants are considered justice herbs or arrow plants, reflecting his role as the hunter and bringer of fairness. The Archer's Wood includes trees and plants with straight, flexible branches, as well as most vines and climbing plants, all of which are strongly associated with this Orisha. Vines and climbing plants are especially sacred, symbolizing the hunter's skill, precision, and deep connection to the environment, weaving through it much like the hunter navigates the forest.

Most vines and climbing plants are sacred to Ochosi, symbolizing the hunter's connection to the environment and the flow of movement, as the vines stretch and climb toward the sun.

Arrowroot – (*Maranta arundinacea* **)** - The leaves are often lance-shaped (like an arrowhead). Used in works involving "aiming" one's intentions, towards something like an arrow.

Palo Justicia / Justice Stick – (*Ebelingia\ spp.)* - A hard wood often included in *resguardos* (amulets) to weight the scales of justice in your favor.

Caa-pía / Contrayerva) – (*Dorstenia / contrajerva)* - A powerful root used to "neutralize" spiritual traps or false testimony set by an opponent.

Guaco / Mikania) – (*Mikania / micrantha* **)** - A climbing vine used to "untangle" complex legal or personal problems that feel like a thicket.

Helecho Macho / Male Fern – (*Dryopteris\ filix-mas)* - Believed to provide "spiritual camouflage," making the practitioner invisible to enemies or predators if it is worn in a sachet or pouch around one's neck.

Pine – (*Pinus\ caribaea)* - The needles are used to sharpen the intellect and gain a "birds-eye view" of a problem.

Ebony - (*Diospyros spp.)* - A dense, dark wood used to carve the tools of Ochosi (his bow and arrow). This plant symbolizes his strength.

Bloodleaf – (*Iresine/ diffusa)* - Used to fortify the physical body and provide the stamina needed for a long "hunt" or a difficult trial if worn in a medicine pouch around the neck.

Pear (Pyrus communis) - Often used as *Addimu* (a food offering) to cool his energy and ask for a peaceful resolution to a conflict.

Palo Santo / Holy Wood (*Bursera graveolens)* - A sacred tree native to South America, primarily Peru and Ecuador and is a close botanical relative of Frankincense and Myrrh. In spiritual and traditional practices, its primary use is for purification and cleaning the air. Unlike Sage, which is often used to "strip" all energy from a space (both good and bad), Palo Santo is believed to clear negative energy while bringing in positive vibrations.

* * *

<u>The Orisha Babalu-aye</u>

Plants associated with Babalu-Ayé are typically characterized by their bitter, thorny, or wiry textures, which serve as spiritual detergents to "sweep" and "burn" away illness and stagnant energy. These botanicals often mirror the physical appearance of skin ailments, such as pock-marked seeds, bumpy pods, or blistering vines, allowing them to absorb disease and ground it back into the earth for transformation.

Some Common Plants Associated with Babalu-aye

Bitter Broom – (*Parthenium\ hysterophorus* **)** - This is the most iconic herb for Babalu-Aye. A bundle of these stalks is used to physically "sweep" a sick person from head to toe. Afterward, the bundle is traditionally discarded at a crossroads or in the trash far from the home to carry the sickness away.

White Sage (*Salvia apiana/ officinalis***)** – Salvia clears negative energy from spaces and auras, serving as a powerful tool for smudging and spiritual renewal. When burned, its cooling smoke is sacred to Obatala for silencing chaos and restoring peace. In baths or teas, it is associated with Babalu-Aye for physical healing and purging toxins from the body.

Mugwort (*Artemisia vulgaris***)** – Used for protection, divination, and spiritual insight and healing; commonly burned as incense, added to ritual baths, or carried as a charm to enhance dreams, intuition and help healing from disease. This plant is also connected to Oya and used to help communicate with the dead in dreams.

Purple Basil) – (*Ocimum basilicum)* - Purple Basil is used in *Sarayeye* (spiritual sweeping) to physically brush illness and "heavy" luck off the body, which is then discarded at the crossroads. In bitter baths or floor washes, it is boiled with dry wine to act as a spiritual disinfectant that "burns off" envy and parasitic energy. It is also a key ingredient in Omiero, the sacred herbal water used to wash and "feed" the stones and vessel of Babalu-Aye.

Garlic - (*Allium sativum*) - Used to "dry out" infections and pull systemic toxins from the blood. In Sarayeye (spiritual sweeping), the whole bulbs are used to absorb physical illness and "spiritual parasites" before being discarded at the crossroads or in the woods. Sometimes used in bitter baths to rid the body of illness.

Nettle (*Urtica dioica*) is a "warrior" botanical sacred to Babalu-Aye and Ogun, used for its stinging "heat" to aggressively repel parasitic spirits and envy. In bitter baths, it acts as a spiritual caustic that "burns off" sorcery and the stagnant energy of chronic illness.

Spinach (*Spinacia oleracea*) – Provides strength, vitality, and protection; used in spiritual work for energy, endurance, and safeguarding.

* * *

CONCLUSION

Plants provide healing and nourishment to life, supporting both physical well-being and spiritual practice through their natural properties. Their presence in ritual and tradition reflects a lasting connection between humanity and the natural world.

* * *

CHAPTER 18

THE SACRED WATERS OF TRANSFORMATION

THE PRACTICE OF RITUAL BATHING IN ORISHA TRADITION

From the earliest stages of initiation in Orisha traditions, ritual bathing is a basic and important practice. It shows a key idea: purification and spiritual balance do not come from belief alone, but from intentional actions. In this tradition, spirituality is something you actively do by working with natural forces that carry Ase, the spiritual force in all things. Water is central to this practice. It is not seen as just a physical substance, but as something that can receive, hold, and carry spiritual energy. Because of this, bathing is more than simple cleaning it is a way to restore balance to the body and spirit. Water becomes more powerful when combined with plants and sacred leaves, known as *ewe*. Each plant is believed to have its own energy and purpose. Some herbs are used to calm and cool the body, while others increase energy and help movement within the body. Some are used for protection, while others are meant to bring clarity or attract positive outcomes.

The use of these herbs follows a structured system of knowledge. Many plants are connected to specific Orishas, ancestors, or spiritual purposes, and their effects depend on how they are selected and prepared. This process is often guided by a trained herbalist, called an *Onisegun*, or by an Orisha priest. In some cases, guidance is also based on spiritual consultation or communication with the spirits. For this reason, ritual baths are not made randomly. They are carefully prepared with clear knowledge and purpose. Using the wrong herbs or preparing them incorrectly is believed to be ineffective and, in some cases, harmful.

The History Carried in Water

Long before the forced migration of Africans to the Americas, many African traditions recognized the spiritual and healing power of natural bodies of water. Rivers were seen as places of strong spiritual presence. Among the Yoruba, specific Orishas are connected to certain bodies of water, such as the Orisha Yemoja to the sea, Oshun to rivers, and Oya to the Niger River. Many believed that these natural bodies of water held the healing power of the Orishas, carrying their ase, within them and by entering these sacred waters it was believed that a person would encounter the Orishas ase and be spiritually renewed from it. This belief continued across the Atlantic, where African descendants in places like Brazil and Cuba maintained a deep respect for nature and the natural bodies of water within the local landscape. Indigenous peoples in the Americas also held similar beliefs about water as sacred and spiritually powerful. Like many African traditions, they saw rivers and natural bodies of water as living spaces connected to healing, ceremony, and spiritual forces. When Africans were brought to the Americas through the transatlantic slave trade, their traditions came into contact with the Indigenous cultures. In many places, both the Africans and Indigenous peoples shared ideas about nature, spirit, and healing. These similarities, along with shared experiences of hardship and resistance, helped create cultural bond and connection. Over time, some practices influenced one another and blended into the larger Yoruba diaspora.

RITUAL BATHING
Removal and Restoration

Ritual bathing in Orisha traditions serves two main purposes: *removal* and *restoration*. Removal focuses on cleansing away unwanted influences, while restoration focuses on rebuilding balance, strength, and positive energy. These two processes work together and are often used in sequence.

Removal (Discharge Baths)

Discharge baths are used to clear what no longer serves a person spiritually. In daily life, people are believed to absorb different kinds of energetic influence. This may include stress, conflict, emotional heaviness, environmental tension, or the effects of negative interactions. Over time, these influences are thought to build up and affect a person's clarity, emotional balance, and spiritual stability. The purpose of a discharge bath is to release this buildup. It is a cleansing process that restores a sense of lightness and clarity. However, it is not done randomly. The choice of herbs, timing, preparation, and disposal all matter. If done incorrectly, the bath may be ineffective or incomplete.

Simple Discharge Method: Salt Water

One of the most accessible methods is salt water. Coarse sea salt dissolved in water is used after bathing as a rinse. Salt is traditionally understood as a purifying substance that helps draw out unwanted energy when used with intention.

Herbal Discharge Baths

More advanced discharge baths use specific herbs chosen for a particular condition. Some herbs are associated with clearing emotional heaviness, sickness or negativity energy from the body. Often during the bath, it is common for the person remains calm and focused and sometimes they will include prayer or song connected to the herbs or the Orisha invoked to aid in the request. Following the bath, it is sometimes customary not the toss out the herbs used in the cleansing but instead place them somewhere in nature or bury them. This step is important because it completes the process of release. Improper disposal is believed to weaken or interrupt the effect of the bath. These are questions a priest will often ask the spirits when prescribing the bathing ritual for a particular client. It is also important to note that discharge baths can remove both negative and some positive energy as well. For this reason, it is sometimes common for a client to be prescribed herbs for restoration as well, without the restoration aspect, a person may feel drained or unbalanced after a discharge bath depending on type of bathing ritual and herbs prescribed to them.

Restoration (Energizing Baths)

Restoration baths are used to rebuild and strengthen spiritual energy. While discharge baths focus on cleansing, energizing baths focus on activation, balance, and protection. These baths are believed to help restore a person's spiritual energy, their spiritual *ase*.

The Amaci Bath

In the African Brazilian tradition, one of the most important restoration baths is called the *amaci* bath. It is typically given in the early stages of initiation and prepared by an experienced spiritual elder.The amaci bath is made according to a person's Orisha alignment, using herbs connected to that spiritual force. If a person has not yet been identified with a specific Orisha, the bath is often prepared using herbs sacred to the Orisha Obatala. who is understood to have a universal role connected to all heads. The amaci bath is poured over the body from head to toe. It is believed to clear stagnant energy while also strengthening and recharging the spiritual body. Many people report feelings of calm, clarity, warmth, or lightness that can last for days afterward.

Preparing Ritual Baths and Harvesting Sacred Plants

The preparation of ritual baths is itself a spiritual practice, requiring attention, intention, and proper knowledge. Those who are beginning their journey should never experiment with various herbs or plants without guidance. The same plant that heals one condition may aggravate another; the herb that calls the protection of one orisha may be unwelcome in the presence of another. Also, it is important to note that some herbs and plants are toxic and could cause adverse reactions, allergies or interact with various medications. Sometimes plants used in ritual baths are freshly gathered outdoors, while other times dried herbs are used. When harvesting fresh plants, tradition teaches that one should first acknowledge **Orisha Osain,** who is associated with herbal knowledge and the power of plants. Before collecting anything, it is customary to touch the ground with the hands to release any excess or disruptive energy and to show respect to Osain.

Metal tools are often avoided when harvesting because they are believed to interfere with the flow of ase, within the plant. Instead, herbs are typically gathered by hand. When tools are needed, materials such as wood or stone, like obsidian, may be used. Care is taken to harvest responsibly. Only what is needed is taken, and the plant is never over-harvested. Leaves are preferred over roots so the plant can continue to grow and be used again in the future. Before harvesting, practitioners often invoke Orisha Osain and ask for his blessing. In some cases, an *oríkì* (praise prayer) associated with Osain is recited before collecting herbs in the forest. The Oriki (Praise) below is found in the Odu *Ogunda Meji* and can be said before collecting the herbs in the forest.

(Yoruba)
Òsanyìn, bàbá ewé,
Mo ké pe e,
Kí ewé yìí ó dàra fún ètò mi,
Kí ó má bà mí jé,
Kí ó gbé mí sókè.
Ase o

Translation:
Òsanyìn, father of the leaves,
I call upon you,
May this leaf work well for my purpose,
May it not harm me,
May it lift me up.
Ashay oh

After picking the herbs they are then washed in clean, running water before preparation. The preparation itself follows established forms. Water ideally spring or filtered water is placed in a basin with the herbs, which are gently macerated to release their essence. The mixture is allowed to rest for a couple hours following this if the plant materials are soft like flowers or leaves but with the materials are hard like stems, barks and roots they are often left for days maybe even a week before being used. During this resting period, the practitioner maintains focused intention, often singing the songs associated with the herbs or the Orisha to whom the bath is dedicated. Osain is also often invoked during this process as well. Different lineages have different traditions regarding this, and it is best to follow your lineage and get guidance from your elders on this topic. Another incantation, we commonly recite is one in the Odu Osa Meji, (verse invoking herbs for cleansing and transformation)

(Yoruba)
Òsá méjì níí mọ ewé gbogbo,
Òsá méjì ló mọ'ní bá a se fi nṣe òrìsà.
Ewé níí wẹ ara,
Ewé níí mú èèyàn mọ́,
Ewé níí dá ibi sílẹ̀,
Ewé níí mú ire wọlé.
Ase o

Translation:
Òsá Méjì knows all the leaves,
Òsá Méjì knows how to use them for the Òrìṣà.
Leaves wash the body,
Leaves make a person pure,
Leaves remove misfortune,
Leaves bring blessings home.
Ashay oh

For baths requiring heated water, gentle warming is used never boiling, which destroys the volatile essences that carry the herbs' spiritual properties. The herbs steep beneath a covered vessel for approximately ten minutes, preserving their potency. Sometimes the herbs are boiled in water to release the essence from them and to eliminate bacteria, but the mixture is always left to cool down before use. Certain times are traditionally avoided for ritual bathing as well. The hours of sunrise and noon and midafternoon, are considered times of energetic transition and are less stable, making the outcome of any ritual work less predictable. After the bath is taken, the body is not rubbed vigorously but gently patted dry, allowing the properties of the bath to continue their work as the water evaporates naturally. The practitioner then wears white or light-colored clothing, avoiding dark colors that may absorb or interfere with the energies that have been established.

The Living Waters of the Natural World

Not all sacred baths require preparation. The natural environment offers its own sources of spiritual cleansing and restoration, forces that have been recognized since before recorded history, requiring only the willingness to receive them. Rain for an example, carries a particular power for purification. Falling from the sky, it has touched no human hand, received no human intention. It is water in its most primordial form, carrying the energy of the sky and the winds. Standing in rain, the practitioner receives cleansing directly from heavens. The sea also offers both discharge and energizing properties. Its salt content naturally draws impurities, while the oceans vastness and constant movement transform and disperse whatever is released. Rivers, too, carry their own power. Moving water is living water, water that does not stagnate, water that carries the ase of the orisha who claims dominion over it. To enter a river with respect and intention is to enter a temple constructed not by human hands but by the forces of nature.

Protocols, Precautions, and the Wisdom of Lineage

Knowledge in Orisha traditions is never complete without guidance. The same system that preserves herbal knowledge also preserves the wisdom of how, when, and for whom it should be used. A bath that benefits one person may not be suitable for another. What is helpful in one situation may be ineffective or even disruptive in another. For this reason, practitioners are encouraged to consult spiritual elders. Through experience and divination when appropriate, an elder can determine which type of bath is needed, which herbs should be used, when it should be taken, and whether additional steps are required.

The Transmission of Sacred Knowledge

Ritual bathing is not a set of fixed instructions, but a living tradition passed from elder to initiate. Each bath carries not only water and herbs, but also the prayers, intention, and accumulated knowledge of those who came before. Songs and prayers are essential parts of the process. They are not optional additions but active components that align the practitioner with spiritual forces, including the Orishas and ancestors. In this way, ritual bathing is understood as part of a continuous flow of knowledge and Ase, that moves from Africa to the Americas and from past generations to the present.

COMMON HERBS AND THEIR USES

- **Sage** – clears negative energy
- **Rosemary** – purifies and improves clarity
- **Lemongrass** – refreshes and removes heaviness
- **Bay leaf** – protection and focus
- **Clove** – spiritual protection and grounding
- **Sea salt / Epsom salt** – cleansing and removal of negativity
- **Lavender** – calm and relaxation
- **Chamomile** – soothing and emotional healing
- **Rose petals** – heart opening and love energy
- **Jasmine** – spiritual uplift and intuition
- **Basil** – prosperity and blessings
- **Cinnamon** – energy, attraction, and success
- **Mint / Peppermint** – renewal and mental clarity
- **Eucalyptus** – clearing and opening perception
- **Citrus peel (lemon, lime, orange)** – cleansing and uplift
- **Honey** – attraction and sweetness in life

* * *

TYPES OF SPIRITUAL BATHS AND THEIR USES

Deep Spiritual Cleansing Bath

- **Ingredients:** basil, rosemary, sage
- **Use:** herbs are steeped in water, cooled, then poured over the body (usually head to toe).
- **Timing:** often used in short cycles such as 3 or 7 days.
- **Association:** commonly linked with Eleguá or Obatalá under guidance.

Obatalá Purification Bath

- **Purpose:** peace, clarity, cooling the mind
- **Ingredients:** coconut water or milk, white flowers, cascarilla (eggshell powder)
- **Use:** gently poured over the body in a quiet setting, often followed by wearing white.

Oshun Love Bath

- **Purpose:** love, attraction, self-esteem, prosperity
- **Ingredients:** honey, cinnamon, orange peel, yellow or gold flowers
- **Use:** poured from the neck down (avoiding the head).

* * *

Yemayá Emotional Healing Bath

- *Purpose: emotional healing and balance*
- *Ingredients: Sea salt, coconut water, watermelon rind, blue or white flowers*

- **Use:** *slow pouring with reflection or prayer, sometimes near the ocean.*

* * *

Road Opener Bath (Eleguá)

- **Purpose:** *removing blockages and opening opportunities*
- **Ingredients:** *basil, mint, citrus peel, brown sugar*
- **Use:** *often taken in the morning before important events; some traditions dispose of remaining water at a crossroads.*

* * *

IMPORTANT SAFETY AND PRACTICE NOTES

1. In traditional practice, exact formulas are often given by an elder after divination
2. Some herbs are restricted or only used by trained initiates
3. Certain plants may cause allergies or irritation; avoid contact with eyes and test skin sensitivity when needed
4. Do not overuse ingredients, typically 3–5 herbs per bath is sufficient
5. Strong cleansing baths are often done in the morning rather than at night
6. Consult a medical professional if there are concerns about skin reactions or health conditions

* * *

Preparation Guidelines and Post-Bath Care

Standard Amounts

Using balanced proportions helps ensure the bath is effective without being overwhelming to the body or skin. Traditional practices favor simplicity and intention over excess.

- **Fresh herbs:** 1–3 handfuls total (lightly crushed to release their essence)
- **Dried herbs:** 2–4 tablespoons total (steeped like a strong tea)
- **Water:** 1–2 gallons (enough to comfortably pour over the body)

These amounts can be adjusted slightly based on personal sensitivity, but it's generally recommended to keep the number of herbs limited (often 3–5) to maintain clarity of purpose and avoid irritation.

After the Bath

What you do after the bath is considered just as important as the bath itself, as it allows the effects to settle and integrate.

Allow the body to air dry when possible: Letting the water dry naturally helps the herbal and spiritual properties remain on the skin. If needed, gently pat dry without fully removing the moisture.

Avoid soap immediately afterward: Washing right away may diminish the intended effects of the bath. If cleansing is needed, it is usually done before the ritual bath rather than after.

Dispose of used water and herbs respectfully: The remnants of the bath are traditionally returned to nature with intention. This may include pouring the water at the base of a tree, placing herbs outdoors, or disposing of them at a crossroads when aligned with the specific practice. The act symbolizes release, completion, and respect for the elements involved.

* * *

CHAPTER 19

EMBODYING SACRED ECOLOGY
LIVING IN HARMONY WITH THE EARTH

THE LIVING EARTH IN YORUBA PHILOSOPHY

Imagine, for a moment, a world where the ground beneath your feet is not inert soil, but a living, conscious organism. This is not a work of fiction; it is the foundational principle of the Yoruba worldview. In this understanding, the Earth is not a resource to be exploited, but a sacred, sentient being. If all of humanity embraced this perspective, how would it change the way we treat our planet? Would we continue to see it as something to own, or would we be compelled to grant it rights similar to those we afford to humans and animals?

This profound relationship with the natural world is rooted in the concept of Ashe, the divine energy that animates all of creation. Every rock, river, wind, and forest is a vessel for this sacred force, connecting all life in a vast, interconnected web. The ancient verses of Ifa do not separate the spiritual from the natural; they are one and the same. They teach that harming the Earth is not merely environmental damage; it is a profound spiritual transgression a wounding of the very fabric of destiny that severs the threads sustaining both human life and the cosmic order. The Yoruba people cultivated this wisdom over millennia, guided by Ifa and their relationships with the Orisha. They understood themselves not as masters of the world, but as active participants within a living community of existence. Today, as humanity confronts mass extinctions, deforestation, and climate instability, this ancient wisdom returns to us. It is not a relic of nostalgia, but an urgent guide for our collective future offering profound insights essential for our survival and the health of the planet we call home.

ONILE

The Orisha of the Earth

In the Yoruba tradition, **Onile** is honored as the Orisha of the Earth, the divine presence that embodies Mother Earth herself. Her name means "Owner of the Land" or "She who owns the Earth," a title that reflects her role as the force that sustains all life. Onile governs fertility, the land, and the growth of all living things. She is not simply the soil, rocks, or physical ground beneath our feet. Rather, she is understood as a living and sacred presence that holds all of creation. Humans, animals, and plants all live within her domain, and she maintains the balance that allows nature to thrive. When the land is mistreated through pollution, overuse, or destruction, that balance is disturbed, and the consequences affect every living being.

In Yoruba ritual practice, offerings follow a sacred sequence that begins with Eshu and ends with Onile. Because all life ultimately depends on the Earth, offerings are usually returned to the ground. Practitioners leave them outside, such as in forests, along riverbanks, or near pathways. This act is a gesture of reciprocity. It honors not only the specific Orisha receiving the offering but also Onile herself, the sacred Mother of the Earth. She is considered the source of the natural elements that other Orishas govern. Iron, for example, belongs to Ogun, and rivers belong to Osun, yet both ultimately come from the Earth that Onile provides. In this way, she offers the materials and sacred spaces that humanity needs for both survival and spiritual practice.

Onile teaches humans the principle of **Ibasepo**, the sacred relationship between humanity and Mother Earth. This teaching reminds us that the Earth does not belong to us. Instead, we belong to her. It is a sacred covenant. Humans live from what Onile provides, the food we eat, the land we walk on, and the resources that sustain our lives. In the end, our bodies return to the Earth. In traditional times, when a body was buried and allowed to decompose naturally, it nourished the soil and fed new life growing from the ground. In this way, death becomes part of the natural cycle of renewal. Our return to the Earth can be understood as a final offering to Onile, a gift given back to the Mother who sustained us throughout our lives.

Because of this sacred relationship, humans carry a responsibility. We must care for the land and honor the Earth through gratitude, respect, and responsible stewardship. By protecting the soil, water, and living world around us, we uphold our covenant with Onile and maintain the balance that supports all life.

The Sacred Relationship of Ibasepo

Ibasepo is a core principle in Yoruba thought that expresses the idea of sacred relationship and reciprocity. The word can be translated as "connection" or "relationship," but within Yoruba spirituality it carries a deeper meaning. It describes the interdependent bonds that link humans, the Earth, and the Orisha. Life is understood as a network of relationships in which every being depends on and affects the others.

At its foundation, Ibasepo teaches that nothing exists in isolation. Humans, animals, rivers, forests, and the spiritual forces of the universe are all part of a living web. Because of this, every action has consequences. The way people treat the land, water, and other forms of life shapes the balance of the world around them. Ibasepo also emphasizes respect and reciprocity. In this worldview, humans do not own the Earth or the forces of nature. Instead, they live from what the Earth provides and are expected to use those gifts with care. What is taken should be balanced with gratitude, offerings, and acts of responsibility toward the land and community.

Another important aspect of Ibasepo is the idea that life is a relationship rather than a transaction. When people gather herbs, collect water, or harvest resources from nature, they approach the source with humility and appreciation. They take only what is needed and acknowledge the spirit of the place through thanks or symbolic offerings. Through this ongoing practice of respect and mindfulness, balance is maintained in both the natural and spiritual worlds. When people honor Ibasepo, harmony is strengthened. When the principle is ignored, imbalance and consequences naturally follow.

In this way, Ibasepo serves as a moral and spiritual framework for life. It guides how humans relate to one another, to nature, and to the divine, encouraging relationships that are respectful, reciprocal, and harmonious.

THE MAIN PRINCIPLES OF IBASEPO

1. Interconnectedness: Nothing exists in isolation. All living things are woven together in a shared web where every action creates a natural ripple effect.

2. Reciprocity: We do not own the Earth, but borrow from it. We must use its resources carefully and give back through care and offerings.

3. Mindful Exchange: Life is a dialogue, not a transaction. Every interaction with nature requires gratitude, mutual respect, and a conscious give-and-take.

4. Conscious Balance: Our intentional actions sustain the natural and spiritual order. Neglecting this interconnectedness naturally leads to imbalance.

In the silence of early morning, the Babalawo pours water onto the soil and whispers: "Onile, Mother of the Earth, Guardian of all life, I honor you. May your mercy touch us, Flowing through the land, the rivers, and all that grows beneath your care."

THE DANGER OF DISRESPECT

In Yoruba thought, disrespecting the Earth always carries consequences. Actions taken without reverence invite **Ajogun**, destructive spiritual forces that arise to restore balance. The hunter who enters the forest without greeting its spirits, the farmer who drains the soil without renewing it, or the corporation that strips the land without care for restoration, all violate the sacred order of life.

1. **Physical Consequences** – Ignoring the balance of nature can directly affect health and well-being. Contaminated water, depleted soil, or polluted air can lead to illness, malnutrition, or reduced vitality. In Yoruba understanding, every action has a reaction; harm done to the Earth eventually returns in tangible ways.

2. **Emotional and Spiritual Consequences** – Disrespecting the Earth can disturb inner harmony. Because humans are spiritually connected to the living world, violating nature's balance can cause anxiety, confusion, restlessness, or a sense that "things are not right." Subtle, yet real, these disturbances may signal that **Ajogun** or disruptive forces are present.

3. **Social Consequences** – When people exploit or damage shared resources, through over harvesting, pollution, or neglect, it doesn't just harm the land, it harms the community.

4. **Destiny and Life Flow** – In the teachings of Ifa, a person's destiny is woven into the web of life. Disrespecting the Earth can create obstacles, delays, or hardships within the person's own life as a punishment.

Ultimately, to disrespect the Earth is to harm ourselves. When we create imbalance in the natural world, that disruption inevitably ripples back to the individual and the collective, manifesting as physical, emotional, and spiritual distress. This aligns with the fundamental Yoruba teaching that our personal well-being is inseparable from the health of our environment. When we honor this interconnected web, the result is *Itelorun*: a state of true harmony and flourishing. Conversely, when greed or ignorance severs these threads, the result is ***arun***, (sickness). This imbalance does not remain external; it migrates from the land into our communities and personal destinies. Human beings do not stand above this web; we are entirely dependent upon its integrity at every moment. The Odu ***Oyeku Meji*** contains one of the tradition's most direct ecological warnings: *"He who cuts down the forest without greeting its spirits has already cut his own life short."* while the Odu ***Irosun Meji*** says: *"The one who honors the Earth will never be left without shelter".* This means the earth will continue to provide for us as long as we honor her.

Oshun (Rivers): Embodies fresh water and abundance. Protecting waterways is an act of love for a living, divine being.

Yemoja (Oceans): Governs the global water system. Reverence for her is a commitment to planetary survival.

Osain (Forests): The essence of plant medicine. He *is* the forest, requiring a relationship of gratitude and sustainable resource management.

Oya (Atmosphere): Governs winds and storms. She represents the necessary cycles of atmospheric renewal and transformation.

Obatala (Mountains): Represents purity and the ethical foundation of life. He calls for the preservation of the world's structural integrity.

Olokun (Deep Sea): Guardian of the ocean's depths. Olokun reminds us to respect the vast, hidden reserves of the planet.

* * *

IWA PELE
Gentle Character

At the very core of Ifa, shaping its ethics and guiding its wisdom, lies the concept of Iwa Pele, often translated as "gentle character." It is far more than a simple personality trait; it is the foundational principle of right relationship with all of creation. To embody Iwa Pele is to move through the world with a profound sense of balance, respect, and restraint. It is to understand that one's actions ripple outward, touching the human, the animal, the mineral, and the divine alike.

A person of Iwa Pele walks lightly upon the earth. They are mindful of their footsteps, aware that every step lands upon the body of Onile. They do not take more than they need, for they recognize that greed is a disruption of the natural order. They do not destroy what they cannot restore, honoring the principle that life is a cycle of reciprocity, not a one-way extraction. This gentle character is not weakness; it is a cultivated strength, a conscious choice to live in harmony rather than domination, to prioritize connection over accumulation. In a modern world, and particularly within an economic system built upon the relentless logic of unlimited extraction and endless growth, Iwa Pele emerges not as a quaint ideal but as a radical and transformative vision. It challenges the very foundation of an economy that treats the Earth as a warehouse of resources to be emptied and a landfill for waste to be hidden. Against the prevailing culture of more, Iwa Pele offers a philosophy of enough. It redefines abundance, shifting its meaning away from the quantity of possessions and toward the quality of relationships: our connection to the land, to our communities, to the Orisha, and to ourselves.

THE PATH FORWARD
Embodying Sacred Ecology

In conclusion, the path forward lies not in mere belief but in living these principles every day. The diviner's shrine becomes more than a place of ritual; it is a sanctuary of ecological mindfulness where sustainability is itself a form of sacred order. In this understanding, every tree planted becomes a living reservoir of Ashe, and every act of restraint an offering made directly to Onile. The integration of Yoruba ecological wisdom with modern efforts to protect our planet is not an abstract ideal but a practical necessity.

The growing legal movement to grant rivers and forests "rights of nature" is, from this perspective, not a novel invention but a rediscovery of what Onile has always represented: a living being, not a resource to be consumed. Meanwhile, scientific revelations that forests communicate through intricate fungal networks only confirm what the Yoruba have long maintained: *the natural world is not a collection of separate parts, but a conscious, interconnected whole.*

* * *

GLOSSARY

A

- **Aganju**: Orisha of strength, transformation, and perseverance, associated with volcanoes, deserts, and mountains. Called upon for stability in difficult times.
- **Aje-Shaluga**: Orisha of wealth, prosperity, and abundance, governing financial success and commerce. Invoked for business blessings.
- **Ajogun**: Negative spirits believed to cause misfortune. They are often seen as obstacles to personal and communal well-being in Yoruba belief.
- **Arun**: Sickness, a type of imbalance.
- **Ayangalu**: Orisha of the talking drum, seen as the first drummer and conveys spiritual messages through rhythm.
- **Ayelalá**: An Orisha of justice and truth, known for punishing criminals and exposing lies. She is invoked to seek justice and fight against injustice and criminality.

B

- **Baba**: "Father" (a respectful term used in family and religious contexts).
- **Babaloricha/Babalocha**: A respected Santero with extensive initiation knowledge.
- **Babalawo**: A skilled diviner and spiritual guide, also known as a priest of Orula.

- **Babalú-Aye**: Orisha of earth, illness, and healing, with the power to cure or bring diseases. Tied to death and nature's cycles.
- **Batá**: A set of three double headed drums resembling an hourglass, each with specific roles and spiritual significance.
- **Bembé**: A lively drumming ceremony held in honor of the Orishas.
- **Boveda**: An altar dedicated to ancestors and spirits, used for offerings and prayers.
- **Burukú**: Moral flaws or bad character ("iwá burukú").

C

- **Cowrie**: A type of seashell used in divination and ceremonies, symbolizing wealth, money and used as currency by the ancient Yoruba.

D

- **Dada**: Orisha of motherhood, fertility, and the well-being of unborn children. Revered for her role in childbirth and nurturing.
- **Derecho**: Payment made to Olorisha or Babalawo for their services or out or respect.

E

- **Egbe:** Refers to a group, society, or community in heaven.
- **Egún**: Spirits of deceased ancestors, often honored and revered for their guidance and protection.
- **Egungun**: Masquerade costumes worn to honor the Egun (ancestor) spirits in ceremonies.
- **Erinle**: Orisha of health, medicine, hunting, and estuaries. Syncretized with Archangel Raphael, protector of marginalized communities.
- **Esu/Elegua**: Messenger of the Orishas, owner of all roads and

paths. A trickster and gatekeeper who facilitates
communication between realms.

I

- **Ibasepo**: Sacred relationship and reciprocity
- **Ibeji**: Orisha of twins, symbolizing duality and balance.
  Revered for the sacred bond between twins.
- **Igbo Orisa**: Sacred grove
- **Iroko**: Spirit inhabiting the Iroko tree, linked to spiritual
  connection. Harm to the tree brings misfortune.
- **Itelorun:** Yoruba concept, translates to contentment,
  satisfaction, or the fulfillment of a good, disciplined life
- **Iyami Osoronga**: powerful female spirits in Yoruba tradition
  who guard nature, enforce justice, and punish those who act
  disrespectfully or unjustly.

N

- **Nana Buluku**: Supreme goddess of creation, grandmother of
  all life and Orishas. Rules over life cycles, fertility, and
  abundance.

O

- **Oba**: Orisha of marriage and relationships, known for her
  tragic story with Shango. Transformed into the Oba River.
- **Obatala**: Father of all Orishas, symbolizing purity, wisdom,
  and justice. Creator of humans and associated with moral
  character.
- **Ochosi**: Orisha of hunting, justice, and truth. Protector of
  hunters, called upon for fairness and protection.
- **Oduduwa**: Father of the Yoruba people and civilization,
  credited with world creation and establishing order.
- **Ogun**: Orisha of war, iron, and technology. Known for strength
  and endurance, Ogun serves as a protector and guide.

- **Oke**: Orisha of high mountains and elevated places, often linked to Obatala. A protector during travel.
- **Oko**: Orisha of agriculture, farming, and abundance. Invoked for prosperous harvests.
- **Olodumare** : The supreme creator deity, also referred to as God in Yoruba tradition.
- **Olokun**: Orisha of the deep ocean, wealth, and prosperity. Associated with hidden treasures, beauty, and the ocean's mysteries.
- **Olori-Merin**: Orisha who governs the four cardinal points and maintains balance across all creation.
- **Onile:** Orisha of the Earth, Mother Earth
- **Ori**: The head or spiritual consciousness of an individual. It represents one's destiny and essence.
- **Oro**: Historical king and an Orisha of justice. Also represents a spiritual force associated with divine communication.
- **Orunmila**: Orisha of wisdom, knowledge, and divination. The first Babalawo, consulted for guidance on destiny.
- **Osain**: Orisha of herbs, healing plants, and herbal medicine. Protector of healers and the forest, with knowledge of all plants' healing properties.
- **Oshun**: Orisha of love, beauty, and sensuality. Protector of women and children, bringing wealth and emotional healing.
- **Osumare**: Orisha of rainbows and serpents, symbolizing renewal and transformation. Protects children and creative individuals.
- **Oya**: Orisha of wind, tornadoes, and hurricanes. Known for her fierce protection of the dead and as a guardian of the marketplace, she is associated with sudden changes and heightened intuition.

S

- **Santería:** also known as Santería or Lucumí, is an Afro-Cuban religion rooted in Yoruba traditions. It originated in Cuba and spread to other parts of the Americas, blending elements of

Catholicism, Taino (Indigenous Caribbean) beliefs, and other
spiritual traditions alongside its Yoruba foundation.
- **Shango**: Orisha of thunder, lightning, fire, and drumming. A
symbol of masculinity and protection, revered for his power to
overcome obstacles.

T

- **Taiwo:** A name often given to the first-born of twins.
- **Tutu**: Coolness.

U

- **Umbanda:** Originating in Brazil, Umbanda combines elements
of African, indigenous, and Christian beliefs. It centers on the
worship of the orishás.

V

- **Vodou**: Also known as Voodoo, Vodou is a syncretic religion
that originated in Haiti. It centers on the worship of loas,
spirits who represent various aspects of nature and human life
and incorporates elements of West African religions.

W

- **Warriors**: An initiation ceremony where the Orishas Elegua,
Ogun, Ochosi, and Osun are bestowed upon individuals to
assist them on their spiritual journey.

Y

- **Yemaya**: Orisha of the ocean and motherhood. Represents
fertility, protection, and nurturing, often invoked by women
seeking to conceive.
- **Yewa**: Orisha associated with earth and death. Guards the

boundary between life and death and governs the
decomposition of corpses.

* * *

May Olodumare continue to bless you,
give you support and guide you on your journey.

THE END

* * *

ABOUT THE AUTHOR

Michael Perez, also known as *Awo Ayodele Ifagbemi,* is a priest of the Yoruba spiritual tradition and a devoted practitioner of Orisha spirituality and Ifá divination. With a background in social work and over twenty years of experience exploring philosophies, spiritual practices, and personal healing, he combines professional insight with profound spiritual knowledge. Through his work, he shares the wisdom of the Orishas, guiding others on a path of self-discovery, spiritual growth, and alignment with their true essence. He is the author of several books and is passionate about preserving and teaching the rich traditions of the Yoruba people.

OTHER BOOKS BY THIS AUTHOR

THE YORUBA SPIRITUAL TRAINING MANUAL – *The Ultimate Resource Guide to the Yoruba Religion – Awo Ifagbemi:* A practical, hands-on guide for both beginners and experienced practitioners, offering clear, step-by-step instructions for learning and practicing Yoruba spirituality. This book offers guidance on connecting with the Orishas and integrating Yoruba spiritual principles into daily life, enabling readers to deepen their spiritual practice, foster personal growth, and cultivate balance and purpose.

THE SACRED TEACHINGS OF THE ORISHAS – *Explore Over 50 Stories, Prayers, Rituals, and Insights from the Yoruba Spiritual Tradition – Awo Ifagbemi:* Delve into the wisdom, symbolism, and spiritual lessons of the Orishas. This book presents over 50 sacred stories, prayers, rituals, and practices designed to help readers connect with the Orishas and integrate their teachings into everyday life.

* * *

Keep learning and growing.

Best Wishes!

Awo Ifagbemi